DYNASTIES OF THE WORLD

Think, in this batter'd Caravanserai
Whose Portals are alternate Night and Day,
How Sultán after Sultán with his Pomp
Abode his destined Hour, and went his way.

The Rubáiyát of Omar Khayyám

Là sont les devanciers joints à leurs descendants;
Tous les règnes y sont, on y voit tous les temps...

Pierre Le Moyne (1602–1672)

Time expounded, not by generations or centuries, but by the vast periods of conquests and dynasties; by cycles of Pharaohs and Ptolemies, Antiochi and Arsacides!

Thomas De Quincey

DYNASTIES OF THE WORLD

A Chronological and Genealogical Handbook

JOHN E. MORBY

Oxford New York
OXFORD UNIVERSITY PRESS
1989

Oxford University Press, Walton Street, Oxford OX2 6DP

Oxford New York Toronto
Delhi Bombay Calcutta Madras Karachi
Petaling Jaya Singapore Hong Kong Tokyo
Nairobi Dar es Salaam Cape Town
Melbourne Auckland
and associated companies in
Berlin Ibadan

Oxford is a trade mark of Oxford University Press

British Library Cataloguing-in-Publication Data

Morby, J. E.
Dynasties of the world: a chronological and genealogical handbook
1. Royal families. Genealogies
I. Title.
929.7
ISBN 0-19-215872-4

Library of Congress Cataloging-in-Publication Data

Morby John E.
Dynasties of the world: a chronological and genealogical handbook
John E. Morby.
Includes bibliographies and index.
1. Kings and rulers—Genealogy. I. Title.
CS27.M67 1989 909—dc19 87-36438
ISBN 0-19-215872-4

Set by Graphicraft Typesetters Ltd.
Printed in Great Britain by
Bookcraft (Bath) Ltd
Midsomer Norton, Avon

To my family, friends,
and teachers

PREFATORY NOTE

THE present work provides clearly designed chronological tables giving years of rule, family relationships, and other information for the major dynasties of the world. The format should enable the reader not only to document each individual reign, but to grasp at once each royal line's pattern of succession and temporal span. Though coverage is global, it has not been possible to include all states conceivably of interest; but there is comprehensive treatment of Europe and its roots in the ancient world. Some dynasties have been left out because of a lack of reliable data; among these are the kingdom of the Medes, the Seljuqids of Iconium, and most Hindu Indian royal lines. The information given in this book, however, attains to the highest level of accuracy, and rests on a thorough examination of the sources.

Countries are arranged in broad territorial groupings, and are denoted by their monarchs' highest title; Poland is styled a kingdom, though its rulers began as princes. A family such as the Bavarian Wittelsbachs, which ruled a series of states, may give its name to the table. European dynastic groups are termed *houses*, which may ramify into *lines* (these last collateral branches, in the German states ruling subdivided territories); non-European reigning families are termed *dynasties*.

Dates are Julian to the later sixteenth century, when the Gregorian calendar was introduced. Those that follow are Gregorian, even where the earlier year (from ten to thirteen days behind) remained in use. Thus, Mary II of England dies in 1695, not 1694; Elizabeth of Russia dies in 1762, not the previous year. So as not to burden the tables with *circa*s, question marks, and slashes, information regarding approximate dates and margins of error will be found in the notes. Where months and days are known, non-western dates are rendered precisely in western terms; Islamic, Japanese, and similar years are not rounded off to their nearest Christian equivalents.

Names are given either in versions as faithful as possible to the originals, or in English equivalents in normal use. Complete consistency is scarcely possible, and would flout accepted practice; thus, the reader will confront Philip of Spain but Lorenzo of Florence; Francis of France but Francesco of Milan. Arabic names are shown as written, not as pronounced (al-Nāṣir, not an-Nāṣir); Ottoman names are in Turkish, not Arabic versions. Chinese names are emphatically Wade-Giles, and not Pinyin. Hellenized versions of Mesopotamian and Egyptian names are sparingly used; Greek names are rendered in Latinized equivalents (Constantine, not Konstantinos).

Descent is shown in the male line unless stated otherwise; thus, 'grandson' means son's son, 'nephew' means brother's son, 'tenth in descent' means through males; further, 'brother-in-law' means specifically wife's brother. Collaterals are traced from the nearest reigning member of a dynasty;

bastardy is given only if a factor in the succession. For more detailed European lineages, see *Europäische Stammtafeln*, ed. D. Schwennicke (11 vols. in 13 pts., Marburg, 1978–88), or, for the modern period, *Burke's Royal Families of the World, Volume I: Europe and Latin America* (London, 1977).

Titles pertaining to one member of a dynasty hold good for subsequent members unless otherwise noted. Simultaneous rule by one prince in two or more states is cross referenced. In the context of European history, 'emperor' alone means Holy Roman emperor; 'caliph' by itself denotes the original direct line from 632 to 1258.

Sobriquets, most colourful and most abundant for the western world, follow the rulers' names. As observed by W. Kienast, *Historische Zeitschrift*, CCV (1967), 1–14, the epithet 'the Great', from the Latin *magnus*, may actually mean 'the Elder'. For medieval sobriquets, see also my own article in *Canadian Journal of History*, XIII (1978), 1–16.

Co-regencies are shown, either explicitly or by means of overlapping dates; regencies normally appear only where the regent also held the sovereign title. Abdications and depositions are given, together with the year of death (if known) of former monarchs; captured rulers are termed deposed. Interregna of over a year are recorded, as are beatifications and canonizations in the major churches. Dynastic realignments, as during the Napoleonic years in Europe, are indicated; so are mandates and protectorates, progress from autonomy to independence, dynastic unions, and finally the end of monarchic rule through conquest or overthrow.

The *notes* contain supplementary information regarding chronological problems and uncertainties, calendars and dating systems, and names and royal style. They will be most detailed where the questions are greatest, and for those states most distant from the modern western world in space and time.

The *bibliographies* list books and articles most likely to assist the reader in search of additional information, or which deal in detail with chronology and lineage. They do not comprise the sum of works consulted, nor do they list auxiliary materials such as newspapers and coins.

The *index* contains references to the major sections and subsections of the work, to each named dynasty or line, with an indication of the area it ruled, and to countries or geographical regions linking references scattered throughout the book.

ACKNOWLEDGEMENTS

IN compiling this work, I have received most generous help from scholars in many fields. Some have allowed me access to valuable unpublished material; some have answered inquiries so numerous as to stretch the bounds of academic courtesy; others have combed unfamiliar sources in little-known languages in order to send me the data I required. I wish there were space to list each contribution in detail; my gratitude far exceeds the compass of this brief acknowledgement. For help with dates, relationships, and titles, I am deeply indebted to Ludwig W. Adamec, Thanom Anarmwat, Robert L. Backus, Klaus Baer, Peter Hunter Blair, C. E. Bosworth, John A. Brinkman, A. A. M. Bryer, David P. Chandler, John P. Chiapuris, Roger Collins, George T. Dennis, Martin Dimnik, Audrey Droop, Björn Englund, J. L. I. Fennell, John V. A. Fine, Richard N. Frye, Hans Gillingstam, Vasil Giuzelev, N. G. L. Hammond, Kenneth Harrison, Patricia Herbert, Tomoyuki Inoue, Peter Jackson, Paul W. Knoll, Dimitŭr Kosev, Luc Kwanten, P.-B. Lafont, Erle Leichty, Eric Macro, Robert D. McChesney, W. F. Mkhonza, William J. Murnane, princess Nhu May of Annam, John R. Perry, J.-P. Poly, Michael C. Rogers, Wilfrid J. Rollman, Robert W. Stookey, Kevin L. Sykes, Marc Szeftel, Hugh Toye, Denis Twitchett, Wilhelm Volkert, F. W. Walbank, W. L. Warren, Edward F. Wente, David Williamson, John E. Woods, Dietrich Wörn, David K. Wyatt, Malcolm E. Yapp, and Norman Yoffee.

For the translation of material in languages I cannot read, I am happy to acknowledge the help of Meyer Galler, my late father, Edwin S. Morby, Eugenia V. Nomikos, Richard C. Raack, and Helen Schulak.

For calling my attention to valuable books and articles, and for other references, I am most grateful to Stephen Album, John F. Benton, Frank D. Gilliard, Rudi P. Lindner, and Peter Topping.

I also thank most sincerely the inter-library loan staff of California State University, Hayward, headed by Ruth Jaeger and Barbara Kwan, who have tirelessly obtained the hundreds of items I required; the auxiliary foundation, CSUH, for a small grant to defray the costs of photocopying; Peva Keane, for the preparation of a most excellent index; and lastly my several editors at Oxford University Press, whose support and encouragement have never flagged since my original typescript (so many times since enlarged and revised) was first accepted for publication.

J. E. M.

Dutch Flat and Hayward, Calif.
December 1988

CONTENTS

I

The Ancient Near East

ANCIENT EGYPT

EARLY DYNASTIC PERIOD

First Dynasty (Thinite): *c*.3100–2905 BC

c.34	Horus Aha	Meni (Menes)
c.46	Horus Djer	Iti
c.7	Horus Wadji	Iterti
c.14	Horus Dewen	Khasti
c.52	Horus Anedjib	Merpibia
c.8	Horus Semerkhet	Irynetjer
c.30	Horus Qaa	Qaa
c.2?	Horus Seneferka	

Second Dynasty (Thinite): *c*.2905–2755 BC

c.41	{Horus Hetep-sekhemwy Horus Nebre}	Hotep
c.37	Horus Nynetjer	Nynetjer
c.6		Weneg
c.20		{Sened Nubnefer}
c.8	Seth Peribsen	
c.11		Sekhemib-perenmaat
c.27	Horus-and-Seth Khase-khemwy	Hetep-netjerwiimef

OLD KINGDOM

Third Dynasty (Memphite): *c*.2755–2680 BC

c.18	Horus Sanakht	Nebka I
c.20	Horus Netjerykhet	Djoser
c.7	Horus Sekhemkhet	Djoser-Teti
c.6	Horus Qahedjet	
c.24	Horus Khaba	Hu(ni)

Fourth Dynasty (Memphite): *c*.2680–2544 BC

c.40	Snefru
c.2	Nebka II(?)
c.25	Khufwy (Cheops)
c.10	Djedefre
c.25	Khafre (Chephren)
c.25	Menkaure (Mycerinus)
c.2	Wehemka
c.7	Shepseskaf

Fifth Dynasty (Memphite): *c*.2544–2407 BC

c.12	Userkaf
16	Sahure
c.10	Neferirkare Kakai
c.15	{Shepsikare Isi Neferefre}

c.10	Nyuserre Ini
9	Menkauhor Akauhor
44	Djedkare Isesi
21	Unas

Sixth Dynasty (Memphite): *c*.2407–2255 BC

c.12	Teti
c.35	Meryre Pepi I (son)
c.10	Merenre Nemtyemsaf I (son)
c.90	Neferkare Pepi II (brother)
c.5?	Merenre Nemtyemsaf II (son)

FIRST INTERMEDIATE PERIOD

Seventh–Eighth Dynasties (Memphite): *c*.2255–2235 BC

Sixteen kings, six to nine known from contemporary sources:

Neferkare
Horus Kha[bau]
Qakare Ibi
Neferkauhor Kapuibi
Horus Demedjibtawy(?)

Order uncertain:

Sekhemkare
Wadjkare
Iti(?)
Imhotep(?)

Ninth–Tenth Dynasties (Heracleopolitan): *c*.2235–2035 BC

Eighteen kings, eight known from contemporary sources:

	Meryibre Akhtoy
	Neferkare
fl. 2075	Nebkaure Akhtoy
	Merykare (son?)

Order uncertain:

Khui
Iytjenu
Wahkare Akhtoy
Mery[..]re Akhtoy

MIDDLE KINGDOM

Eleventh Dynasty (Theban): *c*.2134–1991 BC

2134–2118	{Tepya Mentuhotep I Sehertawy Inyotef I (son)}
2118–2069	Wahankh Inyotef II (brother)
2069–2061	Nakhtnebtepnefer Inyotef III (son)
2061–2010	Nebhepetre Mentuhotep II (son)
2010–1998	Sankhkare Mentuhotep III (son)
1998–1991	{Qakare Inyotef IV(?) Nebtawyre Mentuhotep IV}

Twelfth Dynasty (Theban): *c*.1991–1786 BC

1991–1962	Sehetepibre Amenemhat I
1971–1926	Kheperkare Senwosret I (son)
1929–1895	Nubkaure Amenemhat II (son)
1897–1878	Khakheperre Senwosret II (son)
1878–1842	Khakaure Senwosret III (son)
1842–1797	Nymare Amenemhat III (son)
1798–1789	Makherure Amenemhat IV (son)
1789–1786	Sebekkare Sebeknefru (sister)

SECOND INTERMEDIATE PERIOD

Thirteenth Dynasty (Theban): *c*.1786–1668 BC

At least sixty-five kings, about forty known from contemporary sources:

1786–1784	Khutawyre Wegaf
1784–?	Sekhemkare Amenemhatsonbef
?–1774	Sekhemre-khutawy Pentjini(?)
1774–1772	Sekhemkare Amenemhat V
1772–1771	Sehetepibre [. . .]
1771–?	Sankhibre Amenemhat VI
	Hetepibre Hornedjheryotef
	[. . .] Ameni-Qemau
	[. . .] Khuyoqer
	Khaankhre Sebekhotep I
	Awibre Hor
	Sedjefakare Amenemhat VII
	Sekhemre-khutawy Sebekhotep II
	Userkare Khendjer
	Semenkhkare Mermesha
?–1754	Nerkare [. . .]
1754–1751	Sekhemre-sewadjtawy Sebekhotep III
1751–1740	Khasekhemre Neferhotep I
1740	Menwadjre Sihathor (brother)
1740–1730	Khaneferre Sebekhotep IV (brother)
1730–1725	Khahetepre Sebekhotep V (son?)
1725–1714	Wahibre Ibya
1714–1700	Merneferre Ay
1700–1698	Merhetepre Sebekhotep VI
1698–?	Mersekhemre Neferhotep II
	Sewadjkare Hori
?–1693	Merkaure Sebekhotep VII

Order uncertain, *c*.1693–1668 BC:

Seneferibre Senwosret IV
Merankhre Mentuhotep V
Djedankhre Mentuemsaf
Djedhetepre Dedumose I
Djedneferre Dedumose II
Sewahenre Senebmiu
Sekhemre-sankhtawy Neferhotep III
Sekhemre-seusertawy Sebekhotep VIII
Mershepsesre Ini

	[. . .] Mentuwoser
	Menkhaure Senaaib
	Sekhemre-neferkhau Wepwawetemsaf

Fourteenth Dynasty (Xoite): *c.*1720–1665 BC

Perhaps as many as seventy-six kings, one known from a contemporary source:

*fl.*1720	Nehasi

Fifteenth Dynasty (Hyksos): *c.*1668–1560 BC

1668–1652	Sekhaenre(?) Shalik
1652–1638	Maibre Sheshi
1638–1630	Meruserre Yaqob-her
1630–1610	Seuserenre Khayan
1610–1569	Auserre Apopi
1569–1560	Asehre(?) Khamudi

Sixteenth Dynasty (Hyksos): *c.*1665–1565 BC

About seventeen kings known from contemporary sources, including:

	Nubuserre
	Yakboam
	Wadjed
	Yakbaal
	Nubankhre
	Anath-her
	Khauserre

Seventeenth Dynasty (Theban): *c.*1668–1570 BC

1668–1663	Nubkheperre Inyotef V
1663–1660	Sekhemre-wahkhau Rahotep (son)
1660–1644	Sekhemre-wadjkhau Sebekemsaf I
1644–1643	Sekhemre-sementawy Djehuti
1643–1642	Sankhenre Mentuhotep VI
1642–1623	Sewadjenre Nebiryerau I
1623	Neferkare Nebiryerau II
1623–1622	Semenenre
1622–1610	Seuserenre Senwosret V(?)
1610–1601	Sekhemre-shedtawy Sebekemsaf II
1601–1596	Sekhemre-wepmaat Inyotef VI (son?)
1596	Sekhemre-herhermaat Inyotef VII (brother)
1596–1591	Senakhtenre Tao I
1591–1576	Seqenenre Tao II (son)
1576–1570	Wadjkheperre Kamose (son or brother)

NEW KINGDOM

Eighteenth Dynasty (Theban): *c.*1570–1293 BC

1570–1546	Nebpehtyre Ahmose I (son or brother)
1551–1524	Djeserkare Amenhotep I (son)
1524–1518	Akheperkare Thutmose I
1518–1504	Akheperenre Thutmose II (son)
1503–1483	Makare Hatshepsut (sister)

1504–1450	Menkheperre Thutmose III (son of Thutmose II)
1453–1419	Akheprure Amenhotep II (son)
1419–1386	Menkheprure Thutmose IV (son)
1386–1349	Nebmare Amenhotep III (son)
1350–1334	Neferkheprure Amenhotep IV/Akhenaten (son)
1336–1334	Ankhkheprure Semenkhkare (son)
1334–1325	Nebkheprure Tutankhamun (brother)
1325–1321	Kheperkheprure Ay
1321–1293	Djeserkheprure Horemheb

Nineteenth Dynasty (Theban): *c*.1293–1185 BC

1293–1291	Menpehtyre Ramesses I
1291–1279	Menmare Seti I (son)
1279–1212	Usermare Ramesses II (son)
1212–1202	Baenre Merenptah (son)
1202–1199	Menmire Amenmesses (brother?)
1199–1193	Userkheprure Seti II (son of Merenptah)
1193–1187	Akhenre Merenptah-Siptah (son?)
1193–1185	Sitre-meryetamun Tawosret (widow of Seti II)

Twentieth Dynasty (Theban): *c*.1185–1070 BC

1185–1182	Userkhaure Setnakht
1182–1151	Usermare Ramesses III (son)
1151–1145	Heqamare Ramesses IV (son)
1145–1141	Usermare Ramesses V (son)
1141–1133	Nebmare Ramesses VI (son of Ramesses III)
1133–1127	Usermare-meryamun Ramesses VII
1127–1126	Usermare-akhenamun Ramesses VIII
1126–1108	Neferkare Ramesses IX
1108–1098	Khepermare Ramesses X
1098–1070	Menmare Ramesses XI

THIRD INTERMEDIATE PERIOD

Twenty-first Dynasty (Tanite): *c*.1070–946 BC

At Tanis:

1070–1044	Hedjkheperre Smendes
1044–1040	Neferkare Amenemnisu
1040–992	Akheperre Psusennes I
994–985	Usermare Amenemope
985–979	Akheperre Osochor
979–960	Nutekheperre Siamun
960–946	Tyetkheprure Psusennes II

High priests of Amun at Thebes:

1070–1055	Pinudjem I
1055–1047	Masahart (son)
1047–1046	Djedkhonsefankh (brother)
1046–993	Menkheperre (brother)
993–991	Smendes (son)

991–970	Pinudjem II (brother)
970–946	Psusennes (son)

Twenty-second Dynasty (Bubastite): *c*.946–712 BC

946–913	Hedjkheperre Shoshenq I
916–904	Sekhemkheperre Osorkon I (son)
?–904	Heqakheperre Shoshenq II (son)
904–890	Usermare(?) Takelot I (brother)
890–860	Usermare Osorkon II (son)
860–835	Hedjkheperre Takelot II (son)
835–783	Usermare Shoshenq III
783–773	Usermare Pami
773–735	Akheperre Shoshenq V (son)
735–712	Akheperre Osorkon IV (son?)

Twenty-third Dynasty (Tanite): *c*.828–720 BC

At Thebes:

828–803	Usermare Pedubast
803–797	Usermare Shoshenq IV
797–769	Usermare Osorkon III
774–767	Usermare Takelot III (son)
767–765	Usermare Amenrud (brother)

At Leontopolis:

814–790	Yuput I
. . .	(several kings?)
745–720	Usermare Yuput II

Twenty-fourth Dynasty (Saite): *c*.740–712 BC

740–718	Shepsesre Tefnakht
718–712	Wahkare Bakenranef

Twenty-fifth Dynasty (Nubian): *c*.767–656 BC

767–753	Nymare Kashta
753–713	Seneferre Piye (son)
713–698	Neferkare Shabako (brother)
701–690	Djedkaure Shebitku (son of Piye)
690–664	Khunefertemre Taharqa (brother)
664–656	Bakare Tanwetamani (son of Shebitku)

SAITE PERIOD

Twenty-sixth Dynasty (Saite): 664–525 BC

664–610	Wahibre Psamtik I
610–595	Wehemibre Necho (son)
595–589	Neferibre Psamtik II (son)
589–570	Haibre Wahibre (son)
570–526	Khnemibre Ahmose II
526–525	Ankhkaenre Psamtik III (son)

LATER DYNASTIC PERIOD

Twenty-seventh Dynasty (Persian Kings): 525–405 BC

See Persia: Achaemenid Dynasty (p. 25)

Twenty-eighth Dynasty (Saite): 405–399 BC

405–399	Amyrtaeus

Twenty-ninth Dynasty (Mendesian): 399–380 BC

399–393	Baenre Nepherites I
393	Userre Psammuthis
393–380	Khnemmare Hagor
380	Nepherites II (son)

Thirtieth Dynasty (Sebennytic): 380–343 BC

380–362	Kheperkare Nectanebo I
365–360	Irmaenre Djehor (son)
360–343	Senedjemibre Nectanebo II (nephew)

Thirty-first Dynasty (Persian Kings): 343–332 BC

See Persia: Achaemenid Dynasty

(Macedonian conquest 332 BC)

NOTES

Chronology For a discussion of sources and problems, see the *Cambridge Ancient History*, I: 1, 173–93. Radiocarbon material suggests a date of 3100 BC ±120 years for Horus Aha (Hassan); the reign of Pepi II may be set at 2350–2260 ±25 years on the basis of contemporary evidence (Baer, 'Tentative Chronology'). Middle Kingdom dates rest on an observation of Sothis (Sirius) in the seventh year of Senwosret III (Parker, 180). For the beginning of the New Kingdom, see Wente and Van Siclen; lunar dates support an accession year of 1504 or 1479 for Thutmose III and of 1290 or 1279 for Ramesses II (ibid.). Shoshenq I became king very close to 946; dates are accurate to the year from 690.

Dates, sequence of kings, and lengths of reign for Dynasties I-XX are those of Baer, 'Chronology', adjusted for Dynasty XII as in Murnane, for the Second Intermediate Period as in Beckerath, *Untersuchungen*, and for the New Kingdom as in Wente and Van Siclen. Dynasties XXI-XXVI follow Baer, 'Egyptian Chronology', but cf. Kitchen. For Dynasty XXX, see Johnson.

For New Kingdom relationships, see most recently J. E. Harris and E. F. Wente, *An X-Ray Atlas of the Royal Mummies* (Chicago, 1980), ch. iv.

Calendar and Dating The Egyptian civil year was a vague year of 365 days; the beginning of the solar year, marked by the rising of the star Sothis (Sirius), coincided with the civil new year's day only at the start of a 'Sothic cycle' of 1460 (4 × 365) years. For the restatement of dated Sothic sightings in terms of the Julian calendar, see Parker.

In the Old Kingdom, regnal years were numbered in terms of the biennial cattle count; a reign's fourth count was its eighth year. In Dynasty VI, the count was held more often, so that a 71st occasion is attested for Pepi II (Baer, 'Tentative Chronology'). For dating by regnal year in the Middle Kingdom and afterwards, see A. H. Gardiner, *Egypt of the Pharaohs* (Oxford, 1961), 69–71.

Names and Titles The earliest monarchs had two names, the first identifying them with the sky-god Horus; for some kings only one name is known, while for others the proper pairing is uncertain. In the Old Kingdom there appeared a new royal name, compounded with that of the sun-god Re. By Dynasty XII the title had five standard elements, of which the last two, the throne name or praenomen and the personal name or nomen, are generally used today: the former was preceded by hieroglyphs reading 'king of Upper and Lower Egypt', the latter by the epithet 'son of Re'. See A. H. Gardiner, *Egyptian Grammar* (3rd edn., London, 1957), 71–6.

BIBLIOGRAPHY

Baer, K., 'Egyptian Chronology' (unpublished, 1976); 'Tentative Chronology of the Old Kingdom based on Contemporary Sources' (unpublished, 1979).

Beckerath, J. von, *Handbuch der ägyptischen Königsnamen* (Munich, 1984).

——*Untersuchungen zur politischen Geschichte der zweiten Zwischenzeit in Ägypten* (Glückstadt, 1964).

Cambridge Ancient History, ed. I. E. S. Edwards (3rd edn., 2 vols. in 4 pts., Cambridge, 1970–5).

Hassan, F. A., 'Radiocarbon Chronology of Archaic Egypt', *Journal of Near Eastern Studies*, XXXIX (1980), 203–7.

Johnson, J. H., 'The Demotic Chronicle as an Historical Source', *Enchoria*, IV (1974), 1–17.

Kitchen, K. A., 'On the Princedoms of Late-Libyan Egypt', *Chronique d'Egypte*, LII (1977), 40–8.

Murnane, W. J., *Ancient Egyptian Coregencies* (Chicago, 1977).

Parker, R. A., 'The Sothic Dating of the Twelfth and Eighteenth Dynasties', *Studies in Honor of George R. Hughes* (Chicago, 1976), 177–89.

Traunecker, C., 'Essai sur l'histoire de la XXIXe Dynastie', *Bulletin de l'institut français d'archéologie orientale*, LXXIX (1979), 395–436.

Wente, E. F., and C. C. Van Siclen III, 'A Chronology of the New Kingdom', *Studies in Honor of George R. Hughes* (Chicago, 1976), 217–61. Review by K. A. Kitchen, *Serapis*, IV (1977–8), 65–80.

EARLY MESOPOTAMIA

First Dynasty of Ur: *c*.2563–2387 BC

2563–2524	Mesannepadda
2523–2484	A'annepadda (son)
2483–2448	Meskiagnunna (son)
2447–2423	Elulu
2422–2387	Balulu

Dynasty of Lagash: *c*.2494–2342 BC

2494–2465	Ur-Nanshe
2464–2455	Akurgal (son)
2454–2425	Eannatum (son)
2424–2405	Enannatum I (brother)
2404–2375	Entemena (son)
2374–2365	Enannatum II (son)
2364–2359	Enentarzi
2358–2352	Lugal-anda
2351–2342	Uru-inim-gina

Dynasty of Uruk: *c*.2340–2316 BC

2340–2316	Lugal-zaggesi

Dynasty of Akkad: *c*.2334–2154 BC

2334–2279 (56)	Sargon
2278–2270 (9)	Rimush (son)
2269–2255 (15)	Manishtushu (brother)
2254–2218 (37)	Naram-Suen (son)
2217–2193 (25)	Shar-kali-sharri (son)
2192–2190 (3)	(period of anarchy)
2189–2169 (21)	Dudu
2168–2154 (15)	Shu-Turul

Third Dynasty of Ur: *c*.2112–2004 BC

2112–2095 (18)	Ur-Nammu
2094–2047 (48)	Shulgi (son)
2046–2038 (9)	Amar-Suena (son)
2037–2029 (9)	Shu-Suen (brother)
2028–2004 (25)	Ibbi-Suen (son or brother)

Dynasty of Isin: *c*.2017–1794 BC

2017–1985 (33)	Ishbi-Erra
1984–1975 (10)	Shu-ilishu (son)
1974–1954 (21)	Iddin-Dagan (son)
1953–1935 (19)	Ishme-Dagan (son)
1934–1924 (11)	Lipit-Ishtar (son)
1923–1896 (28)	Ur-Ninurta
1895–1875 (21)	Bur-Ṣin (son)
1874–1870 (5)	Lipit-Enlil (son)
1869–1863 (7)	Erra-imitti
1862–1839 (24)	Enlil-bani

1838–1836 (3)	Zambiya
1835–1832 (4)	Iter-pisha
1831–1828 (4)	Ur-dukuga
1827–1817 (11)	Sin-magir
1816–1794 (23)	Damiq-ilishu (son)

(Conquest by Larsa *c.*1794 BC)

Dynasty of Larsa: *c.*2026–1763 BC

2026–2006 (21)	Naplanum
2005–1978 (28)	Emisum
1977–1943 (35)	Samium
1942–1934 (9)	Zabaya (son)
1933–1907 (27)	Gungunum (brother)
1906–1896 (11)	Abi-sare
1895–1867 (29)	Sumu-el
1866–1851 (16)	Nur-Adad
1850–1844 (7)	Sin-iddinam (son)
1843–1842 (2)	Sin-eribam
1841–1837 (5)	Sin-iqisham (son)
1836 (1)	Silli-Adad
1835–1823 (13)	Warad-Sin
1822–1763 (60)	Rim-Sin (brother)

(Babylonian conquest *c.*1763 BC)

NOTES

Chronology and Dating See, in general, the *Cambridge Ancient History*, I: 1, 193–239. Relative chronology depends on surviving lists of year-names, each year being named after an outstanding event within each reign, and upon the numerous copies, giving years of reign, of the Sumerian king-list. The First Dynasty of Isin began about midway through the last reign of Ur III; absolute chronology for Isin and Larsa rests on synchronisms with the First Dynasty of Babylon.

All dates are approximate. Those of Ur I and Lagash are Sollberger and Kupper's; those of the remaining dynasties follow Brinkman, adjusted for Isin and Larsa as in Stol, ch. i. Reigns are given in whole calendar years, on the accession-year system (see under Babylonia). For a shorter interval between Akkad and Ur III, see *Reallexikon der Assyriologie*, III, 713–14.

Names and Titles The Sumerian city-state rulers prior to the Dynasty of Akkad were styled city-governor or king. The designation 'king of the four regions' was first assumed by Naram-Suen of Akkad; the titles 'king of Ur' and 'king of Sumer and Akkad' were first employed by the monarchs of Ur III. See M.-J. Seux, *Epithètes royales akkadiennes et sumériennes* (Paris, 1967).

BIBLIOGRAPHY

Brinkman, J. A., 'Mesopotamian Chronology of the Historical Period', in A. L. Oppenheim, *Ancient Mesopotamia* (rev. edn., Chicago, 1977), 335–48.

Cambridge Ancient History, ed. I. E. S. Edwards (3rd edn., 2 vols. in 4 pts., Cambridge, 1970–5).

Reallexikon der Assyriologie und vorderasiatischen Archäologie, ed. E. Ebeling *et al.* (6 vols. to date, Berlin, 1928–83).

Sollberger, E., and J.-R. Kupper, *Inscriptions royales sumériennes et akkadiennes* (Paris, 1971).

Stol, M., *Studies in Old Babylonian History* (Leiden, 1976) (*Publications de l'institut historique et archéologique néerlandais de Stamboul*, XL).

ASSYRIA

	Sulili
	Kikkiya
	Akiya
	Puzur-Ashur I
1939–1900 BC	Shalim-ahum (son)
	Ilu-shuma (son)
	Erishum I (son)
	Ikunum (son)
	Sargon I (son)
	Puzur-Ashur II (son)
	Naram-Sin
	Erishum II (son)
1813–1781 (33)	Shamshi-Adad I
1780–1741 (40)	Ishme-Dagan I (son)
	Mut-Ashkur (son)
	Rimush
	Asinum
(6)	Ashur-dugul
	Ashur-apla-idi
	Nasir-Sin
	Sin-namir
	Ipqi-Ishtar
	Adad-salulu
	Adasi
1698–1689 (10)	Belu-bani (son)
1688–1672 (17)	Libaya (son)
1671–1660 (12)	Sharma-Adad I (son)
1659–1648 (12)	Iptar-Sin (son)
1647–1620 (28)	Bazaya (son of Belu-bani)
1619–1614 (6)	Lullaya
1613–1600 (14)	Shu-Ninua (son of Bazaya)
1599–1597 (3)	Sharma-Adad II (son)
1596–1584 (13)	Erishum III (brother)
1583–1578 (6)	Shamshi-Adad II (son)
1577–1562 (16)	Ishme-Dagan II (son)
1561–1546 (16)	Shamshi-Adad III (grandson of Shu-Ninua)
1545–1520 (26)	Ashur-nirari I (son of Ishme-Dagan II)
1519–1496 (24)	Puzur-Ashur III (son)
1495–1483 (13)	Enlil-nasir I (son)
1482–1471 (12)	Nur-ili (son)
1471 (1 m.)	Ashur-shaduni (son)
1470–1451	Ashur-rabi I (son of Enlil-nasir I)
1450–1431	Ashur-nadin-ahhe I (son)
1430–1425 (6)	Enlil-nasir II (brother)
1424–1418 (7)	Ashur-nirari II (brother)
1417–1409 (9)	Ashur-bel-nisheshu (son)
1408–1401 (8)	Ashur-ra'im-nisheshu (brother)
1400–1391 (10)	Ashur-nadin-ahhe II (son)
1390–1364 (27)	Eriba-Adad I (son of Ashur-bel-nisheshu)

1363–1328 (36)	Ashur-uballit I (son)
1327–1318 (10)	Enlil-nirari (son)
1317–1306 (12)	Arik-den-ili (son)
1305–1274 (32)	Adad-nirari I (son)
1273–1244 (30)	Shalmaneser I (son)
1243–1207 (37)	Tukulti-Ninurta I (son)
1206–1203 (4)	Ashur-nadin-apli (son)
1202–1197 (6)	Ashur-nirari III (nephew)
1196–1192 (5)	Enlil-kudurri-usur (son of Tukulti-Ninurta I)
1191–1179 (13)	Ninurta-apil-Ekur (descendant of Eriba-Adad I)
1178–1133 (46)	Ashur-dan I (son)
	Ninurta-tukulti-Ashur (son)
	Mutakkil-Nusku (brother)
1132–1115 (18)	Ashur-resh-ishi I (son)
1114–1076 (39)	Tiglath-Pileser I (son)
1075–1074 (2)	Ashared-apil-Ekur (son)
1073–1056 (18)	Ashur-bel-kala (brother)
1055–1054 (2)	Eriba-Adad II (son)
1053–1050 (4)	Shamshi-Adad IV (son of Tiglath-Pileser I)
1049–1031 (19)	Ashurnasirpal I (son)
1030–1019 (12)	Shalmaneser II (son)
1018–1013 (6)	Ashur-nirari IV (son)
1012–972 (41)	Ashur-rabi II (son of Ashurnasirpal I)
971–967 (5)	Ashur-resh-ishi II (son)
966–935 (32)	Tiglath-Pileser II (son)
934–912 (23)	Ashur-dan II (son)
911–891 (21)	Adad-nirari II (son)
890–884 (7)	Tukulti-Ninurta II (son)
883–859 (25)	Ashurnasirpal II (son)
858–824 (35)	Shalmaneser III (son)
823–811 (13)	Shamshi-Adad V (son)
810–783 (28)	Adad-nirari III (son)
782–773 (10)	Shalmaneser IV (son)
772–755 (18)	Ashur-dan III (brother)
754–745 (10)	Ashur-nirari V (brother)
744–727 (18)	Tiglath-Pileser III
726–722 (5)	Shalmaneser V (son)
721–705 (17)	Sargon II
704–681 (24)	Sennacherib (son)
680–669 (12)	Esarhaddon (son)
668–627 (42)	Ashurbanipal (son)
626–?	Ashur-etil-ilani (son)
	Sin-shumu-lishir
?–612	Sin-shar-ishkun (son of Ashurbanipal)
611–609 (3)	Ashur-uballit II

(Median-Babylonian conquest 609 BC)

NOTES

Chronology Assyrian chronology is the most solidly established of any in the ancient Near East; see the *Cambridge Ancient History*, I: 1, 193–239; I: 2, 740–52. It is based on lists of eponymous officials, serving for one year, and on a king-list which survives in three principal copies; a solar eclipse of 763 BC provides a fixed point. The king-list is largely intact from about 1700 BC, though years of reign are missing for four kings and at variance for six others (Brinkman, 'Comments', 311).

Dates follow the *Cambridge Ancient History* and Brinkman, 'Mesopotamian Chronology'; for Erishum I and Shamshi-Adad I, cf. Oates, ch. ii. The reigns of two twelfth-century kings, Ninurta-tukulti-Ashur and Mutakkil-Nusku, are probably to be reckoned as zero. For the later seventh century, see Reade; for variant relationships, see Brinkman, 'Comments', 312–13.

Names and Titles The earliest Assyrian rulers were styled lieutenants or stewards (of the god Ashur); the title of king is first encountered under Ashur-uballit I. The epithets 'king of the four regions', 'king of kings' and 'great king' came into use slightly later. See J. A. Brinkman, 'Notes on Mesopotamian History in the Thirteenth Century BC', *Bibliotheca Orientalis*, XXVII (1970), 301–14.

BIBLIOGRAPHY

Brinkman, J. A., 'Comments on the Nassouhi Kinglist and the Assyrian Kinglist Tradition', *Orientalia*, new series, XLII (1973), 306–19.
——'Mesopotamian Chronology of the Historical Period', in A. L. Oppenheim, *Ancient Mesopotamia* (rev. edn., Chicago, 1977), 335–48.
Cambridge Ancient History, ed. I. E. S. Edwards (3rd edn., 2 vols. in 4 pts., Cambridge, 1970–5).
Oates, D., *Studies in the Ancient History of Northern Iraq* (London, 1968).
Reade, J., 'The Accession of Sinsharishkun', *Journal of Cuneiform Studies*, XXIII (1970), 1–9.

BABYLONIA

First Dynasty of Babylon (Amorite): *c*.1894–1595 BC

1894–1881 (14)	Sumu-abum
1880–1845 (36)	Sumulael
1844–1831 (14)	Sabium (son)
1830–1813 (18)	Apil-Sin (son)
1812–1793 (20)	Sin-muballit (son)
1792–1750 (43)	Hammurapi (son)
1749–1712 (38)	Samsu-iluna (son)
1711–1684 (28)	Abi-eshuh (son)
1683–1647 (37)	Ammi-ditana (son)
1646–1626 (21)	Ammi-saduqa (son)
1625–1595 (31)	Samsu-ditana (son)

Kassite Dynasty: *c*.1729–1155 BC

1729–1704 (26)	Gandash
1703–1682 (22)	Agum I (son)
1681–1660 (22)	Kashtiliashu I (son?)
	(2 kings: names uncertain)
	Urzigurumash
	Harba-[x]
	(2 kings: names uncertain)
	Burna-Buriash I
	(4 kings: names uncertain)
	Kara-indash
	Kadashman-Harbe I
	Kurigalzu I (son)
1374–1360 (15)	Kadashman-Enlil I
1359–1333 (27)	Burna-Buriash II (son)
1333	Kara-hardash
1333	Nazi-Bugash
1332–1308 (25)	Kurigalzu II (son of Burna-Buriash II)
1307–1282 (26)	Nazi-Maruttash (son)
1281–1264 (18)	Kadashman-Turgu (son)
1263–1255 (9)	Kadashman-Enlil II (son)
1254–1246 (9)	Kudur-Enlil (son?)
1245–1233 (13)	Shagarakti-Shuriash (son)
1232–1225 (8)	Kashtiliashu IV (son)
1225	Tukulti-Ninurta I of Assyria
1224 (1)	Enlil-nadin-shumi
1223 (1)	Kadashman-Harbe II
1222–1217 (6)	Adad-shuma-iddina
1216–1187 (30)	Adad-shuma-usur (son of Kashtiliashu IV)
1186–1172 (15)	Meli-Shipak (son)
1171–1159 (13)	Merodach-Baladan I (son)
1158 (1)	Zababa-shuma-iddina
1157–1155 (3)	Enlil-nadin-ahi (Enlil-shuma-usur)

Second Dynasty of Isin: *c*.1157–1026 BC

1157–1140 (18)	Marduk-kabit-ahheshu
1139–1132 (8)	Itti-Marduk-balatu (son)
1131–1126 (6)	Ninurta-nadin-shumi
1125–1104 (22)	Nebuchadrezzar I (son)
1103–1100 (4)	Enlil-nadin-apli (son)
1099–1082 (18)	Marduk-nadin-ahhe (son of Ninurta-nadin-shumi)
1081–1069 (13)	Marduk-shapik-zeri (son)
1068–1047 (22)	Adad-apla-iddina
1046 (1)	Marduk-ahhe-eriba
1045–1034 (12)	Marduk-zer?-[x]
1033–1026 (8)	Nabu-shumu-libur

Second Dynasty of the Sealand: *c*.1025–1005 BC

1025–1008 (18)	Simbar-Shipak
1008 (5 m.)	Ea-mukin-zeri
1007–1005 (3)	Kashshu-nadin-ahhe

Dynasty of Bazi: *c*.1004–985 BC

1004–988 (17)	Eulmash-shakin-shumi
987–985 (3)	Ninurta-kudurri-usur I
985 (3 m.)	Shirikti-Shuqamuna (brother?)

Dynasty of Elam: *c*.984–979 BC

984–979 (6)	Mar-biti-apla-usur

Undetermined or Mixed Dynasties: *c*.978–732 BC

978–943 (36)	Nabu-mukin-apli
943 (8 m.)	Ninurta-kudurri-usur II (son)
942–?	Mar-biti-ahhe-iddina (brother)
	Shamash-mudammiq
	Nabu-shuma-ukin I
(33+)	Nabu-apla-iddina (son)
(27+)	Marduk-zakir-shumi I (son)
?–813	Marduk-balassu-iqbi (son)
812–?	Baba-aha-iddina
	(interregnum)
	Ninurta-apl?-[x]
	Marduk-bel-zeri
	Marduk-apla-usur
(9+)	Eriba-Marduk
?–748 (13+)	Nabu-shuma-ishkun
747–734 (14)	Nabonassar
733–732 (2)	Nabu-nadin-zeri (son)
732 (1 m.)	Nabu-shuma-ukin II

'*Ninth Dynasty of Babylon*': 731–626 BC

731–729 (3)	Nabu-mukin-zeri
728–727 (2)	Tiglath-Pileser III of Assyria (Pulu)
726–722 (5)	Shalmaneser V of Assyria (Ululayu)
721–710 (12)	Merodach-Baladan II
709–705 (5)	Sargon II of Assyria

704–703 (2)	Sennacherib of Assyria
703 (1 m.)	Marduk-zakir-shumi II
703 (9 m.)	Merodach-Baladan II (again)
702–700 (3)	Bel-ibni
699–694 (6)	Ashur-nadin-shumi (son of Sennacherib)
693 (1)	Nergal-ushezib
692–689 (4)	Mushezib-Marduk
688–681 (8)	Sennacherib of Assyria (again)
680–669 (12)	Esarhaddon of Assyria
668 (1)	Ashurbanipal of Assyria
667–648 (20)	Shamash-shuma-ukin (son of Esarhaddon)
647–627 (21)	Kandalanu
626 (1)	(interregnum)

Neo-Babylonian Dynasty: 625–539 BC

625–605 (21)	Nabopolassar
604–562 (43)	Nebuchadrezzar II (son)
561–560 (2)	Amel-Marduk (son)
559–556 (4)	Neriglissar
556 (3 m.)	Labashi-Marduk (son)
555–539 (17)	{Nabonidus {Belshazzar (son; regent)

(Persian conquest 539 BC)

NOTES

Chronology For a discussion of sources and problems, see the *Cambridge Ancient History*, I: 1, 193–239. Astronomical evidence suggests a date of 1651 or 1595 BC for the end of the First Dynasty (Weir, ch. i); from *c.*1332, dates depend on synchronisms with Assyria (Brinkman, *Materials*, 30–3; *Political History*, 75–6).

The scheme above is that of Brinkman, 'Mesopotamian Chronology'; dates are accurate to the year from Nabonassar. For the 'First Dynasty of the Sealand', here omitted, see ibid., 346–7. Overlapping dates show rival claims.

Calendar and Dating The Babylonians employed a highly accurate lunisolar calendar, with the civil year beginning in the spring (1 Nisannu). This calendar replaced indigenous systems in Assyria, Israel, and Persia, and remained in use under the Seleucids and the Parthians (see below). See E. J. Bickerman, *Chronology of the Ancient World* (2nd edn., Ithaca, 1980), 22–6.

On the accession-year or post-dating system as used in Babylonia, a king's first numbered year began the new year's day, 1 Nisannu, following accession; length of rule was expressed in whole calendar years (Brinkman, *Political History*, 63–7). On the nonaccession-year or ante-dating system, used in Egypt and in Israel at certain periods, the king was in his first year at accession, his second year beginning on the subsequent new year's day.

Names and Titles As the heirs of their Sumerian and Akkadian predecessors, Babylonian monarchs were styled 'king of Ur', 'king of Sumer and Akkad' and 'king of the four regions'; the titles 'king of Babylon' and 'king of Karduniash' (the Kassite name for Babylonia) were also in use. See Brinkman, *Political History*, 123–4.

BIBLIOGRAPHY

Brinkman, J. A., *Materials and Studies for Kassite History, Volume I* (Chicago, 1976).

——'Mesopotamian Chronology of the Historical Period', in A. L. Oppenheim, *Ancient Mesopotamia* (rev. edn., Chicago, 1977), 335–48.

——*A Political History of Post-Kassite Babylonia, 1158–722 BC* (Rome, 1968) (*Analecta Orientalia*, XLIII).

Cambridge Ancient History, ed I. E. S. Edwards (3rd edn., 2 vols. in 4 pts., Cambridge, 1970–5).

Weir, J. D., *The Venus Tablets of Ammizaduga* (Istanbul, 1972) (*Publications de l'institut historique et archéologique néerlandais de Stamboul*, XXIX).

THE HITTITE KINGDOM

Old Kingdom

1650 BC–?	Labarna
	Hattushili I (sister's son)
?–1590	Murshili I (grandson)
1590–?	Hantili I (sister's husband)
	Zidanta I (son-in-law)
	Ammuna (son)
	Huzziya I (son?)
	Telipinu (sister's husband?)
?–1525	Alluwamna (son-in-law?)
	Hantili II (?)
	Zidanta II (?)
	Huzziya II (?)

New Kingdom

1430–1406	Tudhaliya I
1410–1386	Arnuwanda I (son)
1385–1381	Tudhaliya II (son)
1380–1358	Hattushili II (brother)
1357–1323	Shuppiluliuma I (son)
1322	Arnuwanda II (son)
1321–1297	Murshili II (brother)
1296–1271	Muwatalli (son)
1270–1264	Murshili III (son)
1263–1245	Hattushili III (son of Murshili II)
1244–1220	Tudhaliya III (son)
1219–1218	Arnuwanda III (son)
1217–1200	Shuppiluliuma II (brother)

(Destruction of the Hittite kingdom *c.*1200 BC)

NOTES

Chronology All dates are approximate. In the absence of king-lists or documents dated by regnal year, Hittite chronology depends almost wholly on synchronisms with neighbouring countries; dates for Murshili II, however, may be confirmed through astronomical evidence (Sykes, 93–5). Old Kingdom dates are those of Kammenhuber; New Kingdom dates follow Sykes, sec. 3.

The order of the first nine rulers is established, as is the succession of kings from Shuppiluliuma I. Early New Kingdom relationships are in dispute; Güterbock's scheme, given above, is followed by Gurney and Sykes.

BIBLIOGRAPHY

Gurney, O. R., 'The Hittite Line of Kings and Chronology', *Anatolian Studies presented to Hans Gustav Güterbock*, ed. K. Bittel (Istanbul, 1974), 105–11.

Güterbock, H. G., 'Ḫattušili II Once More', *Journal of Cuneiform Studies*, XXV (1973), 100–4.

Kammenhuber, A., 'Die Vorgänger Šuppiluliumas I.', *Orientalia*, new series, XXXIX (1970), 278–301.

Sykes, K. L., 'Assyro-Hittite Foreign Relations, 1450–1200 BC' (uncompleted Ph.D. dissertation, University of Chicago), ch. ii.

THE HEBREW KINGDOMS

United Monarchy of Israel

1020–1010 BC	Saul
1010–970	David
970–931	Solomon (son)

Kingdom of Judah

930–914	Rehoboam (son)
913–911	Abijah (son)
911–871	Asa (son or brother)
871–847	Jehoshaphat (son)
847–841	Jehoram (son; co-regent 853)
841	Ahaziah (son)
841–836	Athaliah (mother)
835–796	Jehoash (son of Ahaziah)
795–767	Amaziah (son; co-regent 798)
766–740	Uzziah (Azariah) (son; co-regent 791)
739–732	Jotham (son; co-regent 750)
730–715	Ahaz (son; co-regent 734)
714–686	Hezekiah (son; co-regent 729)
685–641	Manasseh (son; co-regent 695)
640–639	Amon (son)
639–609	Josiah (son)
609	Jehoahaz (Shallum) (son; deposed)
608–598	Jehoiakim (Eliakim) (brother)
598–597	Jehoiachin (son; deposed)
596–586	Zedekiah (Mattaniah) (son of Josiah; deposed)

(Babylonian conquest 586 BC)

Kingdom of Israel

931–910	Jeroboam I
910–909	Nadab (son)
909–886	Baasha
886–885	Elah (son)
885	Zimri
885–881	Tibni
885–874	Omri (rival king)
874–853	Ahab (son)
853–852	Ahaziah (son; co-regent 855)
852–841	Jehoram (brother)
841–814	Jehu
813–797	Jehoahaz (son)
796–781	Jehoash (son; co-regent 799)
781–754	Jeroboam II (son; co-regent 794)
754–753	Zechariah (son)
753	Shallum
753–742	Menahem

742–741	Pekahiah (son)
740–731	Pekah
731–723	Hoshea (deposed)

(Assyrian conquest 722 BC)

NOTES

Chronology, Calendar, and Dating For the chronological problems, see Gray, 55–75, and Malamat, ch. iii. Modern interpretations of the biblical data presuppose the alternation of ante-dating and post-dating at various points in the history of the Divided Monarchy (see under Babylonia), and are at variance over the beginning of the calendar and regnal year (whether spring or autumn). 'Interregna' in the tables above denote accession-years.

Dates of reign, which are approximate to 609 BC, are those of Gray. For the Assyrian conquest of Israel late in 722, see Hayes and Miller, 433. The first Babylonian capture of Jerusalem took place in March 597 (Malamat, 210); the final fall of the city occurred in July 587 (Andersen) or 586 (Malamat). For further bibliography on the Divided Monarchy, see Hayes and Miller, 678–9.

Names and Titles Uzziah, Jehoahaz (in Judah), Jehoiakim, and Zedekiah are throne names, and the same may be true of David (for Elhanan) and Solomon (for Jedidiah). A. M. Honeyman, 'The Evidence for Regnal Names among the Hebrews', *Journal of Biblical Literature*, LXVII (1948), 13–25.

BIBLIOGRAPHY

Andersen, K. T., 'Die Chronologie der Könige von Israel und Juda', *Studia Theologica*, XXIII (1969), 69–114.

Gray, J., *I and II Kings: a Commentary* (2nd edn., Philadelphia, 1970).

Hayes, J. H., and J. M. Miller, *Israelite and Judaean History* (Philadelphia, 1977).

Malamat, A, ed., *The Age of the Monarchies* (2 vols., Jerusalem, 1979) (*World History of the Jewish People*, first series, IV: 1–2).

THE KINGDOM OF LYDIA

Mermnad Dynasty

680–645	Gyges (son of Dascylus; traditional founder of a new royal dynasty *c*.680 BC)
645–624	Ardys (son)
624–610	Sadyattes (son)
610–560	Alyattes (son)
560–547	Croesus (son; conquest of Lydia by Cyrus the Great of Persia *c*.547 BC)

NOTES

Chronology Dates are approximate. The traditional year of Gyges' death, 652, can be lowered on the basis of Assyrian evidence. On the date of the Persian conquest, see J. Cargill, *American Journal of Ancient History*, II (1977), 97–116.

BIBLIOGRAPHY

Pedley, J. G., *Sardis in the Age of Croesus* (Norman, Okla., 1968).

Spalinger, A. J., 'The Date of the Death of Gyges and its Historical Implications', *Journal of the American Oriental Society*, XCVIII (1978), 400–9.

THE PERSIAN EMPIRE

Achaemenid Dynasty

559–530	Cyrus the Great (fourth in descent from Achaemenes; king of Anshan *c.*559 BC; conquered Media 550)
529–522	Cambyses (son)
522	Smerdis (Bardiya) (brother)
521–486	Darius I, the Great (fifth in descent from Achaemenes)
485–465	Xerxes I (son)
464–424	Artaxerxes I, Longimanus (son)
424	Xerxes II (son)
424	Sogdianus (brother)
423–405	Darius II, Nothus (brother)
404–359	Artaxerxes II, Mnemon (son)
358–338	Artaxerxes III (Ochus) (son)
337–336	Arses (son)
335–330	Darius III (Codomannus) (great-grandson of Darius II; Macedonian conquest of the Persian empire 330)

NOTES

Chronology From Cambyses, reigns are given in whole calendar years, on the post-dating system which the Persians adopted from Babylonia. The traditional genealogy of Cyrus and Darius I presents problems; see Cook, 8–10.

Names and Titles The standard Achaemenid title in inscriptions was 'king of the lands' (*Reallexikon der Assyriologie*, IV, 356); the Assyrian titles 'great king' and 'king of kings' were also in use. For throne names, see Cook, 133.

BIBLIOGRAPHY

Cambridge History of Iran, Volume II, ed. I. Gershevitch (Cambridge, 1985).
Cook, J. M., *The Persian Empire* (London, 1983).

II

The Hellenistic World

THE KINGDOM OF MACEDONIA

Temenid Dynasty

c.650–?	Perdiccas I (descendant of Temenus; traditional founder of Macedonian royal house *c*.650 BC)
	Argaeus I (son)
	Philip I (son)
	Aëropus I (son)
	Alcetas (son)
?–495	Amyntas I (son)
495–452	Alexander I (son)
452–413	Perdiccas II (son)
413–399	Archelaus (son)
399–397	Orestes (son)
397–394	Aëropus II (son of Perdiccas II)
394–393	Amyntas II (grandson of Alexander I)
394–393	Pausanias (son of Aëropus II; rival king)
393–385	Amyntas III (great-grandson of Alexander I; deposed)
385–383	Argaeus II (son of Archelaus; deposed)
383–370	Amyntas III (restored)
370–368	Alexander II (son)
368–365	Ptolemy of Alorus (son of Amyntas II; regent)
365–359	Perdiccas III (son of Amyntas III)
359–336	Philip II (brother)
336–323	Alexander III, the Great (son; conquered Egypt 332; Babylonia 331; Persia 330)
323–317	Philip III (Arrhidaeus) (brother)
317–309	Alexander IV (son of Alexander III: interregnum 309–306)

Antigonid Dynasty

306–301	Antigonus I, the One-eyed (strategos of Asia 321; claimed the empire of Alexander the Great)

Dynasty of Cassander

305–297	Cassander (son of Antipater, strategos of Europe; claimed Macedonia)
297	Philip IV (son)
297–294	Alexander V (brother)
297–294	Antipater I (brother; deposed, died 287)

Antigonid Dynasty

294–287	Demetrius I, the Besieger (son of Antigonus I; co-regent 306; deposed, died 283)
287–285	Pyrrhus of Epirus (deposed)
285–281	Lysimachus (satrap of Thrace 323; king 305)
281–279	Ptolemy Ceraunus (son of Ptolemy I of Egypt)
279	Meleager (brother; deposed)
279	Antipater II, Etesias (nephew of Cassander; deposed)
279–277	Sosthenes (strategos only)
277–239	Antigonus II, Gonatas (son of Demetrius I; deposed by Pyrrhus of Epirus 274–272)

239–229	Demetrius II (son)
227–221	Antigonus III, Doson (grandson of Demetrius I; regent 229–227)
221–179	Philip V (son of Demetrius II)
179–168	Perseus (son; deposed, died 162; Roman conquest of Macedonia)

NOTES

Chronology Dates and relationships down to Philip II, many of which are uncertain, follow Hammond and Griffith; but for Argaeus II, see J. R. Ellis, *Makedonika*, IX (1969), 1–8. Some third-century dates may vary by a year; for Demetrius I, cf. Shear, 98–100, and Habicht, 60. From Cassander, the dates given are those of *de facto* rule in Macedonia.

Names and Titles Before Cassander, who assumed the royal title of *basileus* in 305/4, the monarch was known simply by his personal name. See Hammond, II, 387–8, with references.

BIBLIOGRAPHY

Habicht, C., *Untersuchungen zur politischen Geschichte Athens im 3. Jahrhundert v. Chr.* (Munich, 1979).
Hammond, N. G. L., *et al.*, *A History of Macedonia* (3 vols., Oxford, 1972–88).
Shear, T. L., Jr., *Kallias of Sphettos and the Revolt of Athens in 286 BC* (Princeton, 1978) (*Hesperia*, supplement XVII).
Walbank, F. W., *A Historical Commentary on Polybius* (3 vols., Oxford, 1957–79).

THE KINGDOM OF SYRACUSE

Tyrants of Gela

505–498	Cleander (son of Pantares; tyrant of Gela after fall of the oligarchy 505 BC)
498–491	Hippocrates (brother)

Tyrants of Syracuse

491–478	Gelon I (son of Deinomenes; tyrant of Gela 491; captured Syracuse 485)
478–466	Hiero I (brother; Gela 485)
466–465	Thrasybulus (brother; deposed; democratic rule 465–405)
405–367	Dionysius I
367–357	Dionysius II (son; deposed)
357–354	Dion (son-in-law of Dionysius I)
354–353	Callippus (deposed, died 351)
353–351	Hipparinus (son of Dionysius I)
351–347	Nysaeus (brother; deposed)
347–344	Dionysius II (restored; deposed)
344–337	Timoleon (abdicated; democratic rule 337–317)

Kings of Syracuse

317–289	Agathocles (assumed the title of king 304; democratic rule 289–270)
270–215	Hiero II
?–216	Gelon II (son; co-regent)
215–214	Hieronymus (son; Roman siege and capture of Syracuse 213–212)

NOTES

Chronology The dates of the early tyrants follow Miller, 59–64; for Dionysius I and his successors, see Beloch, III: 2, ch. xxxv; for Hiero II, Walbank, I, 54–5. Olympiad years have been rounded off to the nearest Julian equivalents.

Names and Titles The word *tyrannos* meant simply an unconstitutional ruler, and was not an official designation; Dionysius I and his successors had the title *strategos autocrator*, or general with supreme power.

BIBLIOGRAPHY

Beloch, K. J., *Griechische Geschichte* (2nd edn., 4 vols. in 8 pts., Strassburg and Berlin, 1912–27).

Miller, M., *The Sicilian Colony Dates* (Albany, NY, 1970) (*Studies in Chronography*, I).

Walbank, F. W., *A Historical Commentary on Polybius* (3 vols., Oxford, 1957–79).

THE PTOLEMAIC DYNASTY

323–282	Ptolemy I, Soter (son of Lagus; satrap of Egypt 323 BC; assumed the title of king 305)
282–246	Ptolemy II, Philadelphus (son; co-regent 284)
246–222	Ptolemy III, Euergetes (son)
222–204	Ptolemy IV, Philopator (son)
204–180	Ptolemy V, Epiphanes (son; co-regent 210)
180–145	Ptolemy VI, Philometor (son; deposed 164–163)
145	Ptolemy VII, Neos Philopator (son; co-regent 145)
145–116	Ptolemy VIII, Euergetes II (Physcon) (son of Ptolemy V; co-regent 170–164; sole king 164–163)
116–107	Ptolemy IX, Soter II (Lathyrus) (son; deposed)
107–88	Ptolemy X, Alexander I (brother)
88–80	Ptolemy IX, Soter II (restored)
80	Ptolemy XI, Alexander II (son of Ptolemy X)
80–51	Ptolemy XII, Neos Dionysus (Auletes) (son of Ptolemy IX; in exile 58–55)
51–47	Ptolemy XIII, Philopator (son)
51–30	Cleopatra Philopator (sister)
47–44	Ptolemy XIV, Philopator (brother)
36–30	Ptolemy XV Caesar, Philopator Philometor (Caesarion) (son of Cleopatra and Julius Caesar; Roman rule 30 BC)

NOTES

Chronology and Dating Dates follow Samuel, *Ptolemaic Chronology*. For the possible concealment of Philopator's death and delayed accession of Epiphanes, see ibid., 108–14; Walbank, II, 435–7. Dates for Caesarion follow Samuel, 'Joint Regency'; cf. Pestman, 82. For additional works on Ptolemaic chronology see H. Heinen, *Bibliotheca Orientalis*, XXVII (1970), 209–10.

In Macedonian usage, the regnal year began with the actual accession day; Greek scribes dated the reign of Soter from the death of Alexander the Great. Egyptian scribes equated the regnal with the calendar year; as in pharaonic Egypt, the king was in his first numbered year at accession. See Samuel, *Ptolemaic Chronology*, ch. i.

Names and Titles The title of *basileus* was followed by the name and honorary epithet(s); for the latter, see A. D. Nock, 'Notes on Ruler-Cult, I–IV', *Journal of Hellenic Studies*, XLVIII (1928), 21–43.

BIBLIOGRAPHY

Pestman, P. W., *Chronologie égyptienne d'après les textes démotiques (332 av. J.-C.–453 ap. J.-C.)* (Leiden, 1967).

Samuel, A. E., *Ptolemaic Chronology* (Munich, 1962) (*Münchener Beiträge zur Papyrusforschung und antiken Rechtsgeschichte*, XLIII).

——'The Joint Regency of Cleopatra and Caesarion', *Etudes de papyrologie*, IX (1971), 73–9.

Walbank, F. W., *A Historical Commentary on Polybius* (3 vols., Oxford, 1957–79).

THE SELEUCID DYNASTY

312–281	Seleucus I, Nicator (satrap of Babylonia 321 BC; dated his reign from 312; assumed the title of king 305)
281–261	Antiochus I, Soter (son; co-regent 292)
280–267	Seleucus (son; co-regent)
261–246	Antiochus II, Theos (brother; co-regent 266)
246–226	Seleucus II, Callinicus (son)
226–223	Seleucus III, Soter (Ceraunus) (son)
223–187	Antiochus III, the Great (brother)
210–193	Antiochus (son; co-regent)
187–175	Seleucus IV, Philopator (brother; co-regent 189)
175–170	Antiochus (son; co-regent)
175–164	Antiochus IV, Epiphanes (son of Antiochus III)
164–162	Antiochus V, Eupator (son; co-regent 165)
162–150	Demetrius I, Soter (son of Seleucus IV)
150–145	Alexander I, Theopator Euergetes (Balas) (pretended son of Antiochus IV)
145–142	Antiochus VI, Epiphanes Dionysus (son)
145–139	Demetrius II, Nicator (son of Demetrius I; deposed)
142–138	Tryphon (Diodotus) (usurper)
139–129	Antiochus VII, Euergetes (Sidetes) (son of Demetrius I)
129–125	Demetrius II (restored)
128–122	Alexander II (Zabinas) (pretended son of Alexander I)
125–120	Cleopatra Thea (daughter of Ptolemy VI of Egypt)
125	Seleucus V (son of Cleopatra and Demetrius II)
125–96	Antiochus VIII, Philometor (Grypus) (brother)
113–95	Antiochus IX, Philopator (Cyzicenus) (son of Cleopatra and Antiochus VII)
96–95	Seleucus VI, Epiphanes Nicator (son of Antiochus VIII)
95–88	Demetrius III, Philopator Soter (Eucaerus) (brother; deposed)
95–83	Antiochus X, Eusebes Philopator (son of Antiochus IX; deposed)
95	Antiochus XI, Epiphanes Philadelphus (son of Antiochus VIII)
95–83	Philip I, Epiphanes Philadelphus (brother)
87–84	Antiochus XII, Dionysus (brother)
83–69	Tigranes the Great (king of Armenia *c*.95–55; deposed)
69–64	Philip II (son of Philip I; deposed)
69–64	Antiochus XIII, Philadelphus (Asiaticus) (son of Antiochus X; deposed; Roman rule of Syria 64 BC)

NOTES

Chronology, Calendar, and Dating For the bases of Seleucid chronology, see Schürer, I, 126–36; for cuneiform evidence, of particular importance down to Antiochus IV, see Parker and Dubberstein. Much of the dynasty's later history is obscure; for the last two kings, see Vérilhac and Dagron, 241–2. Where only the Seleucid year is known, it has been rounded off to its nearest Julian equivalent.

The accession of the dynasty's founder was the starting-point for the Seleucid era. In the Macedonian calendar, this began in autumn 312 BC; in the Babylonian calendar, it ran from the following spring (1 Nisannu). The coinage was dated by the Macedonian count. The Seleucid era was borrowed by the Parthians (see below), by the authors of I and II Maccabees, and by Josephus. Le Rider, ch. ii; A. E. Samuel, *Greek and Roman Chronology: Calendars and Years in Classical Antiquity* (Munich, 1972), 245–6.

Names and Titles The title of *basileus* was followed by the name and honorary epithet(s), as in Ptolemaic Egypt. For Antiochus 'the Great', see E. R. Bevan, *Journal of Hellenic Studies*, XXII (1902), 241–4.

BIBLIOGRAPHY

Le Rider, G., *Suse sous les Séleucides et les Parthes: les trouvailles monétaires et l'histoire de la ville* (Paris, 1965).

Parker, R. A., and W. H. Dubberstein, *Babylonian Chronology, 626 BC–AD 75* (Providence, 1956).

Schürer, E., *History of the Jewish People in the Age of Jesus Christ* (rev. edn., 3 vols. in 4 pts., Edinburgh, 1973–87).

Vérilhac, A.-M., and G. Dagron, 'Une nouvelle inscription du temple de Zeus à Diocésarée Uzuncaburç (Cilicie)', *Revue des études anciennes*, LXXVI (1974), 237–42.

BITHYNIA AND PONTUS

328–280	Zipoites (autonomous dynast of Bithynia *c.*328 BC; assumed the title of king 297)
280–250	Nicomedes I (son)
250–230	Ziaelas (son)
230–182	Prusias I (son)
182–149	Prusias II (son)
149–127	Nicomedes II, Epiphanes (son)
127–94	Nicomedes III, Euergetes (son)
94–74	Nicomedes IV, Philopator (son; bequeathed the kingdom to the Roman People)

Mithridatid Dynasty

302–266	Mithridates I (nephew of Mithridates of Cius; autonomous dynast of Pontus *c.*302 BC; king 281)
266–256	Ariobarzanes (son)
256–220	Mithridates II (son)
220–185	Mithridates III (son)
185–159	Pharnaces I (son)
159–150	Mithridates IV, Philopator Philadelphus (brother)
150–120	Mithridates V, Euergetes (son of Pharnaces I)
120–63	Mithridates VI, Eupator (son)
63–47	Pharnaces II (son; king of Bosporus only; Roman rule of Pontus 63 BC)

NOTES

Chronology Dates for Pontus down to *c.*120 BC, and for Bithynia down to *c.*94, are approximate.

BIBLIOGRAPHY

Magie, D., *Roman Rule in Asia Minor to the End of the Third Century after Christ* (2 vols., Princeton, 1950).

Perl, G., 'Zur Chronologie der Königreiche Bithynia, Pontos und Bosporos', *Studien zur Geschichte und Philosophie des Altertums*, ed. J. Harmatta (Amsterdam, 1968), 299–330.

PERGAMUM: THE ATTALIDS

Dynasts of Pergamum

283–263	Philetaerus (son of Attalus of Tieum; autonomous dynast following revolt 283 BC)
263–241	Eumenes I (nephew)

Kingdom of Pergamum

241–197	Attalus I, Soter (grandnephew of Philetaerus; assumed the title of king 238/7)
197–159	Eumenes II, Philadelphus (son)
159–138	Attalus II, Philadelphus (brother; co-regent 160)
138–133	Attalus III, Philometor Euergetes (son of Eumenes II; bequeathed the kingdom to the Roman People)

BIBLIOGRAPHY

Allen, R. E., *The Attalid Kingdom: a Constitutional History* (Oxford, 1983).
Hansen, E. V., *The Attalids of Pergamon* (2nd edn., Ithaca, 1971).

THE PARTHIAN EMPIRE

Arsacid Dynasty

247–211	Arsaces I (king or chief of the Parni *c*.247 BC; conquered Parthia *c*.238)
211–191	Arsaces II (son)
191–176	Priapatius (son)
176–171	Phraates I (son)
171–138	Mithridates I (brother)
138–128	Phraates II (son)
128–123	Artabanus I (son of Priapatius)
123–87	Mithridates II, the Great (son)
90–80	Gotarzes I
80–77	Orodes I
77–70	Sinatruces
70–57	Phraates III (son)
57–54	Mithridates III (son)
57–38	Orodes II (brother)
38–2	Phraates IV (son)
2–AD 4	Phraates V (son)
4–7	Orodes III
7–12	Vonones I (son of Phraates IV)
12–38	Artabanus II
38–51	Gotarzes II (son)
39–45	Vardanes I (brother)
51	Vonones II
51–78	Vologases I (son)
55–58	Vardanes II (son)
77–80	Vologases II
80–81	Artabanus III
78–105	Pacorus
105–147	Vologases III
109–129	Osroes
129–147	Mithridates IV
147–191	Vologases IV
191–208	Vologases V
208–222	Vologases VI (son)
213–224	Artabanus IV (brother; Sasanid conquest of the Parthian empire 224)

NOTES

Chronology, Calendar, and Dating Dates are approximate. Names and lineage of the earliest kings follow the *Cambridge History of Iran*, ch. viii; for a different reconstruction, cf. chs. ii, xix. On the much-debated 'dark age' from *c*.90 to 57, cf. Mørkholm, with references.

The Arsacid coinage, a major historical source, is dated by the Macedonian Seleucid era (Le Rider, ch. ii). An Arsacid era was also in use, which probably ran from the beginning of the dynasty; in the Babylonian calendar, its starting-point was spring (1 Nisannu) 247 (ibid., 36).

Names and Titles The Parthian monarchs used the oriental titles 'great king' and 'king of kings'. Most coins bear the dynastic name Arsaces instead of the ruler's personal name (Sellwood).

BIBLIOGRAPHY

Cambridge History of Iran, Volume III, ed. E. Yarshater (2 pts., Cambridge, 1983).

Le Rider, G., *Suse sous les Séleucides et les Parthes: les trouvailles monétaires et l'histoire de la ville* (Paris, 1965).

Mørkholm, O., 'The Parthian Coinage of Seleucia on the Tigris, *c.*90–55 BC', *Numismatic Chronicle*, CXL (1980), 33–47.

Sellwood, D. G., *An Introduction to the Coinage of Parthia* (London, 1971).

THE HASMONAEAN DYNASTY

Hasmonaean Dynasty

166–160	Judas Maccabaeus (son of Mattathias the Hasmonaean; led Jewish revolt against Seleucid rule 166 BC)
160–143	Jonathan (brother; high priest 152; deposed, died 142)
143–135	Simon (brother; ethnarch 140)
135–104	Hyrcanus I (John) (son)
104–103	Aristobulus I (Judas) (son; king)
103–76	Alexander Jannaeus (Jonathan) (brother)
76–67	Alexandra (Salome) (widow)
67	Hyrcanus II (John) (son; high priest only 76; deposed)
67–63	Aristobulus II (Judas) (brother; deposed, died 49)
63–40	Hyrcanus II (restored; high priest only 63; ethnarch 47; deposed, died 30)
40–37	Antigonus (Mattathias) (son of Aristobulus II; Herodian conquest of Judaea 37 BC)

NOTES

Chronology and Dating The chief sources for early Hasmonaean history, I and II Maccabees, are dated by the Seleucid era. The first book employs both the Macedonian and Babylonian reckonings; the second book is dated by the Babylonian count (Jepsen and Hanhart, 55–84; Mørkholm, 160–1). Dates down to Simon follow Bunge, ch. x; later dates are those of Schürer.

Names and Titles The later Hasmonaeans had both Greek and Hebrew names; Jannaeus (Iannaios) is a Hellenization of Yannai, short for Jonathan. The title of high priest was hereditary from 140, that of king (except for the restored Hyrcanus II) from 104. Schürer, I, 216–17.

BIBLIOGRAPHY

Bunge, J., *Untersuchungen zum zweiten Makkabäerbuch* (Bonn, 1971).

Jepsen, A., and R. Hanhart, *Untersuchungen zur israelitisch-jüdischen Chronologie* (Berlin, 1964).

Mørkholm, O., *Antiochus IV of Syria* (Copenhagen, 1966).

Schürer, E., *History of the Jewish People in the Age of Jesus Christ* (rev. edn., 3 vols. in 4 pts., Edinburgh, 1973–87).

III

The Roman and Byzantine Worlds

THE ROMAN EMPIRE

The Julio-Claudian Emperors

27 BC–AD 14	Augustus (C. Julius Caesar Octavianus) (son of C. Octavius; maternal grandson of Julia, sister of C. Julius Caesar)
14–37	Tiberius (Ti. Claudius Nero) (son of Livia, later married to Augustus, and Ti. Claudius Nero)
37–41	Caligula (C. Caesar) (grandnephew; maternal grandson of Julia, daughter of Augustus)
41–54	Claudius (Ti. Claudius Drusus) (uncle; maternal grandson of Octavia, sister of Augustus)
54–68	Nero (Nero Claudius Caesar) (son of Agrippina, sister of Caligula, and Cn. Domitius Ahenobarbus)
68–69	Galba (Ser. Sulpicius Galba)
69	Otho (M. Salvius Otho)
69	Vitellius (A. Vitellius)

The Flavian Emperors

69–79	Vespasian (T. Flavius Vespasianus)
79–81	Titus (T. Flavius Vespasianus) (son)
81–96	Domitian (T. Flavius Domitianus) (brother)

The Five Good Emperors

96–98	Nerva (M. Cocceius Nerva)
98–117	Trajan (M. Ulpius Trajanus)
117–138	Hadrian (P. Aelius Hadrianus)
138–161	Antoninus Pius (T. Aurelius Fulvus Boionius Arrius Antoninus)
161–169	Lucius Verus (L. Aurelius Verus)
161–180	Marcus Aurelius (M. Aurelius Antoninus)
180–192	Commodus (M. Aurelius Commodus Antoninus) (son; co-regent 177)
193	Pertinax (P. Helvius Pertinax)
193	Didius Julianus (M. Didius Severus Julianus)

The Severi

193–211	Septimius Severus (L. Septimius Severus)
211	Geta (L. or P. Septimius Geta) (son; co-regent 209)
211–217	Caracalla (M. Aurelius Antoninus) (brother; co-regent 198)
217–218	Macrinus (M. Opellius Macrinus)
218	Diadumenian (M. Opellius Diadumenianus) (son; co-regent)
218–222	Elagabalus (M. Aurelius Antoninus) (maternal grandson of Julia Maesa, sister-in-law of Septimius Severus)
222–235	Severus Alexander (M. Aurelius Alexander) (maternal grandson of Julia Maesa)

The Soldier-Emperors

235–238	Maximinus the Thracian (C. Julius Verus Maximinus)
238	Gordian I (M. Antonius Gordianus Sempronianus) Gordian II (M. Antonius Gordianus Sempronianus) (son)
238	Balbinus (D. Caelius Calvinus Balbinus) Pupienus Maximus (M. Clodius Pupienus Maximus)

238–244	Gordian III (M. Antonius Gordianus) (maternal grandson of Gordian I)
244–249	Philip I, the Arabian (M. Julius Philippus)
247–249	Philip II (M. Julius Severus Philippus) (son)
249–251	Decius (C. Messius Quintus Decius)
251	Herennius Etruscus (Q. Herennius Etruscus Messius Decius) (son; co-regent)
251	Hostilian (C. Valens Hostilianus Messius Quintus) (brother; co-regent with Trebonianus Gallus)
251–253	Trebonianus Gallus (C. Vibius Trebonianus Gallus)
251–253	Volusian (C. Vibius Afinius Gallus Veldumnianus Volusianus) (son)
253	Aemilian (M. Aemilius Aemilianus)
253–260	Valerian (P. Licinius Valerianus) (deposed)
253–268	Gallienus (P. Licinius Egnatius Gallienus) (son)
260	Saloninus (P. Licinius Cornelius Saloninus Valerianus) (son)
268–270	Claudius II, Gothicus (M. Aurelius Claudius)
270	Quintillus (M. Aurelius Quintillus) (brother)
270–275	Aurelian (L. Domitius Aurelianus)
275–276	Tacitus (M. Claudius Tacitus)
276	Florian (M. Annius Florianus)
276–282	Probus (M. Aurelius Probus)
282–283	Carus (M. Aurelius Carus)
283–284	Numerian (M. Aurelius Numerianus) (son)
283–285	Carinus (M. Aurelius Carinus) (brother; co-regent 283)

The 'Gallic Empire'

260–269	Postumus (M. Cassianius Latinius Postumus)
269	Laelian (Ulpius Cornelius Laelianus)
269	Marius (M. Aurelius Marius)
269–271	Victorinus (M. Piavonius Victorinus)
271–274	Tetricus (C. Pius Esuvius Tetricus) (deposed)

Diocletian and the Tetrarchy

284–305	Diocletian (C. Aurelius Valerius Diocletianus) (abdicated, died 311)
286–305	Maximian (M. Aurelius Valerius Maximianus) (Caesar 285; abdicated; resumed the title of Augustus 307–8, 309–10)
305–306	Constantius I, Chlorus (Fl. Valerius Constantius) (Caesar 293)
305–311	Galerius (C. Galerius Valerius Maximianus) (Caesar 293)
306–307	Severus (Fl. Valerius Severus) (Caesar 305; deposed, died 307)
307–312	Maxentius (M. Aurelius Valerius Maxentius) (son of Maximian)

Dynasty of Constantine

307–337	Constantine I, the Great (Fl. Valerius Constantinus) (son of Constantius I; Caesar 306)
308–324	Licinius (Valerius Licinianus Licinius) (deposed, died 325)
310–313	Maximinus II (Galerius Valerius Maximinus) (son of Galerius' sister; Caesar 305)

316–317	Valerius Valens (C. Aurelius Valerius Valens)
324	Martinian (M. Martinianus) (deposed, died 325)
337–340	Constantine II (Fl. Claudius Constantinus) (son of Constantine I)
337–350	Constans (Fl. Julius Constans) (brother)
337–361	Constantius II (Fl. Julius Constantius) (brother)
350–353	Magnentius (Fl. Magnus Magnentius)
360–363	Julian the Apostate (Fl. Claudius Julianus) (nephew of Constantine I)
363–364	Jovian (Fl. Jovianus)

Dynasty of Valentinian

364–375	Valentinian I (Fl. Valentinianus)
364–378	Valens (Fl. Valens) (brother)
375–383	Gratian (Fl. Gratianus) (son of Valentinian I; co-regent 367)
375–392	Valentinian II (Fl. Valentinianus) (brother)

Dynasty of Theodosius

379–395	Theodosius I, the Great (Fl. Theodosius)
383–388	Maximus (Magnus Maximus)
387–388	Victor (Fl. Victor) (son)
392–394	Eugenius (Fl. Eugenius)

Western Roman Emperors

395–423	Honorius (Fl. Honorius) (son of Theodosius I; co-regent 393)
421	Constantius III (Fl. Constantius)
423–425	John (Johannes)
425–455	Valentinian III (Fl. Placidus Valentinianus) (son of Constantius III; maternal grandson of Theodosius I)
455	Petronius Maximus
455–456	Avitus (Eparchius Avitus) (deposed, died 456)
457–461	Majorian (Julius Valerius Majorianus)
461–465	Libius Severus
467–472	Anthemius (Procopius Anthemius)
472	Olybrius (Anicius Olybrius)
473–474	Glycerius (deposed)
474–480	Julius Nepos
475–476	Romulus Augustus (deposed; end of direct imperial rule in the west 476/80)

NOTES

Chronology For Geta's death in December 211, see T. D. Barnes, *Journal of Theological Studies*, new series, XIX (1968), 522–4; for the date of Valerian's capture, *Aufstieg und Niedergang*, 818–20. Dates for the 'Gallic Empire' follow ibid., 853–1012; other regional usurpers and pretenders are omitted.

Calendar and Dating For the Julian year of 365 days, with an intercalary day every fourth year, see A. E. Samuel, *Greek and Roman Chronology: Calendars and Years in Classical Antiquity* (Munich, 1972), 155–8. Under Augustus, the Egyptian vague year was synchronized with the Julian year, so that the Egyptian new year's day, 1 Thoth, fell on 29 August. Ibid., 177.

Roman emperors numbered not their regnal years, but their years of tribunician power (*tribunicia potestas*); this was renewed annually, either on the anniversary of its first conferment, or on a fixed date. H. Mattingly, '"Tribunicia Potestate"', *Journal of Roman Studies*, XX (1930), 78–91. Egyptian materials are dated by regnal years, beginning 29 August (see above).

Names and Titles As many emperors changed their names on adoption or accession, or both, it has not been possible to present them in a fully consistent manner. The names given are relatively familiar forms, and do not include elements of the imperial style: Nero Claudius Caesar rather than L. Domitius Ahenobarbus, M. Ulpius Trajanus and not Imp. Caesar Nerva Trajanus Augustus. For details on nomenclature, see the biographical articles in *Paulys Realencyclopädie*.

The style was complex, and included both 'republican' and 'imperial' elements; the basic title of emperor was Imperator Caesar [name] Augustus. See M. Hammond, 'Imperial Elements in the Formula of the Roman Emperors during the First Two and a Half Centuries of the Empire', *Memoirs of the American Academy in Rome*, XXV (1957), 17–64. Co-regents with full powers had the title of Augustus; rulers denoted above as Caesars were junior partners in Diocletian's tetrarchic system.

Latin praenomina

A.: Aulus	M.: Marcus
C.: Gaius	P.: Publius
Cn.: Gnaeus	Q.: Quintus
D.: Decimus	Ser.: Servius
Fl.: Flavius	T.: Titus
L.: Lucius	Ti.: Tiberius

BIBLIOGRAPHY

Aufstieg und Niedergang der römischen Welt, ed. H. Temporini and W. Haase, II: *Principat*, pt. 2 (Berlin, 1975).

Barnes, T. D., *The New Empire of Diocletian and Constantine* (Cambridge, Mass., 1982).

Mattingly, H. *et al.*, eds., *The Roman Imperial Coinage* (9 vols. in 12 pts., London, 1926–84).

Paulys Realencyclopädie der classischen Altertumswissenschaft, ed. G. Wissowa *et al.* (49 vols. in 83 pts., Stuttgart and Munich, 1893–1978).

Schwartz, J., 'Chronologie du IIIe s. p. C.', *Zeitschrift für Papyrologie und Epigraphik*, XXIV (1977), 167–77.

THE KINGDOM OF NUMIDIA

Dynasty of Masinissa

203–148	Masinissa (son of Gaia, chief of the Massyli; king of Numidia under Roman protection 203 BC)
148–140	Gulussa (son)
148–140	Mastanabal (brother)
148–118	Micipsa (brother)
118–116	Hiempsal I (son)
118–112	Adherbal (brother)
118–105	Jugurtha (son of Mastanabal; deposed, died 104)
105–?	Gauda (brother)
88–60	Hiempsal II (son)
60–46	Juba I (son; Roman rule 46 BC)

Kingdom of Mauretania

25–AD 23	Juba II (son; king of Mauretania under Roman protection 25 BC)
23–40	Ptolemy (son; maternal grandson of Cleopatra and Mark Antony; Roman rule AD 40)

NOTES

Chronology Some dates may vary by a year or so; Hiempsal II's are approximate.

Names and Titles Masinissa, not Massinissa: Gsell, III, 178.

BIBLIOGRAPHY

Gsell, S., *Histoire ancienne de l'Afrique du Nord* (8 vols., Paris, 1914–28).
Mazard, J., *Corpus nummorum Numidiae Mauretaniaeque* (Paris, 1955).

THE HERODIAN KINGDOMS

Herodian Dynasty

37–4 BC	Herod the Great (son of Antipater; king of Judaea under Roman protection; captured Jerusalem 37)
4 BC–AD 6	Herod Archelaus (son; ethnarch of Judaea, Idumaea, and Samaria; deposed; Roman rule 6–41)
4 BC–AD 34	Philip (brother; tetrarch of Auranitis, Batanaea, Trachonitis, Gaulanitis, and Paneas)
4 BC–AD 39	Herod Antipas (brother; tetrarch of Galilee and Peraea; deposed)
37–44	Agrippa I (M. Julius Agrippa) (nephew; king of Philip's lands 37; given Antipas' lands 40; king of Judaea 41; Roman rule 44)
41–48	Herod (brother; king of Chalcis)
49–92	Agrippa II (M. Julius Agrippa) (son of Agrippa I; king of Chalcis 49; exchanged it for Philip's lands 53; Roman rule 92/3)

NOTES

Chronology Herod the Great died in December 5 BC (Barnes) or March/April 4 BC (Schürer, I, 326–8), after the birth of Jesus according to Matthew 2:1. Filmer's date of 1 BC for the monarch's demise is improbable. For Agrippa II see Smallwood, appendix F.

Names and Titles For the use of Herod as a dynastic name, see H. W. Hoehner, *Herod Antipas* (Cambridge, 1972), 105–9.

BIBLIOGRAPHY

Barnes, T. D., 'The Date of Herod's Death', *Journal of Theological Studies*, new series, XIX (1968), 204–9.

Filmer, W. E., 'The Chronology of the Reign of Herod the Great', *Journal of Theological Studies*, new series, XVII (1966), 283–98.

Schürer, E., *History of the Jewish People in the Age of Jesus Christ* (rev. edn., 3 vols. in 4 pts., Edinburgh, 1973–87).

Smallwood, E. M., *The Jews under Roman Rule: from Pompey to Diocletian* (Leiden, 1976).

PERSIA: THE SASANIDS

Sasanid Dynasty

224–241	Ardashīr I (son or descendant of Sāsān; king of Persis; conquered Iran 224)
241–272	Shāpūr I (son; co-regent 240)
272–273	Hormizd I (son)
273–276	Bahrām I (brother)
276–293	Bahrām II (son)
293	Bahrām III (son; deposed)
293–302	Narseh (son of Shāpūr I)
302–309	Hormizd II (son)
309–379	Shāpūr II (son)
379–383	Ardashīr II (nephew; deposed)
383–388	Shāpūr III (son of Shāpūr II)
388–399	Bahrām IV (son)
399–420	Yazdgard I (son)
420–438	Bahrām V, the Wild Ass (son)
438–457	Yazdgard II (son)
457–459	Hormizd III (son)
459–484	Pērōz (brother)
484–488	Balāsh (brother; deposed)
488–497	Kavād I (son of Pērōz; deposed)
497–499	Zāmāsp (brother; deposed)
499–531	Kavād I (restored)
531–579	Khusrau I, Anūshīrvān (son)
579–590	Hormizd IV (son; deposed)
590–591	Bahrām VI, Chōbīn (usurper; deposed)
590–628	Khusrau II, the Victorious (son of Hormizd IV; deposed, died 628)
628	Kavād II, Shīroe (son)
628–630	Ardashīr III (son)
630	Shahrbarāz (usurper)
630–631	Bōrān (daughter of Khusrau II)
631–632	Āzarmēdukht (sister; pretenders and rival kings in various parts of the empire)
632–651	Yazdgard III (nephew; Arab conquest of the Sasanid empire 651)

NOTES

Chronology, Calendar, and Dating The basic treatment of Sasanid chronology is still that of Nöldeke, 400–36. The Persian civil year was a vague year of 365 days. Reigns were dated from the new year's day prior to accession; before Khusrau I, who became king late in 531, actual accession dates are unknown (Altheim and Stiehl, tables 1–12). For the co-regency of Shāpūr I, see Henrichs and Koenen, 125–32; for the last kings, cf. M. I. Mochiri, *Numismatic Chronicle*, CXLIII (1983), 221–3.

Names and Titles Like their Arsacid predecessors, the Sasanid monarchs used the oriental title 'king of kings' (*shāhānshāh*). For titles on the coinage, see Altheim and Stiehl, ch. ii.

BIBLIOGRAPHY

Altheim, F., and R. Stiehl, *Ein asiatischer Staat: Feudalismus unter den Sasaniden und ihren Nachbarn* (Wiesbaden, 1954).

Cameron, A., 'Agathias on the Sassanians', *Dumbarton Oaks Papers*, XXIII–XXIV (1969–70), 67–183.

Henrichs, A., and L. Koenen, 'Ein griechischer Mani-Codex', *Zeitschrift für Papyrologie und Epigraphik*, V (1970), 97–216.

Nöldeke, T., tr., *Geschichte der Perser und Araber zur Zeit der Sasaniden aus der arabischen Chronik des Ṭabarī* (Leiden, 1879).

THE EASTERN ROMAN EMPIRE

Dynasty of Theodosius

395–408	Arcadius (Fl. Arcadius) (son of the Roman emperor Theodosius I; co-regent 383)
408–450	Theodosius II (Fl. Theodosius) (son; co-regent 402)
450–457	Marcian (married Pulcheria, daughter of Arcadius)

Dynasty of Leo

457–474	Leo I, the Thracian
474	Leo II (son of Ariadne, daughter of Leo I, and Zeno the Isaurian; co-regent 473)
474–475	Zeno the Isaurian (co-regent 474; deposed)
475–476	Basiliscus
476–491	Zeno (restored)
491–518	Anastasius I (second husband of Ariadne)

Dynasty of Justin

518–527	Justin I
527–565	Justinian I, the Great (sister's son; co-regent 527)
565–578	Justin II (sister's son)
578–582	Tiberius II Constantine (co-regent 578)
582–602	Maurice (co-regent 582)
602–610	Phocas

Dynasty of Heraclius

610–641	Heraclius
641	Constantine III (son; co-regent 613)
641	Heraclonas (brother; co-regent 638; deposed)
641–668	Constans II, Pogonatus (son of Constantine III; co-regent 641)
668–685	Constantine IV (son; co-regent 654)
685–695	Justinian II, Rhinotmetus (son; deposed)
695–698	Leontius (deposed, died 706?)
698–705	Tiberius III (Apsimar) (deposed, died 706?)
705–711	Justinian II (restored)
711–713	Philippicus (Bardanes) (deposed)
713–715	Anastasius II (Artemius) (deposed, died 719)
715–717	Theodosius III (deposed)

Isaurian Dynasty

717–741	Leo III, the Isaurian
741	Constantine V, Copronymus (son; co-regent 720; deposed)
741–743	Artavasdus (deposed)
743–775	Constantine V (restored)
775–780	Leo IV, the Khazar (son; co-regent 751)
780–797	Constantine VI (son; co-regent 776; deposed)
797–802	Irene (mother; co-regent 780–90, 792–7; deposed, died 803)
802–811	Nicephorus I
811	Stauracius (son; co-regent 803; deposed, died 812)

811–813	Michael I Rangabè (deposed, died 844)
813–820	Leo V, the Armenian

Amorian Dynasty

820–829	Michael II, the Amorian
829–842	Theophilus (son; co-regent 821)
842–867	Michael III, the Drunkard (son; co-regent 840)

Macedonian Dynasty

867–886	Basil I, the Macedonian (co-regent 866)
886–912	Leo VI, the Wise (son; co-regent 870)
912–913	Alexander (brother; co-regent 879)
913–959	Constantine VII, Porphyrogenitus (son of Leo VI; co-regent 908)
920–944	Romanus I Lecapenus (deposed, died 948)
921–931	Christopher (son)
959–963	Romanus II (son of Constantine VII; co-regent 945)
963–969	Nicephorus II Phocas
969–976	John I Tzimisces
976–1025	Basil II, Bulgaroctonus (son of Romanus II; co-regent 960)
1025–1028	Constantine VIII (brother; co-regent 962)
1028–1034	Romanus III Argyrus (married Zoë, daughter of Constantine VIII)
1034–1041	Michael IV, the Paphlagonian (second husband of Zoë)
1041–1042	Michael V, Calaphates (sister's son; deposed)
1042	Zoë (daughter of Constantine VIII; co-regent 1028–50) and Theodora (sister)
1042–1055	Constantine IX Monomachus (third husband of Zoë)
1055–1056	Theodora (again; co-regent 1042)
1056–1057	Michael VI, Stratioticus (deposed)
1057–1059	Isaac I Comnenus (abdicated, died 1060)

Ducas Dynasty

1059–1067	Constantine X Ducas
1067–1068	Eudocia Macrembolitissa (widow)
1068–1071	Romanus IV Diogenes (second husband; deposed, died 1072)
1071	Eudocia (again; deposed)
1071–1078	Michael VII, Parapinaces (son of Eudocia and Constantine X; co-regent 1060; deposed)
1078–1081	Nicephorus III Botaniates (deposed)

Comnenian Dynasty

1081–1118	Alexius I Comnenus (nephew of Isaac I)
1118–1143	John II (son; co-regent 1092)
1143–1180	Manuel I (son)
1180–1183	Alexius II (son)
1183–1185	Andronicus I (grandson of Alexius I; co-regent 1183)

Angelus Dynasty

1185–1195	Isaac II Angelus (deposed)
1195–1203	Alexius III (brother; deposed)
1203–1204	Isaac II (restored)
1203–1204	Alexius IV (son; deposed, died 1204)
1204	Alexius V Ducas, Murtzuphlus (deposed, died 1204)

Lascarid Dynasty

1204–1222	Theodore I Lascaris (despot only 1204–8)
1222–1254	John III Vatatzes
1254–1258	Theodore II Lascaris (son of Irene, daughter of Theodore I, and John III)
1258–1261	John IV (son; deposed, died 1305?)

Palaeologan Dynasty

1261–1282	Michael VIII Palaeologus (co-regent 1259)
1282–1328	Andronicus II (son; co-regent 1272; deposed, died 1332)
1294–1320	Michael IX (son)
1328–1341	Andronicus III (son; co-regent 1325)
1341–1376	John V (son; deposed)
1347–1354	John VI Cantacuzenus (deposed, died 1383)
1353–1357	Matthew (son; deposed, died 1383)
1376–1379	Andronicus IV (son of John V; deposed, died 1385)
1379–1390	John V (restored; deposed)
1390	John VII (son of Andronicus IV; deposed)
1390–1391	John V (restored)
1391–1425	Manuel II (son; co-regent 1373)
1399–1408	John VII (restored)
1425–1448	John VIII (son of Manuel II; co-regent 1421)
1448–1453	Constantine XI, Dragases (brother; Turkish capture of Constantinople 1453)

NOTES

Calendar and Dating Dating in the eastern empire was from the creation of the world; the most widespread eras were the Alexandrian, which began in 5492 BC, and the Byzantine, which ran from 5508 (Grumel, chs. vi, viii). The Julian civil year started on 1 September.

Names and Titles From Heraclius, the imperial title was the Greek *basileus*; from the early ninth century, this was used with the epithet 'of the Romans' (Ostrogorsky, 106, 198–9). Family names follow the number directly; sobriquets follow a comma.

BIBLIOGRAPHY

Bellinger, A. R., and P. Grierson, eds., *Catalogue of the Byzantine Coins in the Dumbarton Oaks Collection and in the Whittemore Collection* (3 vols. in 5 pts., Washington, DC, 1966–73).

Grierson, P., 'The Tombs and Obits of the Byzantine Emperors (337–1042)', *Dumbarton Oaks Papers*, XVI (1962), 1–63.

Grumel, V., *La chronologie* (Paris, 1958) (*Traité d'études byzantines*, ed. P. Lemerle, I).

Cambridge Medieval History, Volume IV: the Byzantine Empire, ed. J. M. Hussey (2 pts., Cambridge, 1966–7).

Ostrogorsky, G., *History of the Byzantine State* (rev. edn., New Brunswick, NJ, 1969).

THE KINGDOM OF ARMENIA

Bagratid Dynasty

884–890	Ashot I, the Great (prince of princes of Armenia 863; crowned king 884)
890–914	Smbat I, the Martyr (son)
914–928	Ashot II, the Iron (son)
928–952	Abas (brother)
952–977	Ashot III, the Merciful (son)
977–989	Smbat II, the Conqueror (son)
989–1020	Gagik I (brother)
1020–1041	John Smbat III (son)
1021–1040	Ashot IV, the Valiant (brother)
1041–1045	Gagik II (son; deposed, died 1080?; Byzantine, then Seljuqid rule)

Kingdom of Kars

962–984	Musheḷ (son of Abas; received the appanage of Kars *c*.962)
984–1029	Abas I (son)
1029–1064	Gagik Abas II (son; deposed, died 1080?; Byzantine, then Seljuqid rule)

Kingdom of Loṛi

980–989	Gurgēn I (son of Ashot III; received the appanage of Loṛi *c*.980)
989–1048	David the Landless (son)
1048–1089	Gurgēn II (Kiurike) (son; Seljuqid rule of Loṛi, 1089/1100 or later)

NOTES

Chronology and Calendar Some dates may vary by a year or so depending on the source; those given above follow Grousset. Armenia used a vague year; the starting-point of the Armenian era was 11 July 552.

The Bagratid dynasty can be traced as far back as the fourth century, and reigned in Georgia as late as the beginning of the nineteenth. For all of its branches and possessions in the Caucasus, consult C. Toumanoff, *Manuel de généalogie et de chronologie pour l'histoire de la Caucasie chrétienne* (Rome, 1976).

BIBLIOGRAPHY

Grousset, R., *Histoire de l'Arménie des origines á 1071* (Paris, 1947).

Hakobian, V., 'La date de l'avènement d'Ašot, premier roi bagratide', *Revue des études arméniennes*, new series, II (1965), 273–82.

THE EMPIRE OF THESSALONICA

House of Montferrat – Kingdom of Thessalonica

1204–1207	Boniface (marquis of Montferrat as Boniface I; captured Thessalonica 1204)
1207–1224	Demetrius (son; deposed, died 1230)

Angelus Dynasty – Empire of Thessalonica

1224–1230	Theodore (captured Thessalonica 1224; crowned emperor 1225; deposed)
1230–1237	Manuel (brother; deposed, died 1241)
1237–1244	John (son of Theodore; despot only 1242)
1244–1246	Demetrius (brother; despot only; deposed; Byzantine capture of Thessalonica)

NOTES

Chronology Coronation of Theodore: A. Karpozilos, *Byzantina*, VI (1974), 251–61.

BIBLIOGRAPHY

Longnon, J., *L'empire latin de Constantinople* (Paris, 1949).
Nicol, D. M., *The Despotate of Epiros* (Cambridge, 1984).

THE EMPIRE OF TREBIZOND

Comnenian Dynasty

1204–1222	Alexius I (grandson of Andronicus I, East Roman emperor; captured Trebizond 1204)
1222–1235	Andronicus I, Gidos (son-in-law)
1235–1238	John I, Axouchos (son of Alexius I)
1238–1263	Manuel I (brother)
1263–1266	Andronicus II (son)
1266–1280	George (brother; deposed)
1280–1284	John II (brother; deposed)
1284–1285	Theodora (sister; deposed)
1285–1297	John II (restored)
1297–1330	Alexius II (son)
1330–1332	Andronicus III (son)
1332	Manuel II (son; deposed, died 1333)
1332–1340	Basil (son of Alexius II)
1340–1341	Irene Palaeologina (widow; deposed)
1341	Anna Anachoutlou (daughter of Alexius II; deposed)
1341	Michael (son of John II; deposed)
1341–1342	Anna (restored)
1342–1344	John III (son of Michael; deposed, died 1362)
1344–1349	Michael (restored; deposed)
1349–1390	Alexius III (son of Basil)
1390–1417	Manuel III (son)
1417–1429	Alexius IV (son)
1429–1458	John IV, Calojoannes (son)
1458–1461	David (brother; deposed, died 1463; Turkish capture of Trebizond)

BIBLIOGRAPHY

Janssens, E., *Trébizonde en Colchide* (Brussels, 1969).

Kuršanskis, M., 'L'usurpation de Théodora Grande Comnène', *Revue des études byzantines*, XXXIII (1975), 187–210.

IV

The Barbarian West

THE VISIGOTHIC KINGDOM

395–410	Alaric I (elected king or chieftain of the Visigoths in Thrace 395)
410–415	Athaulf (brother-in-law)
415	Sigeric
415–418	Wallia
418–451	Theoderic I (son-in-law of Alaric I)
451–453	Thorismund (son)
453–466	Theoderic II (brother)
466–484	Euric (brother)
484–507	Alaric II (son)
507–511	Gesalic (son)
511–531	Amalaric (brother)
531–548	Theudis
548–549	Theudigisel
549–555	Agila I
555–567	Athanagild
567–572	Liuva I (Septimania 568)
568–586	Leovigild (brother; Spain 568; sole king 572)
586–601	Reccared I (son)
601–603	Liuva II (son)
603–610	Witteric
610–612	Gundemar
612–621	Sisebut
621	Reccared II (son)
621–631	Suinthila (deposed)
631–636	Sisenand
636–639	Chintila
639–642	Tulga (son; deposed)
642–653	Chindasuinth
653–672	Reccesuinth (son; co-regent 649)
672–680	Wamba (deposed)
680–687	Erwig
687–702	Egica (son-in-law)
702–710	Wittiza (son; co-regent 698)
710–711	Roderic
711–714	Agila II (son of Wittiza?; Muslim conquest of Visigothic Spain 714)

BIBLIOGRAPHY

Miles, G. C., *Coinage of the Visigoths of Spain* (New York, 1952).

Sánchez-Albornoz, C., 'El senatus visigodo: Don Rodrigo, rey legítimo de España', *Cuadernos de historia de España*, VI (1946), 5–99.

Thompson, E. A., 'The Visigoths from Fritigern to Euric', *Historia*, XII (1963), 105–26.

Zeumer, K., 'Die Chronologie der Westgothenkönige des Reiches von Toledo', *Neues Archiv der Gesellschaft fur ältere deutsche Geschichtskunde*, XXVII (1902), 409–44.

THE VANDAL KINGDOM

Hasding House

439–477	Geiseric (invaded north Africa 429; dated his reign from his capture of Carthage 439)
477–484	Huneric (son)
484–496	Gunthamund (nephew)
496–523	Thrasamund (brother)
523–530	Hilderic (son of Huneric; deposed, died 533)
530–533	Gelimer (nephew of Thrasamund; deposed; Byzantine conquest of the Vandal kingdom)

BIBLIOGRAPHY

Courtois, C., *Les Vandales et l'Afrique* (Paris, 1955).
Schmidt, L., *Geschichte der Wandalen* (2nd edn., Munich, 1942).

THE FRANKISH KINGDOM

Merovingian House

460–482	Childeric I (son of Merovech; chief or king of the Salian Franks of Tournai *c*.460)
482–511	Chlodovech (Clovis) I (son)
511–524	Chlodomer (son; king of Orléans)
511–533	Theuderic I (brother; Reims)
511–558	Childebert I (brother; Paris)
511–561	Chlothar I (brother; Soissons; sole king 558)
533–547	Theudebert I (son of Theuderic I; Reims)
547–555	Theudebald (son; Reims)
561–567	Charibert I (son of Chlothar I; Paris)
561–575	Sigebert I (brother; Reims (Austrasia))
561–584	Chilperic I (brother; Soissons (Neustria))
561–593	Guntramn (brother; Burgundy)
575–596	Childebert II (son of Sigebert I; Austrasia; Burgundy 593)
584–629	Chlothar II (son of Chilperic I; Neustria; sole king 613)
596–612	Theudebert II (son of Childebert II; Austrasia; deposed, died 612)
596–613	Theuderic II (brother; Burgundy; Austrasia 612)
613	Sigebert II (son; Austrasia and Burgundy)
629–639	Dagobert I (son of Chlothar II; Austrasia 623; sole king 632)
630–632	Charibert II (brother; Aquitaine)
639–656	St Sigebert III (son of Dagobert I: Austrasia 634)
639–657	Chlodovech II (brother; Neustria and Burgundy)
656–661	Childebert (adopted son of Sigebert III; Austrasia)
657–673	Chlothar III (son of Chlodovech II; Neustria and Burgundy)
662–675	Childeric II (brother; Austrasia; sole king 673)
676–679	St Dagobert II (son of Sigebert III: Austrasia)
676–690	Theuderic III (son of Chlodovech II; Neustria and Burgundy; sole king 679)
690–694	Chlodovech III (son)
694–711	Childebert III (brother)
711–715	Dagobert III (son)
715–721	Chilperic II (son of Childeric II?)
717–719	Chlothar IV (son of Theuderic III?; rival king; Austrasia)
721–737	Theuderic IV (son of Dagobert III; interregnum 737–43)
743–751	Childeric III (probable son; deposed; start of Carolingian rule)

NOTES

Chronology Some dates may vary by a year. For the period from 561 to 596, see Eckhardt, 57–71; for Childebert the Adoptive, see Ewig. Childeric III was deposed either in November 751 (Tangl), or at the turn of the year 751/2 (Levison, 51–3). For additional references, see R. Schneider, *Königswahl und Königserhebung im Frühmittelalter* (Stuttgart, 1972), 66.

Names and Titles The Merovingian royal title, inherited by the Carolingian rulers, was 'king of the Franks' (*rex Francorum*). For this, and for royal style in the other barbarian kingdoms, see H. Wolfram, *Intitulatio, I: Lateinische Königs- und Fürstentitel bis zum Ende des 8. Jahrhunderts* (Graz, 1967), chs. ii–iii.

BIBLIOGRAPHY

Eckhardt, W. A., 'Die Decretio Childeberti und ihre Überlieferung', *Zeitschrift der Savigny-Stiftung für Rechtsgeschichte*, Germanistische Abteilung, LXXXIV (1967), 1–71.

Ewig, E., 'Noch einmal zum "Staatsstreich" Grimoalds', *Speculum Historiale*, ed. C. Bauer (Munich, 1965), 454–7.

Krusch, B., 'Chronologica regum Francorum stirpis Merowingicae', *Monumenta Germaniae historica: Scriptorum rerum Merovingicarum*, VII (Hanover, 1920), 468–516.

Levison, W., 'Das Nekrologium von Dom Racine und die Chronologie der Merowinger', *Neues Archiv der Gesellschaft für ältere deutsche Geschichtskunde*, XXXV (1910), 15–53.

Tangl, M., 'Die Epoche Pippins', *Neues Archiv der Gesellschaft für ältere deutsche Geschichtskunde*, XXXIX (1914), 257–77.

THE OSTROGOTHIC KINGDOM

Amal House

493–526	Theoderic the Great (invaded Italy 489; recognized as king 493)
526–534	Athalaric (maternal grandson)
534–536	Theodahad (son of Theoderic's sister)
536–540	Witigis (married a sister of Athalaric; deposed, died 542)
540–541	Ildibad
541	Eraric
541–552	Totila (Baduila) (nephew of Ildibad)
552	Teias (Byzantine conquest of the Ostrogothic kingdom in Italy 552)

BIBLIOGRAPHY

Romano, G., and A. Solmi, *Le dominazioni barbariche in Italia (395–888)* (Milan, 1940) (*Storia politica d'Italia*, V).

Stein, E., *Histoire du Bas-Empire* (2 vols. in 3 pts., Amsterdam, 1968).

THE LOMBARD KINGDOM

569–572	Alboin (invaded Italy 568; dated his reign from his capture of Milan 569)
572–574	Cleph (interregnum 574–84)
584–590	Authari (son; married Theudelinda, daughter of Garibald, duke of Bavaria)
590–616	Agilulf (second husband of Theudelinda)
616–626	Adaloald (son; co-regent 604)
626–636	Arioald (married Gundiperga, daughter of Agilulf)
636–652	Rothari (second husband of Gundiperga)
652–653	Rodoald (son)
653–661	Aripert I (nephew of Theudelinda)
661–662	Godepert (son)
662–671	Grimoald (son-in-law of Aripert I)
671	Garibald (son; deposed)
671–688	Perctarit (son of Aripert I)
688–700	Cunipert (son; co-regent 680)
700–701	Liutpert (son; deposed, died 702)
701	Raginpert (son of Godepert)
701–712	Aripert II (son)
712	Ansprand
712–744	Liutprand (son)
744	Hildeprand (nephew; co-regent 735; deposed)
744–749	Ratchis (deposed)
749–756	Aistulf (brother)
756–757	Ratchis (restored; deposed)
757–774	Desiderius (deposed with his son Adalgis, co-regent since 759; Frankish conquest of the Lombard kingdom)

BIBLIOGRAPHY

Bethmann, L., and O. Holder-Egger, 'Langobardische Regesten', *Neues Archiv der Gesellschaft für ältere deutsche Geschichtskunde*, III (1878), 225–318.

Romano, G., and A. Solmi, *Le dominazioni barbariche in Italia (395–888)* (Milan, 1940) (*Storia politica d'Italia*, V).

THE ANGLO-SAXON KINGDOMS

Kingdom of Kent

455–488	Hengest (son of Wihtgils; traditional founder of Kentish royal house)
488–512	Oisc (son)
512–522	Octa (son)
522–560	Eormenric (son)
560–616	Aethelbert I (son)
616–640	Eadbald (son)
640–664	Earconbert (son)
664–673	Egbert I (son)
673–685	Hlothere (brother)
685–686	Eadric (son of Egbert I; West Saxon rule 686–8)
688–690	Oswine (great-grandson of Eadbald?)
689–694	Swaefhard (son of Sebbi, king of Essex)
690–725	Wihtred (son of Egbert I)
725–748	Aethelbert II (son)
748–762	Eadberht I (brother)
762–764	Sigered
764–770	Heaberht
765–784	Egbert II
784–785	Ealhmund (Mercian rule, 785–96)
796–798	Eadberht II (deposed)
798–807	Cuthred (brother of Cenwulf, king of Mercia; Mercian rule 807–23)
823–825	Baldred (deposed; West Saxon annexation of Kent 825 or 827)

Kingdom of Bernicia

547–559	Ida (son of Eoppa; traditional founder of Bernician royal house)
559–560	Glappa
560–568	Adda (son of Ida)
568–572	Aethelric (brother)
572–579	Theoderic (brother)
579–585	Frithuwald
585–592	Hussa

Kingdom of Deira

569–599	Aelle (son of Yffi; traditional founder of Deiran royal house)
599–604	Aethelric

Kingdom of Northumbria

592–616	Aethelfrith (son of Aethelric of Bernicia; unified Bernicia and Deira 604)
616–633	Edwin (son of Aelle)
633–634	Osric (nephew of Aelle; Deira)
633–634	Eanfrith (son of Aethelfrith; Bernicia)
634–642	St Oswald (brother)
642–670	Oswiu (brother)
644–651	St Oswine (son of Osric; Deira)
651–655	Aethelwald (son of Oswald; Deira)

670–685	Ecgfrith (son of Oswiu)
686–705	Aldfrith (brother)
705–706	Eadwulf I
706–716	Osred I (son of Aldfrith)
716–718	Cenred (sixth in descent from Ida)
718–729	Osric (son of Aldfrith)
729–737	Ceolwulf (brother of Cenred; abdicated, died 760)
737–758	Eadberht (sixth in descent from Ida; abdicated, died 768)
758–759	Oswulf (son)
759–765	Aethelwald (deposed)
765–774	Alhred (sixth in descent from Ida; deposed)
774–779	Aethelred I (son of Aethelwald; deposed)
779–788	Aelfwald I (son of Oswulf)
788–790	Osred II (son of Alhred; deposed, died 792)
790–796	Aethelred I (restored)
796	Osbald (deposed, died 799)
796–808	Eardwulf (deposed)
808	Aelfwald II
808–809	Eardwulf (restored)
809–841	Eanred (son)
841–844	Aethelred II (son; deposed)
844	Redwulf
844–848	Aethelred II (restored)
848–866	Osbert (deposed, died 867)
866–867	Aelle
867–873	Egbert I
873–876	Ricsige
876–878	Egbert II
878–913	Eadwulf II
913–927	Aldred (son; deposed; Danish conquest of Deira 867; West Saxon annexation of Bernicia 927)

Kingdom of Mercia

633–655	Penda (son of Pybba; probable founder of Mercian royal house; Northumbrian rule, 655–8)
658–675	Wulfhere (son)
675–704	Aethelred I (brother; abdicated, died 716)
704–709	Cenred (son of Wulfhere; abdicated)
709–716	Ceolred (son of Aethelred I)
716–757	Aethelbald (great-grandson of Pybba)
757	Beornred (deposed, died 769)
757–796	Offa (fifth in descent from Pybba)
796	Ecgfrith (son; co-regent 787)
796–821	Cenwulf (seventh in descent from Pybba)
821–823	Ceolwulf I (brother; deposed)
823–825	Beornwulf
825–827	Ludeca
827–840	Wiglaf (deposed; restored; West Saxon rule 829–30)
840–852	Berhtwulf
852–874	Burgred (deposed)
874–879	Ceolwulf II
879–911	Aethelred II

911–918	Aethelflaed (widow)
918–919	Aelfwyn (daughter; deposed; West Saxon annexation of Mercia)

Kingdom of Wessex

519–534	Cerdic (son of Elesa; traditional founder of West Saxon royal house)
534–560	Cynric (son)
560–591	Ceawlin (son; deposed, died 593)
591–597	Ceol (nephew)
597–611	Ceolwulf (brother)
611–642	Cynegils (son)
642–672	Cenwalh (son)
672–674	Seaxburh (widow)
674–676	Aescwine (fifth in descent from Cynric)
676–685	Centwine (son of Cynegils)
685–688	Caedwalla (fourth in descent from Ceawlin; abdicated, died 689)
688–726	Ine (fifth in descent from Ceawlin; abdicated)
726–740	Aethelheard
740–756	Cuthred
756–757	Sigeberht
757–786	Cynewulf
786–802	Berhtric
802–839	Egbert (ninth in descent from Ceawlin; overlord of all the English kingdoms 829–30)

NOTES

Chronology Most years of reign are those of Fryde. Many early dates and lineages, and later Kentish and Northumbrian dates, are uncertain. Some minor, ill-attested Kentish kings have been omitted. For dating problems in the sources, see K. Harrison, *The Framework of Anglo-Saxon History to AD 900* (Cambridge, 1976).

BIBLIOGRAPHY

Davies, W., 'Annals and the Origin of Mercia', *Mercian Studies*, ed. A. Dornier (Leicester, 1977), 17–29.

Fryde, E. B., ed., *Handbook of British Chronology* (3rd edn., London, 1986).

Miller, M., 'The Dates of Deira', *Anglo-Saxon England 8*, ed. P. Clemoes (Cambridge, 1979), 35–61.

Pagan, H. E., 'Northumbrian Numismatic Chronology in the Ninth Century', *British Numismatic Journal*, XXXVIII (1969), 1–15.

Yorke, B., 'Joint Kingship in Kent, *c.*560–785', *Archaeologia Cantiana*, XCIX (1983), 1–19.

V

Europe

1 THE BRITISH ISLES

THE KINGDOM OF ENGLAND

House of Wessex

802–839	Egbert (king of Wessex 802; annexed Kent 825; overlord of all the English kingdoms 829–30)
839–858	Aethelwulf (son; Kent only 856–8)
856–860	Aethelbald (son; Wessex)
858–865	Aethelbert (brother; Kent 858–60)
865–871	Aethelred I (brother)
871–899	Alfred the Great (brother)
899–924	Edward the Elder (son)
924	Aelfweard (son)
924–939	Aethelstan (brother)
939–946	Edmund I (brother)
946–955	Eadred (brother)
955–959	Eadwig (son of Edmund I; Wessex only 957–9)
957–975	Edgar the Peaceful (brother; Mercia and Northumbria 957–9)
975–978	St Edward the Martyr (son)
978–1016	Aethelred II, the Unready (brother; deposed by Swein Forkbeard 1013–14)
1016	Edmund II, Ironside (son)

House of Denmark

1016–1035	Cnut the Great (son of Swein Forkbeard)
1037–1040	Harold I, Harefoot (son; regent 1035–7)
1040–1042	Harthacnut (brother)

House of Wessex

1042–1066	St Edward the Confessor (son of Aethelred II)
1066	Harold II (son of Godwin, earl of Wessex)

House of Normandy

1066–1087	William I, the Conqueror
1087–1100	William II, Rufus (son)
1100–1135	Henry I (brother)

House of Blois

1135–1154	Stephen (son of Adela, daughter of William I, and Stephen, count of Blois)

House of Plantagenet

1154–1189	Henry II (son of Matilda, daughter of Henry I, and Geoffrey IV, count of Anjou)
1170–1183	Henry (son; co-regent)
1189–1199	Richard I, Coeur-de-Lion (brother)
1199–1216	John (brother)

1216–1272	Henry III (son)
1272–1307	Edward I (son)
1307–1327	Edward II (son; deposed, died 1327)
1327–1377	Edward III (son)
1377–1399	Richard II (grandson; deposed, died 1400)

House of Lancaster

1399–1413	Henry IV (duke of Lancaster; grandson of Edward III)
1413–1422	Henry V (son)
1422–1461, 1470–1471	Henry VI (son; deposed; restored; deposed, died 1471)

House of York

1461–1470, 1471–1483	Edward IV (duke of York; fourth in descent from Edward III; deposed; restored)
1483	Edward V (son; deposed, died 1483)
1483–1485	Richard III (brother of Edward IV)

House of Tudor

1485–1509	Henry VII (son of Margaret, fourth in descent from Edward III, and Edmund Tudor, earl of Richmond)
1509–1547	Henry VIII (son)
1547–1553	Edward VI (son)

House of Suffolk

1553	Jane (daughter of Frances, maternal granddaughter of Henry VII, and Henry, duke of Suffolk; deposed, died 1554)

House of Tudor

1553–1558	Mary I (daughter of Henry VIII; married Philip II of Spain, king consort 1554–8)
1558–1603	Elizabeth I (sister)

House of Stuart

1603–1625	James I (maternal grandson of James V of Scotland, maternal grandson of Henry VII)
1625–1649	Charles I (son)

Commonwealth and Protectorate

1649–1653	Commonwealth
1653–1658	Oliver Cromwell, Lord Protector
1658–1659	Richard Cromwell, Lord Protector (son; abdicated, died 1712)
1659–1660	Commonwealth

House of Stuart

1660–1685	Charles II (son of Charles I)
1685–1688	James II (brother; Scotland 1685–9; deposed, died 1701)

House of Orange

1689–1702	William III (son of Mary, daughter of Charles I, and William II, prince of Orange)
1689–1695	Mary II (daughter of James II; married William III)

House of Stuart

1702–1714	Anne (sister)

House of Hanover

1714–1727	George I (son of Sophia, maternal granddaughter of James I, and Ernest Augustus, elector of Hanover)
1727–1760	George II (son)
1760–1820	George III (grandson)
1820–1830	George IV (son; regent 1811–20)
1830–1837	William IV (brother)
1837–1901	Victoria (niece)

House of Saxe-Coburg-Gotha (Windsor from 1917)

1901–1910	Edward VII (son of Victoria and Albert of Saxe-Coburg-Gotha, prince consort 1857–61)
1910–1936	George V (son)
1936	Edward VIII (son; abdicated, died 1972)
1936–1952	George VI (brother)
1952–	Elizabeth II (daughter)

NOTES

Calendar Until 1752, England used the Julian year beginning 25 March, rather than the Gregorian year starting 1 January; William III was proclaimed on 13 February, 1688 in contemporary terms, but on 23 February, 1689 in modern reckoning. Historians today use either the present calendar throughout, or the Julian month and day with the Gregorian year. See Cheney, 10–11.

Names and Titles Under John, the title 'king of England' (*rex Anglie*) replaced that of 'king of the English' (*rex Anglorum*); the term Great Britain was in use from 1707. The United Kingdom of Great Britain and Ireland was proclaimed in 1801. From 1876 to 1948, the monarch was styled emperor or empress of India; the United Kingdom of Great Britain and Northern Ireland was proclaimed in May 1953. See Fryde, 29f.

BIBLIOGRAPHY

Cheney, C. R., ed., *Handbook of Dates for Students of English History* (London, 1961).

Fryde, E. B., ed., *Handbook of British Chronology* (3rd edn., London, 1986).

THE KINGDOM OF SCOTLAND

House of Alpin

842–858	Kenneth I (son of Alpin; king of Dalriada in western Scotia *c*.840; conquered Pictavia *c*.842)
858–862	Donald I (brother)
862–876	Constantine I (son of Kenneth I)
876–878	Aed (brother)
878–889	Giric (son of Dúngal) and ?Eochaid (maternal grandson of Kenneth I)
889–900	Donald II (son of Constantine I)
900–943	Constantine II (son of Aed; abdicated, died 952)
943–954	Malcolm I (son of Donald II)
954–962	Indulf (son of Constantine II)
962–966	Duf (son of Malcolm I)
966–971	Culén (son of Indulf)
971–995	Kenneth II (son of Malcolm I)
995–997	Constantine III (son of Culén)
997–1005	Kenneth III (son of Duf) and ?Giric (son)
1005–1034	Malcolm II (son of Kenneth II)

House of Dunkeld

1034–1040	Duncan I (son of Bethoc, daughter of Malcolm II, and Crinán, abbot of Dunkeld)

House of Moray

1040–1057	Macbeth (son of Findlaec, mormaer of Moray; married Gruoch, granddaughter of Kenneth II or III)
1057–1058	Lulach (son of Gruoch and Gillecomgan, mormaer of Moray)

House of Dunkeld

1058–1093	Malcolm III, Canmore (son of Duncan I)
1093–1094	Donald III (brother; deposed)
1094	Duncan II (son of Malcolm III)
1094–1097	Donald III (restored; deposed)
1097–1107	Edgar (son of Malcolm III)
1107–1124	Alexander I (brother)
1124–1153	St David I (brother)
1153–1165	Malcolm IV, the Maiden (grandson)
1165–1214	William the Lion (brother)
1214–1249	Alexander II (son)
1249–1286	Alexander III (son)

House of Norway

1286–1290	Margaret (daughter of Margaret, daughter of Alexander III, and Eirik II of Norway; interregnum 1290–2)

House of Balliol

1292–1296	John (son of John Balliol; maternal grandson of Margaret, niece of William; deposed, died 1313; interregnum 1296–1306)

House of Bruce

1306–1329	Robert I (great-grandson of Isabel, niece of William, and Robert Bruce)
1329–1371	David II (son)

House of Balliol

1332–1356	Edward (son of John; rival claimant; abdicated, died 1364)

House of Stewart

1371–1390	Robert II (son of Marjorie, daughter of Robert I, and Walter the High Steward)
1390–1406	Robert III (son)
1406–1437	James I (son)
1437–1460	James II (son)
1460–1488	James III (son)
1488–1513	James IV (son)
1513–1542	James V (son)
1542–1567	Mary (daughter; deposed, died 1587)
1567–1625	James VI (son of Mary and Henry Stuart, earl of Darnley, king consort 1565–7; king of England as James I 1603)

NOTES

Chronology Dates down to the mid-tenth century may vary by a year or so. For a two-year reign of Kenneth I in Dalriada, followed by sixteen years in Pictavia, see Duncan, 58.

Names and Titles The unified Dalriadan (Scottish) and Pictish kingdom was known in Gaelic as Alba, in Latin as Scotia; the royal title was 'king of Scots' (*rex Scotorum*).

BIBLIOGRAPHY

Duncan, A. A. M., *Scotland: the Making of the Kingdom* (Edinburgh, 1975).
Fryde, E. B., ed., *Handbook of British Chronology* (3rd edn., London, 1986).

THE PRINCIPALITY OF WALES

Kingdom of Gwynedd

825–844	Merfyn the Freckled (son of Gwriad; king or chief of Gwynedd 825)
844–878	Rhodri I, the Great (son)
878–916	Anarawd (son)
916–942	Idwal the Bald (son)
942–950	Hywel I, the Good (grandson of Rhodri I; king of Deheubarth)
950–979	Iago I (son of Idwal; deposed)
979–985	Hywel II (nephew)
985–986	Cadwallon (brother)
986–999	Maredudd (grandson of Hywel I; king of Deheubarth)
999–1005	Cynan I (son of Hywel II)
1005–1023	Llywelyn I (son-in-law of Maredudd; king of Deheubarth)
1023–1039	Iago II (great-grandson of Idwal)
1039–1063	Gruffydd I (son of Llywelyn I; king of Deheubarth; rule by Powys, then Arwystli 1063–81)
1081–1137	Gruffydd II (grandson of Iago II)
1137–1170	Owain (son)
1170–1174	Cynan II (son)
1174–1194	David I (brother; east Gwynedd; deposed, died 1203)
1174–1195	Rhodri II (brother; west Gwynedd)
1174–1200	Gruffydd III (son of Cynan II; south Gwynedd)
1194–1240	Llywelyn II, the Great (grandson of Owain; reunited Gwynedd)
1240–1246	David II (son)

Principality of Wales:

1246–1282	Llywelyn III, the Last (nephew; assumed the title prince of Wales 1258)
1282–1283	David III (brother; English conquest of the principality 1283)

NOTES

Chronology Some early dates may vary by a year or so (see Lloyd).

BIBLIOGRAPHY

Davies, W., *Wales in the Early Middle Ages* (Leicester, 1982).
Lloyd, J. E., *A History of Wales* (3rd edn., 2 vols., London, 1939).

THE HIGH KINGSHIP OF IRELAND

House of Uí Néill

445–452	Niall of the Nine Hostages (king of Tara; traditional ancestor of claimants to the high kingship)
452–463	Lóegaire (son)
463–482	Ailill Molt (grandnephew of Niall)
482–507	Lugaid (son of Lóegaire)
507–534	Muirchertach I (CE) (great-grandson of Niall)
534–544	Tuathal Máelgarb (great-grandson of Niall)
544–565	Diarmait I (great-grandson of Niall)
565–566	Forggus (CE) (son of Muirchertach I)
565–566	Domnall Ilchelgach (CE) (brother; co-regent)
566–569	Ainmire (CC) (fourth in descent from Niall)
569–572	Báetán I (CE) (son of Muirchertach I)
569–572	Eochaid (CE) (son of Domnall Ilchelgach; co-regent)
572–586	Báetán II (CC) (fourth in descent from Niall)
586–598	Áed (CC) (son of Ainmire)
598–604	Áed Sláine (AS) (son of Diarmait I)
598–604	Colmán Rímid (CE) (son of Báetán I; co-regent)
604–612	Áed Uaridnach (CE) (son of Domnall Ilchelgach)
612–615	Máel Cobo (CC) (son of Áed)
615–628	Suibne Menn (CE) (grandnephew of Muirchertach I)
628–642	Domnall (CC) (son of Áed)
642–654	Conall Cáel (CC) (son of Máel Cobo)
642–658	Cellach (CC) (brother; co-regent)
658–665	Diarmait II (AS) (son of Áed Sláine)
658–665	Blathmac (AS) (brother; co-regent)
665–671	Sechnussach (AS) (son)
671–675	Cennfáelad (AS) (brother)
675–695	Fínsnechta Fledach (AS) (grandson of Áed Sláine)
695–704	Loingsech (CC) (grandson of Domnall)
704–710	Congal Cennmagair (CC) (grandson of Domnall)
710–722	Fergal (CE) (great-grandson of Áed Uaridnach)
722–724	Fogartach (AS) (great-grandson of Diarmait II)
724–728	Cináed (AS) (fourth in descent from Áed Sláine)
728–734	Flaithbertach (CC) (son of Loingsech; deposed, died 765)
734–743	Áed Allán (CE) (son of Fergal)
743–763	Domnall Midi (CCh) (seventh in descent from Diarmait I)
763–770	Niall Frossach (CE) (son of Fergal; abdicated, died 778)
770–797	Donnchad Midi (CCh) (son of Domnall Midi)
797–819	Áed Oirdnide (CE) (son of Niall Frossach)
819–833	Conchobar (CCh) (son of Donnchad Midi)
833–846	Niall Caille (CE) (son of Áed Oirdnide)
846–862	Máel Sechnaill I (CCh) (nephew of Conchobar)
862–879	Áed Findliath (CE) (son of Niall Caille)
879–916	Flann Sinna (CCh) (son of Máel Sechnaill I)
916–919	Niall Glúndub (CE) (son of Áed Findliath)
919–944	Donnchad Donn (CCh) (son of Flann Sinna)
944–956	Congalach Cnogba (AS) (tenth in descent from Áed Sláine)

956–980	Domnall ua Néill (CE) (grandson of Niall Glúndub)
980–1002	Máel Sechnaill II (CCh) (grandson of Donnchad Donn; deposed)
1002–1014	Brian Bóruma (Dál Cais; king of Munster)
1014–1022	Máel Sechnaill II (restored; interregnum 1022–72)
1072–1086	Tairrdelbach I (grandson of Brian Bóruma; king of Munster)
1086–1119	Muirchertach II (son)
1119–1121	Domnall ua Lochlainn (CE) (fourth in descent from Domnall ua Néill?; king of Ailech)
1121–1156	Tairrdelbach II (Ua Conchobair; king of Connacht)
1156–1166	Muirchertach III (CE) (grandson of Domnall ua Lochlainn)
1166–1186	Ruaidrí (son of Tairrdelbach II; deposed, died 1198; regional kingships under English domination)

NOTES

Chronology Early dates are uncertain, as the annals are not in general agreement until about the middle of the seventh century; the order of succession of the first few kings is debated, and the historicity of two of them has been questioned (Byrne, 102; Mac Niocaill, 12).

Until Brian Bóruma, claims to the kingship of Tara were restricted to descendants of Niall; to the Northern Uí Néill belonged the Cenél Conaill (CC) and Cenél nEógain (CE), to the Southern Uí Néill the Clann Cholmáin (CCh) and Síl nÁedo Sláine (AS). For genealogical charts and for the other Irish kingships, see *A New History of Ireland, IX: Maps, Genealogies, Lists* (Oxford, 1984).

Names and Titles In later theory, Tara was the seat of an immemorial high-kingship, held until Brian's usurpation by descendants of Niall; in fact it was not until the ninth century that the Uí Néill kings of Tara won acceptance as overlords of Ireland, and not until the tenth that the title 'high king of Ireland' (*ard-rí Érenn*) is found. See Byrne, ch. xii.

BIBLIOGRAPHY

Byrne, F. J., *Irish Kings and High-Kings* (New York, 1973).
Mac Niocaill, G., *Ireland before the Vikings* (Dublin, 1972).
Ó Corráin, D., *Ireland before the Normans* (Dublin, 1972).

2 FRANCE

THE KINGDOM OF FRANCE

Carolingian House	
751–768	Pepin the Short (son of Charles Martel; elected king of the Franks 751)
768–771	Carloman (son)
768–814	Charles the Great (Charlemagne) (brother; emperor 800)
814–840	Louis I, the Pious (son; emperor 813)
840–877	Charles I, the Bald (son; king of the West Franks 843; emperor 875)
877–879	Louis II, the Stammerer (son)
879–882	Louis III (son)
879–884	Carloman (brother)
885–888	Charles II, the Fat (grandson of Louis I; emperor 881–7)
Robertian House	
888–898	Eudes (son of Robert, marquis of Neustria)
Carolingian House	
893–923	Charles III, the Simple (son of Louis II; rival king; deposed, died 929)
Robertian House	
922–923	Robert I (brother of Eudes; rival king)
923–936	Rudolf (duke of Burgundy; married Emma, daughter of Robert I)
Carolingian House	
936–954	Louis IV of Outremer (son of Charles III)
954–986	Lothair (son)
986–987	Louis V, the Sluggard (son; co-regent 979)
Capetian House	
987–996	Hugh Capet (grandson of Robert I)
996–1031	Robert II, the Pious (son; co-regent 987)
1017–1025	Hugh (son; co-regent)
1031–1060	Henry I (brother; co-regent 1027)
1060–1108	Philip I (son; co-regent 1059)
1108–1137	Louis VI, the Fat (son)
1129–1131	Philip (son; co-regent)
1137–1180	Louis VII, the Younger (brother; co-regent 1131)
1180–1223	Philip II, Augustus (son; co-regent 1179)
1223–1226	Louis VIII, the Lion (son)
1226–1270	St Louis IX (son)
1270–1285	Philip III, the Bold (son)
1285–1314	Philip IV, the Fair (son)

1314–1316	Louis X, the Stubborn (son)
1316	John I (son)
1316–1322	Philip V, the Tall (son of Philip IV)
1322–1328	Charles IV, the Fair (brother)

House of Valois

1328–1350	Philip VI (count of Valois; grandson of Philip III)
1350–1364	John II, the Good (son)
1364–1380	Charles V, the Wise (son)
1380–1422	Charles VI, the Mad (son)
1422–1461	Charles VII, the Victorious (son)
1461–1483	Louis XI (son)
1483–1498	Charles VIII (son)

Line of Orléans

1498–1515	Louis XII (duke of Orléans; great-grandson of Charles V)

Line of Angoulême

1515–1547	Francis I (count of Angoulême; fourth in descent from Charles V)
1547–1559	Henry II (son)
1559–1560	Francis II (son)
1560–1574	Charles IX (brother)
1574–1589	Henry III (brother)

House of Bourbon

1589–1610	Henry IV (duke of Bourbon-Vendôme; tenth in descent from Louis IX)
1610–1643	Louis XIII (son)
1643–1715	Louis XIV (son)
1715–1774	Louis XV (great-grandson)
1774–1792	Louis XVI (grandson; deposed, died 1793)
1793–1795	Louis XVII (son; never reigned)

First Republic

1792–1795	National Convention
1795–1799	Directory
1799–1804	Consulate: Napoleon Bonaparte, First Consul (consul for life 1802)

House of Bonaparte – First Empire

1804–1814, 1815	Napoleon I (king of Italy 1805; deposed; restored; deposed, died 1821)
1815	Napoleon II (son; deposed, died 1832)

House of Bourbon

1814–1824	Louis XVIII (brother of Louis XVI)
1824–1830	Charles X (brother; deposed, died 1836)

Line of Orléans

1830–1848	Louis Philippe I (duke of Orléans; sixth in descent from Louis XIII; deposed, died 1850)

Second Republic

1848–1852 Louis Napoleon Bonaparte, President (nephew of Napoleon I)

House of Bonaparte – Second Empire

1852–1870 Napoleon III (deposed, died 1873; proclamation of the Third Republic)

NOTES

Chronology For Louis XVII's death in prison in June 1795, see H. G. Francq, *Louis XVII: the Unsolved Mystery* (Leiden, 1970), ch. viii.

Names and Titles From the tenth century, the standard title was 'king of the Franks' (*rex Francorum*); from Louis IX, the monarch was commonly known as king of France. The Capetians from 1285, and the Bourbons to 1791, were styled kings of France and of Navarre. Louis XVI (from 1791) and Louis Philippe were kings of the French; the two Napoleons were emperors of the French; Louis XVIII and Charles X were kings of France.

BIBLIOGRAPHY

Duby, G., ed., *Histoire de la France* (3 vols., Paris, 1970–2).
Lavisse, E., ed., *Histoire de France* (9 vols., Paris, 1900–11).

THE COUNTY AND DUCHY OF ANJOU

First House of Anjou

909–942	Fulk I, the Red (son of Ingelgerius; styled count of Angers by 909)
942–960	Fulk II, the Good (son)
960–987	Geoffrey I, Graymantle (son)
987–1040	Fulk III, Nerra (son)
1040–1060	Geoffrey II, Martel (son)

House of Gâtinais

1060–1068	Geoffrey III, the Bearded (son of Ermengard, daughter of Fulk III, and Geoffrey, count of Gâtinais; deposed)
1068–1109	Fulk IV, the Surly (brother)
1109–1129	Fulk V, the Younger (son; abdicated; king of Jerusalem 1131–43)
1129–1151	Geoffrey IV, the Fair (son)
1151–1189	Henry (son; king of England as Henry II 1154; union with England till French conquest 1205)

House of France

1246–1285	Charles I (son of Louis VIII of France; king of Sicily 1266)
1285–1290	Charles II, the Lame (son; abdicated; king of Naples 1285–1309)
1290–1325	Charles III of Valois (son of Philip III of France; married Margaret, daughter of Charles II)
1325–1350	Philip (son; king of France as Philip VI 1328; union with France)

Dukes of Anjou

1360–1384	Louis I (son of John II of France; titular king of Naples 1383)
1384–1417	Louis II (son)
1417–1434	Louis III (son)
1434–1480	René the Good (brother; king of Naples 1435–42; union with France 1480)

NOTES

Chronology Dates down to 960 may vary by a year or so.

Names and Titles Fulk I was styled viscount by 898, viscount of Tours and Angers by 905, and count of Angers by 909; see K. F. Werner, *Die Welt als Geschichte*, XVIII (1958), 264–79.

BIBLIOGRAPHY

Dornic, F., *Histoire de l'Anjou* (2nd edn., Paris, 1971).
Halphen, L., *Le comté d'Anjou au XIe siècle* (Paris, 1906).

THE DUCHY OF AQUITAINE

House of Auvergne

898–918	William I, the Pious (son of Bernard Hairyfoot, count of Auvergne; styled duke by 898)

House of Razès

918–926	William II, the Younger (son of Adelinda, sister of William I, and Acfrid, count of Razès)
926–927	Acfrid (brother)

House of Poitiers

927–934	Ebalus the Bastard (distant cousin; count of Poitou, 890–2 and from 902)
934–963	William III, Towhead (son)
963–993	William IV, Fierabras (son; abdicated, died 996?)
993–1030	William V, the Great (son)
1030–1038	William VI, the Fat (son)
1038–1039	Eudes (brother)
1039–1058	William VII, the Brave (brother)
1058–1086	William VIII (brother)
1086–1126	William IX, the Troubadour (son)
1126–1137	William X, the Toulousan (son)
1137–1204	Eleanor (daughter; married Henry II of England; union with England till French conquest 1453)

NOTES

Names and Titles William I was styled duke by 898, duke of Aquitaine by 909. W. Kienast, *Die Herzogstitel in Frankreich und Deutschland* (Munich, 1968), ch. v. For some years after the death of Acfrid, the ducal title was contested with Toulouse.

BIBLIOGRAPHY

Auzias, L., *L'Aquitaine carolingienne (778–987)* (Toulouse, 1937).
Richard, A., *Histoire des comtes de Poitou, 778–1204* (2 vols., Paris, 1903).

THE DUCHY OF BOURBONNAIS

House of Bourbon

1310–1342	Louis I (grandson of Louis IX of France; lord of Bourbon 1310; duke of Bourbonnais 1327)
1342–1356	Peter I (son)
1356–1410	Louis II, the Good (son)
1410–1434	John I (son)
1434–1456	Charles I (son)
1456–1488	John II (son)
1488	Charles II (brother; abdicated, died 1488)
1488–1503	Peter II of Beaujeu (brother)
1503–1521	Suzanne (daughter)

Line of Montpensier

1505–1527	Charles III (count of Montpensier; great-grandson of John I; married Suzanne; union with France 1527)

BIBLIOGRAPHY

Dussieux, L., *Généalogie de la maison de Bourbon* (2nd edn., Paris, 1872).
Leguai, A., *Histoire du Bourbonnais* (2nd edn., Paris, 1974).

THE DUCHY OF BRITTANY

House of Nantes	
937–952	Alan I, Wrybeard (leader of revolt against the Norsemen; captured Nantes 937)
952–958	Drogo (son)
960–981	Hoël (brother)
981–988	Guérech (brother)
988–990	Alan II (son)
House of Rennes	
990–992	Conan I, the Crooked (count of Rennes)
992–1008	Geoffrey I (son)
1008–1040	Alan III (son)
1040–1066	Conan II (son)
House of Cornouaille	
1066–1084	Hoël (count of Cornouaille; married Hawisa, daughter of Alan III)
1084–1112	Alan IV, Fergant (son; abdicated, died 1119)
1112–1148	Conan III, the Fat (son)
1148–1156	Eudo of Porhoët (married Bertha, daughter of Conan III; deposed)
1156–1166	Conan IV, the Younger (son of Bertha and Alan of Richmond; deposed, died 1171)
House of Anjou	
1166–1186	Geoffrey II (son of Henry II of England; married Constance, daughter of Conan IV)
1187–1203	Arthur I (son)
1203–1221	Alix (daughter of Constance and Guy of Thouars)
House of Dreux	
1213–1221	Peter I, Mauclerc (son of Robert II of Dreux; married Alix; regent 1221–37; died 1250)
1221–1286	John I, the Red (son)
1286–1305	John II (son; made duke of Brittany by Philip IV of France 1297)
1305–1312	Arthur II (son)
1312–1341	John III, the Good (son)
1341–1345	John (brother; count of Montfort)
1341–1364	Charles of Blois (married Joan, niece of John III; rival claimant; war of the Breton Succession 1341–64)
House of Montfort	
1364–1399	John IV, the Conqueror (son of John, count of Montfort)
1399–1442	John V (son)
1442–1450	Francis I (son)
1450–1457	Peter II (brother)
1457–1458	Arthur III of Richmond (son of John IV)
1458–1488	Francis II (nephew)
1488–1514	Anne (daughter; married Louis XII of France; union with France 1514)

NOTES

Chronology Some dates down to 988 may vary by a year or so.

Names and Titles For the title of duke, formally bestowed in 1297 but in use from Alan I, see W. Kienast, *Der Herzogstitel in Frankreich und Deutschland* (Munich, 1968), ch. iv.

BIBLIOGRAPHY

Durtelle de Saint-Sauveur, E., *Histoire de Bretagne des origines à nos jours* (4th edn., 2 vols., Rennes, 1957).

La Borderie, A. Le Moyne de, and B. Pocquet, *Histoire de Bretagne* (5 vols., Rennes, 1896–1913).

THE COUNTY OF CHAMPAGNE (TROYES)

House of Vermandois

950–975?	Robert (son of Herbert II, count of Vermandois; married Adela, heiress of Troyes *c.*950)
975?–995	Herbert the Younger (son)
995–1021	Stephen I (son)

House of Blois

1021–1037	Eudes I (grandson of Liutgard, sister of Robert, and Thibaut, count of Blois)
1037–1048	Stephen II (son)
1048–1066	Eudes II (son; deposed)
1066–1089	Thibaut I (son of Eudes I)
1089–1093	Eudes III (son)
1093–1125	Hugh (brother; abdicated)
1125–1152	Thibaut II, the Great (nephew)
1152–1181	Henry I, the Liberal (son)
1181–1197	Henry II, the Younger (son; king of Jerusalem 1192)
1197–1201	Thibaut III (brother)
1201–1253	Thibaut IV, the Posthumous (son; king of Navarre 1234)
1253–1270	Thibaut V (son)
1270–1274	Henry III, the Fat (brother)
1274–1305	Joan (daughter)

House of France

1305–1316	Louis (son of Joan and Philip IV of France; king of France as Louis X 1314; union with France)

NOTES

Chronology Robert died some time after 966; remaining dates down to 1048 may vary by a year or more (see Bur). Eudes II survived at least to 1096; see B. English, *The Lords of Holderness, 1086–1260* (Oxford, 1979), 9–13.

Names and Titles Champagne evolved from the county of Troyes in the late eleventh century; the title 'count of Champagne' was in use from the reign of Hugh. See Bur, 259–72.

BIBLIOGRAPHY

Bur, M., *La formation du comté de Champagne (v.950–v.1150)* (Nancy, 1977).

Poinsignon, A. M., *Histoire générale de la Champagne et de la Brie* (2nd edn., 3 vols., Châlons-sur-Marne, 1896–8).

THE DUCHY OF NORMANDY

First House of Normandy

911–925?	Rollo (Norwegian viking chieftain; invested with lands on the lower Seine *c*.911)
925?–942	William I, Longsword (son)
942–996	Richard I, the Fearless (son)
996–1026	Richard II, the Good (son)
1026–1027	Richard III (son)
1027–1035	Robert I, the Magnificent (brother)
1035–1087	William II, the Conqueror (son; king of England 1066)
1087–1106	Robert II, Curthose (son; deposed, died 1134)
1106–1135	Henry I (brother; king of England 1100)

House of Blois

1135–1144	Stephen (son of Adela, daughter of William II, and Stephen, count of Blois; deposed; king of England 1135–54)

House of Anjou

1144–1150	Geoffrey the Fair (count of Anjou; married Matilda, daughter of Henry I; abdicated, died 1151)
1150–1189	Henry II (son; king of England 1154; union with England till French conquest 1204)

NOTES

Chronology Dates down to 925 may vary by a year or so.

Names and Titles On the evolution of the ducal title, see W. Kienast, *Der Herzogstitel in Frankreich und Deutschland* (Munich, 1968), ch. iii.

BIBLIOGRAPHY

Douglas, D. C., *William the Conqueror* (Berkeley, 1964).
Warren, W. L., *Henry II* (Berkeley, 1973).

THE COUNTY OF PROVENCE

House of Barcelona

1112–1131	Raymond Berengar I (count of Barcelona as Raymond Berengar III; married Douce, heiress of Provence, 1112)
1131–1144	Berengar Raymond (son)
1144–1162	Raymond Berengar II (brother; Barcelona 1131)
1162–1166	Raymond Berengar III (son of Berengar Raymond)
1166–1196	Alfonso I (son of Raymond Berengar II; king of Aragon 1164)
1178–1181	Raymond Berengar IV (brother; regent)
1181–1185	Sancho (brother; regent; deposed, died 1223)
1196–1209	Alfonso II (son of Alfonso I)
1209–1245	Raymond Berengar V (son)
1245–1267	Beatrice (daughter)

Capetian House of Anjou

1246–1285	Charles I (count of Anjou; married Beatrice; king of Sicily 1266)
1285–1309	Charles II, the Lame (son)
1309–1343	Robert the Wise (son)
1343–1382	Joan (granddaughter; queen of Naples 1343–81)

Valois House of Anjou

1382–1384	Louis I (adopted son; duke of Anjou)
1384–1417	Louis II (son)
1417–1434	Louis III (son)
1434–1480	René the Good (brother)
1480–1481	Charles III of Maine (nephew; union of Provence and Maine with France 1481)

BIBLIOGRAPHY

Bourrilly, V.-L., and R. Busquet, *La Provence au moyen âge (1112–1481)* (Marseille, 1924).

Busquet, R., *Histoire de Provence* (Monaco, 1954).

THE COUNTY OF TOULOUSE

House of Rouergue

849–852	Fredelon (son of Fulcoald, count of Rouergue; invested with Toulouse 849)
852–863	Raymond I (brother)
863–864	Humfrid of Gothia (deposed)
864–872	Bernard (son of Raymond I)
872–885	Bernard of Auvergne
885–919	Eudes (son of Raymond I)
919–924	Raymond II (son)
924–960	Raymond III Pons (son)
960–1037	William III, Taillefer (son)
1037–1061	Pons (son)
1061–1094	William IV (son)
1094–1105	Raymond IV of St Gilles (brother)
1105–1112	Bertrand (son)
1112–1148	Alfonso Jordan (brother)
1148–1194	Raymond V (son)
1194–1222	Raymond VI (son)
1222–1249	Raymond VII (son)

House of France

1249–1271	Alfonso of Poitiers (son of Louis VIII of France; married Joan, daughter of Raymond VII; union with France 1271)

NOTES

Chronology Down to William IV, dates are approximate; for discussion, see W. Kienast, *Der Herzogstitel in Frankreich und Deutschland* (Munich, 1968), ch. vii. William Taillefer, the *antiquissimus Tolosae comes* of William of Malmesbury, was apparently reigning by 961.

BIBLIOGRAPHY

Auzias, L., *L'Aquitaine carolingienne (778–987)* (Toulouse, 1937).

Vic, C. de, and J. Vaissete, *Histoire générale de Languedoc* (15 vols., Toulouse, 1872–92).

THE PRINCIPALITY OF MONACO

House of Grimaldi

1458–1494	Lambert Grimaldi (married Claudine Grimaldi, heiress of Monaco; lord of Monaco 1458)
1494–1505	John II (son)
1505–1523	Lucien (brother)
1523–1532	Augustine (brother)
1532–1581	Honoré I (son of Lucien)
1581–1589	Charles II (son)
1589–1604	Hercules (brother)

Princes of Monaco

1604–1662	Honoré II (son; assumed the title of prince 1612; French protectorate 1641)
1662–1701	Louis I (grandson)
1701–1731	Anthony (son)
1731	Louise Hippolyte (daughter; married James, duke of Estouteville)
1731–1733	James (widower; abdicated, died 1751)
1733–1793	Honoré III (son; deposed, died 1795; union with France 1793–1814)
1814–1819	Honoré IV (son)
1819–1841	Honoré V (son)
1841–1856	Florestan I (brother)
1856–1889	Charles III (son; recognition of Monégasque sovereignty 1861)
1889–1922	Albert I (son)
1922–1949	Louis II (son)
1949–	Rainier III (son of Charlotte, daughter of Louis II, and Peter, count of Polignac)

BIBLIOGRAPHY

Labande, L.-H., *Histoire de la principauté de Monaco* (Monaco, 1934).

3 THE LOW COUNTRIES

THE COUNTY OF FLANDERS

First House of Flanders

864–879	Baldwin I, Iron Arm (count and marquis in the Scheldt river region 863/4)
879–918	Baldwin II, the Bald (son)
918–965	Arnulf I, the Great (son)
958–962	Baldwin III (son; co-regent)
965–988	Arnulf II, the Younger (son)
988–1035	Baldwin IV, the Bearded (son)
1035–1067	Baldwin V of Lille (son)
1067–1070	Baldwin VI of Mons (son)
1070–1071	Arnulf III, the Unfortunate (son)
1071–1093	Robert I, the Frisian (son of Baldwin V)
1093–1111	Robert II of Jerusalem (son; co-regent 1086)
1111–1119	Baldwin VII, Hapkin (son)

House of Denmark

1119–1127	Bl Charles the Good (son of Adela, daughter of Robert I, and Knud II of Denmark)

House of Normandy

1127–1128	William Clito (grandson of Matilda, daughter of Baldwin V, and William I of England)

House of Lorraine

1128–1168	Thierry of Alsace (son of Gertrude, daughter of Robert I, and Thierry II of Lorraine)
1168–1191	Philip (son; co-regent 1157)

House of Hainault

1191–1194	Baldwin VIII (count of Hainault 1171–95; married Margaret, daughter of Thierry II (died 1194))
1194–1205	Baldwin IX (son; emperor of Constantinople 1205–6)
1205–1244	Joan (daughter)
1244–1278	Margaret I (sister; abdicated; Hainault only 1278–80)

House of Dampierre

1278–1305	Guy (son of Margaret I and William of Dampierre)
1305–1322	Robert III of Béthune (son)
1322–1346	Louis I of Nevers (grandson)
1346–1384	Louis II of Male (son; count of Artois 1382)
1384–1405	Margaret II (daughter; married Philip the Bold, duke of Burgundy; union with Burgundy 1405)

THE COUNTY OF HOLLAND

First House of Holland

916–939	Dirk I (son of Gerulf; count in parts of northern Holland *c*.916)
939–988	Dirk II (son)
988–993	Arnulf (son)
993–1039	Dirk III (son)
1039–1049	Dirk IV (son)
1049–1061	Floris I (brother)
1061–1091	Dirk V (son)
1091–1121	Floris II, the Fat (son)
1121–1157	Dirk VI (son)
1157–1190	Floris III (son)
1190–1203	Dirk VII (son)
1203–1222	William I (brother)
1222–1234	Floris IV (son)
1234–1256	William II (son; king of the Romans 1247)
1256–1296	Floris V (son)
1296–1299	John I (son)

House of Hainault

1299–1304	John II (son of Aleidis, daughter of Floris IV, and John of Avesnes; count of Hainault 1280)
1304–1337	William III, the Good (son)
1337–1345	William IV (son)
1345–1354	Margaret (sister; abdicated; Hainault only 1354–6)

House of Bavaria

1354–1358	William V (son of Margaret and emperor Louis IV; Hainault 1356; deposed, died 1389)
1389–1404	Albert (brother; regent 1358–89)
1404–1417	William VI (son)
1417–1433	Jacqueline (daughter; abdicated, died 1436; union of Holland and Hainault with Burgundy)

NOTES

Chronology Dates down to 939 are approximate (Strubbe and Voet, 368).

Names and Titles The use of the title 'count of Holland' dates from 1101 (Dek, 13).

THE COUNTY AND DUCHY OF LUXEMBURG

House of the Moselle

963–998	Sigefrid (probable son of Wigeric; count of Luxemburg as a vassal of the empire 963)
998–1026	Henry I (son; duke of Bavaria 1004–9, 1017–26)
1026–1047	Henry II (nephew; Bavaria 1042)
1047–1059	Gilbert (brother)
1059–1086	Conrad I (son)
1086–1096	Henry III (son)
1096–1131	William (brother)
1131–1136	Conrad II (son)

House of Namur

1136–1196	Henry IV, the Blind (son of Ermesind, daughter of Conrad I, and Godfrey, count of Namur)
1196–1247	Ermesind (daughter)

House of Limburg

1247–1281	Henry V, the Great (son of Ermesind and Walram III, duke of Limburg)
1281–1288	Henry VI (son)
1288–1310	Henry VII (son; abdicated; king of the Romans 1308–13)
1310–1346	John the Blind (son; king of Bohemia 1310)
1346–1353	Charles (son; abdicated; king of the Romans 1346–78; Bohemia 1346)

Dukes of Luxemburg

1353–1383	Wenceslas I (brother; duke of Luxemburg 1354; duke of Brabant 1355)
1383–1419	Wenceslas II (son of Charles; king of the Romans 1378–1400; Bohemia 1378)
1419–1437	Sigismund (brother; king of Hungary 1387; king of the Romans 1410; Bohemia 1419)

House of Habsburg

1437–1439	Albert of Austria (married Elizabeth, daughter of Sigismund; Hungary and Bohemia 1437; king of the Romans 1438)

House of Wettin

1439–1443	William of Saxony (married Anne, daughter of Albert; abdicated, died 1482; union with Burgundy)

NOTES

Chronology Most dates down to 1136 are approximate (Strubbe and Voet, 379).

THE DUCHY OF LOWER LORRAINE

House of Verdun

1012–1023	Godfrey I (son of Godfrey, count of Verdun; duke of Lower Lorraine as a vassal of the empire 1012)
1023–1044	Gozelo I (brother; duke of Upper Lorraine 1033)
1044–1046	Gozelo II, the Sluggard (son)

House of Luxemburg

1046–1065	Frederick (brother of Henry II, count of Luxemburg)

House of Verdun

1065–1069	Godfrey II, the Bearded (son of Gozelo I; Upper Lorraine 1044–7)
1069–1076	Godfrey III, the Hunchback (son)

Salian House

1076–1087	Conrad (son of emperor Henry IV; king of the Romans 1087–98)

House of Boulogne

1087–1100	Godfrey IV of Bouillon (son of Ida, daughter of Godfrey II, and Eustace II of Boulogne)

House of Limburg

1101–1106	Henry I (count of Limburg; deposed, died 1119?; award of Lower Lorraine to the house of Louvain)

THE COUNTY OF HAINAULT

House of Flanders

1051–1070	Baldwin I of Mons (count of Flanders as Baldwin VI; married Richildis, heiress of Hainault, 1051)
1070–1071	Arnulf the Unfortunate (son; Flanders)
1071–1098	Baldwin II (brother)
1098–1120	Baldwin III (son)
1120–1171	Baldwin IV of Mons (son)
1171–1195	Baldwin V (son; count of Flanders 1191–4; union of Hainault and Flanders 1195–1278)

House of Avesnes

1280–1304	John (grandson of Margaret I of Flanders and Burchard of Avesnes; count of Holland as John II 1299; union with Holland)

THE DUCHY OF BRABANT

House of Louvain

1106–1128	Godfrey I, the Bearded (count of Louvain; duke of Lower Lorraine 1106; deposed, died 1139)
1128–1139	Walram II of Limburg
1139–1142	Godfrey II (son of Godfrey I)
1142–1190	Godfrey III (son)
1190–1235	Henry I (son; co-regent 1183)
1235–1248	Henry II (son)
1248–1261	Henry III (son)
1261–1267	Henry IV (son; abdicated)
1267–1294	John I, the Victorious (brother; duke of Limburg 1288)
1294–1312	John II (son)
1312–1355	John III (son)

House of Luxemburg

1355–1383	Wenceslas (duke of Luxemburg)
1355–1404	Joan (daughter of John III; married Wenceslas; abdicated, died 1406)

House of Burgundy

1406–1415	Anthony (son of Philip the Bold, duke of Burgundy; maternal grandson of Margaret, sister of Joan; regent 1404–6)
1415–1427	John IV (son)
1427–1430	Philip of St Pol (brother; union of Brabant and Limburg with Burgundy 1430)

NOTES

Names and Titles In the twelfth century, the term Brabant came to denote the possessions of the house of Louvain; in the thirteenth, the title 'duke of Brabant' replaced the designation 'duke of (Lower) Lorraine'. W. Kienast, *Der Herzogstitel in Frankreich und Deutschland* (Munich, 1968), 395–404.

THE COUNTY OF ARTOIS

Capetian House

1237–1250	Robert I, the Good (son of Louis VIII of France; invested with Artois 1237)
1250–1302	Robert II, the Noble (son)
1302–1329	Mahaut (daughter)
1329–1330	Joan I (daughter of Mahaut and Otto IV, count of Burgundy)
1330–1347	Joan II (daughter of Joan I and Philip V of France)

House of Burgundy

1347–1361	Philip of Rouvres (grandson of Joan II and Eudes IV of Burgundy; duke of Burgundy 1349)
1361–1382	Margaret (sister of Joan II; married Louis I, count of Flanders; union with Flanders 1382)

BURGUNDY AND THE LOW COUNTRIES

House of Autun

898–921	Richard the Justicer (count of Autun; ruled Frankish Burgundy by 898; styled duke by 918)
921–936	Rudolf (son; king of France 923)
936–952	Hugh the Black (brother)
952–956	Gilbert of Chalon (probable son-in-law)

Robertian House

956–965	Otto (grandson of Robert I of France; married Liutgard, daughter of Gilbert)
965–1002	Henry the Great (brother)
1002–1005	Otto William (stepson; deposed, died 1026; French conquest of Burgundy)

Capetian House

1031–1076	Robert I (son of Robert II of France; recognized as duke 1031)
1076–1079	Hugh I (grandson; abdicated, died 1093)
1079–1102	Eudes I, the Red (brother)
1102–1143	Hugh II (son)
1143–1162	Eudes II (son)
1162–1192	Hugh III (son)
1192–1218	Eudes III (son)
1218–1272	Hugh IV (son)
1272–1306	Robert II (son)
1306–1315	Hugh V (son)
1315–1349	Eudes IV (brother)
1349–1361	Philip of Rouvres (grandson; union of Burgundy with France 1361)

House of Valois

1363–1404	Philip the Bold (son of John II of France; count of Flanders and Artois 1384)
1404–1419	John the Fearless (son)
1419–1467	Philip the Good (son; duke of Brabant 1430; count of Holland 1433; duke of Luxemburg 1443)
1467–1477	Charles the Rash (son)
1477–1482	Mary (daughter; inherited the Low Countries; French conquest of Burgundy 1477)

House of Habsburg

1482–1506	Philip the Handsome (son of Mary and emperor Maximilian I; king of Castile 1504)
1506–1555	Charles (son; king of Spain 1516–56; abdicated, died 1558; union of the Low Countries with Spain)

BIBLIOGRAPHY FOR THE LOW COUNTRIES

Chaume, M., *Les origines du duché de Bourgogne* (2 vols. in 4 pts., Dijon, 1925–37).

Dek, A. W. E., *Genealogie der graven van Holland* (4th edn., Zaltbommel, 1969).

Knetsch, K. G. P., *Das Haus Brabant: Genealogie der Herzoge von Brabant und der Landgrafen von Hessen* (2 vols., Darmstadt, 1931).

Petit de Vausse, E., *Histoire des ducs de Bourgogne de la race capétienne* (9 vols., Dijon, 1885–1905).

Strubbe, E. I., and L. Voet, *De chronologie van de middeleeuwen en de moderne tijden in de Nederlanden* (Antwerp, 1960).

Vannérus, J., 'La première dynastie luxembourgeoise', *Revue belge de philologie et d'histoire*, XXV (1946–7), 801–58.

THE MODERN NETHERLANDS

House of Orange-Nassau – Stadholders of the Northern Provinces

1572–1584	William I, the Silent (son of William of Nassau; prince of Orange 1544; stadholder of Holland, Zealand, and Utrecht)
1585–1625	Maurice (son; Utrecht 1590)
1625–1647	Frederick Henry (brother)
1647–1650	William II (son; interregnum 1650–72)
1672–1702	William III (son; Utrecht 1674; king of England 1689; interregnum 1702–47)
1747–1751	William IV (sixth in descent from William of Nassau)
1751–1795	William V (son; deposed, died 1806; Batavian Republic 1795–1806)

House of Bonaparte – Kingdom of Holland

1806–1810	Louis Napoleon (brother of Napoleon I, emperor of the French; abdicated, died 1846; union with France 1810–13)

House of Orange-Nassau – Kingdom of the Netherlands

1813–1840	William I (son of William V; sovereign prince of the Netherlands 1813; king 1815; abdicated, died 1843)
1840–1849	William II (son)
1849–1890	William III (son)
1890–1948	Wilhelmina (daughter; in exile 1940–5; abdicated, died 1962)
1948–1980	Juliana (daughter of Wilhelmina and Henry of Mecklenburg, prince consort 1901–34; abdicated)
1980–	Beatrix (daughter of Juliana and Bernhard of Lippe, prince consort 1948–80)

BIBLIOGRAPHY

Dek, A. W. E., *Genealogie van het vorstenhuis Nassau* (Zaltbommel, 1970).

Strubbe, E. I., and L. Voet, *De chronologie van de middeleeuwen en de moderne tijden in de Nederlanden* (Antwerp, 1960).

THE KINGDOM OF THE BELGIANS

House of Saxe-Coburg-Gotha

1831–1865	Leopold I (proclaimed king after Belgian secession from the Netherlands 1830)
1865–1909	Leopold II (son; sovereign of the Congo Free State 1885–1908)
1909–1934	Albert (nephew)
1934–1951	Leopold III (son; in exile 1944–50; abdicated, died 1983)
1951–	Baudouin (son; prince royal 1950–1)

BIBLIOGRAPHY

Aronson, T., *Defiant Dynasty: the Coburgs of Belgium* (Indianapolis, Ind., 1968).

THE GRAND DUCHY OF LUXEMBURG

House of Nassau

1890–1905	Adolf (duke of Nassau 1839–66; grand duke of Luxemburg at independence from the Netherlands 1890)
1905–1912	William IV (son)
1912–1919	Marie Adelaide (daughter; abdicated, died 1924)
1919–1964	Charlotte (sister; in exile 1940–5; abdicated, died 1985)
1964–	John (son of Charlotte and Felix of Bourbon-Parma, prince consort 1919–64 (died 1970))

BIBLIOGRAPHY

Dek, A. W. E., *Genealogie van het vorstenhuis Nassau* (Zaltbommel, 1970).

4 ITALY

THE MEDIEVAL KINGDOM OF ITALY

888–924	Berengar I of Friuli (maternal grandson of emperor Louis I; crowned emperor 915)
889–894	Guy of Spoleto (rival king; crowned emperor 891)
894–898	Lambert (son; co-regent 891; crowned emperor 892)
900–905	Louis of Provence (rival king; crowned emperor 901; deposed, died 928)
922–926	Rudolf of Burgundy (rival king; deposed, died 937)
926–948	Hugh of Arles
948–950	Lothair (son; co-regent 931)
950–963	Berengar II of Ivrea (maternal grandson of Berengar I; deposed, died 966)
950–963	Adalbert (son; co-regent; deposed, died 972?; union with the Holy Roman empire)

BIBLIOGRAPHY

Fasoli, G., *I re d'Italia (888–962)* (Florence, 1949).

Mor, C. G., *L'età feudale* (2 vols., Milan, 1952–3) (*Storia politica d'Italia*, VI).

VENICE: THE DOGES

726–737	Orso (chosen *dux* of Venetia following revolt against Byzantine rule)
737–742	Five *magistri militum*, one year each
742–755	Diodato (son of Orso; deposed)
755–756	Galla (deposed)
756–764	Domenico Monegario (deposed)
764–787	Maurizio
787–803	Giovanni (son; deposed)
803–810	Obelerio (deposed, died 831)
810–827	Agnello Particiaco
827–829	Giustiniano Particiaco (son)
829–836	Giovanni Particiaco I (brother; deposed)
836–864	Pietro Tradonico
864–881	Orso Particiaco I
881–887	Giovanni Particiaco II (son; abdicated)
887	Pietro Candiano I
887–888	Giovanni Particiaco II (again; abdicated)
888–911	Pietro Tribuno
911–932	Orso Particiaco II (abdicated)
932–939	Pietro Candiano II
939–942	Pietro Badoer (son of Orso Particiaco II)
942–959	Pietro Candiano III (son of Pietro II)
959–976	Pietro Candiano IV (son)
976–978	St Pietro Orseolo I (abdicated, died 997?)
978–979	Vitale Candiano
979–991	Tribuno Menio
991–1009	Pietro Orseolo II (son of Pietro I)
1009–1026	Ottone Orseolo (son; deposed, died 1031)
1026–1030	Pietro Centranico (deposed)
1030–1031	Orso Orseolo (son of Pietro II; regent; resigned, died 1049)
1031	Domenico Orseolo (deposed)
1031–1041	Domenico Flabiano
1041–1071	Domenico Contarini I
1071–1084	Domenico Silvo (deposed)
1084–1095	Vitale Falier
1095–1101	Vitale Michiel I
1101–1118	Ordelaffo Falier
1118–1130	Domenico Michiel
1130–1148	Pietro Polani
1148–1155	Domenico Morosini
1155–1172	Vitale Michiel II
1172–1178	Sebastiano Ziani
1178–1192	Orio Mastropiero (abdicated, died 1192)
1192–1205	Enrico Dandolo
1205–1229	Pietro Ziani (abdicated, died 1229)
1229–1249	Jacopo Tiepolo (abdicated, died 1249)
1249–1253	Marino Morosini
1253–1268	Renier Zeno
1268–1275	Lorenzo Tiepolo

1275–1280	Jacopo Contarini (deposed, died 1280)
1280–1289	Giovanni Dandolo
1289–1311	Pietro Gradenigo
1311–1312	Marino Zorzi
1312–1328	Giovanni Soranzo
1329–1339	Francesco Dandolo
1339–1342	Bartolomeo Gradenigo
1343–1354	Andrea Dandolo
1354–1355	Marino Falier
1355–1356	Giovanni Gradenigo
1356–1361	Giovanni Dolfin
1361–1365	Lorenzo Celsi
1365–1368	Marco Cornaro
1368–1382	Andrea Contarini
1382	Michele Morosini
1382–1400	Antonio Venier
1400–1413	Michele Steno
1414–1423	Tommaso Mocenigo
1423–1457	Francesco Foscari (deposed, died 1457)
1457–1462	Pasquale Malipiero
1462–1471	Cristoforo Moro
1471–1473	Niccolò Tron
1473–1474	Niccolò Marcello
1474–1476	Pietro Mocenigo
1476–1478	Andrea Vendramin
1478–1485	Giovanni Mocenigo
1485–1486	Marco Barbarigo
1486–1501	Agostino Barbarigo
1501–1521	Leonardo Loredan
1521–1523	Antonio Grimani
1523–1538	Andrea Gritti
1539–1545	Pietro Lando
1545–1553	Francesco Donato
1553–1554	Marcantonio Trevisan
1554–1556	Francesco Venier
1556–1559	Lorenzo Priuli
1559–1567	Girolamo Priuli
1567–1570	Pietro Loredan
1570–1577	Alvise Mocenigo I
1577–1578	Sebastiano Venier
1578–1585	Niccolò da Ponte
1585–1595	Pasquale Cicogna
1595–1605	Marino Grimani
1606–1612	Leonardo Donato
1612–1615	Marcantonio Memmo
1615–1618	Giovanni Bembo
1618	Niccolò Donato
1618–1623	Antonio Priuli
1623–1624	Francesco Contarini
1625–1629	Giovanni Cornaro I
1630–1631	Niccolò Contarini
1631–1646	Francesco Erizzo

1646–1655	Francesco Molin
1655–1656	Carlo Contarini
1656	Francesco Cornaro
1656–1658	Bertuccio Valier
1658–1659	Giovanni Pesaro
1659–1675	Domenico Contarini II
1675–1676	Niccolò Sagredo
1676–1684	Alvise Contarini
1684–1688	Marcantonio Giustinian
1688–1694	Francesco Morosini
1694–1700	Silvestro Valier
1700–1709	Alvise Mocenigo II
1709–1722	Giovanni Cornaro II
1722–1732	Alvise Mocenigo III
1732–1735	Carlo Ruzzini
1735–1741	Alvise Pisani
1741–1752	Pietro Grimani
1752–1762	Francesco Loredan
1762–1763	Marco Foscarini
1763–1778	Alvise Mocenigo IV
1779–1789	Paolo Renier
1789–1797	Ludovico Manin (abdicated, died 1802; French occupation 1797–8, then Austrian rule)

NOTES

Chronology There are basic uncertainties in the chronology of the first four centuries and many dates may vary by a year or so; the scheme above is that of Cessi. On the accession of Vitale Michiel II, see V. Lazzarini, *Archivio veneto*, fifth series, I (1927), 181. Relationships are given only for the period when the dogeship was hereditary; for lineages and family names, many of which are uncertain, see Cessi.

Names and Titles The basic title from the fourteenth century was *dux Venetiarum*; see V. Lazzarini, 'I titoli dei dogi di Venezia', *Archivio veneto*, third series, V (1903), 271–311.

BIBLIOGRAPHY

Cessi, R., *Venezia ducale* (2 vols., Venice, 1963–5).
Kretschmayr, H., *Geschichte von Venedig* (3 vols., Gotha, 1905–34).

THE KINGDOM OF NAPLES AND SICILY

House of Hauteville – Dukes of Apulia

1059–1085	Robert Guiscard (son of Tancred of Hauteville; duke of Apulia as a vassal of the papacy 1059)
1085–1111	Roger Borsa (son)
1111–1127	William (son; union with Sicily 1128)

Counts of Sicily

1072–1101	Roger I (son of Tancred; count of Sicily following capture of Palermo 1072)
1101–1105	Simon (son)

Kings of Naples and Sicily

1105–1154	Roger II, the Great (brother; duke of Apulia 1128; king of Sicily 1130)
1154–1166	William I, the Bad (son; co-regent 1151)
1166–1189	William II, the Good (son)
1190–1194	Tancred of Lecce (grandson of Roger II)
1192–1194	Roger III (son; co-regent)
1194	William III (brother; deposed, died 1198?)

House of Hohenstaufen

1194–1197	Henry (king of the Romans 1190; married Constance, daughter of Roger II)
1197–1250	Frederick I (son; king of the Romans 1212)
1250–1254	Conrad (son; king of the Romans 1250; interregnum 1254–8)
1258–1266	Manfred (bastard brother)

House of Anjou – Kings of Naples

1266–1285	Charles I (count of Anjou; lost Sicily 1282)
1285–1309	Charles II, the Lame (son)
1309–1343	Robert the Wise (son)
1343–1381	Joan I (granddaughter; deposed, died 1382)
1381–1386	Charles III of Durazzo (great-grandson of Charles II; king of Hungary 1385)
1386–1414	Ladislas (son)
1414–1435	Joan II (sister)
1435–1442	René the Good (adopted son; deposed, died 1480)

House of Aragon

1443–1458	Alfonso I, the Magnanimous (king of Aragon 1416)
1458–1494	Ferdinand I (bastard son)
1494–1495	Alfonso II (son; abdicated, died 1495)
1495–1496	Ferdinand II (son)
1496–1501	Frederick (son of Ferdinand I; deposed, died 1504; Aragonese, then Spanish rule 1501–1707; Austrian rule 1707–34)

House of Aragon – Kings of Sicily

1282–1285	Peter I, the Great (king of Aragon 1276; married Constance, daughter of Manfred)
1285–1295	James the Just (son; abdicated; Aragon 1291–1327)
1296–1337	Frederick II (brother; lord of Sicily 1295–6)
1337–1342	Peter II (son; co-regent 1320)
1342–1355	Louis (son)
1355–1377	Frederick III, the Simple (brother)
1377–1401	Mary (daughter)
1390–1409	Martin I, the Younger (son of Martin of Aragon; married Mary)
1409–1410	Martin II, the Humane (father; Aragon 1396; interregnum 1410–12; Aragonese, then Spanish rule 1412–1713)

House of Savoy

1713–1720	Victor Amadeus II (king of Sardinia 1720–30; Austrian rule 1720–34)

House of Bourbon – Kings of Naples and Sicily

1734–1759	Charles (king of Spain 1759–88)
1759–1816	Ferdinand IV (son; lost Naples 1806–15)

House of Bonaparte – Kings of Naples

1806–1808	Joseph Napoleon (brother of Napoleon I, emperor of the French; king of Spain 1808–13)
1808–1815	Joachim Napoleon (married Caroline, sister of Napoleon I; grand duke of Berg 1806–8; deposed, died 1815)

House of Bourbon – Kings of the Two Sicilies

1816–1825	Ferdinand I (formerly Ferdinand IV; kingdom of the Two Sicilies 1816)
1825–1830	Francis I (son)
1830–1859	Ferdinand II (son)
1859–1860	Francis II (son; deposed, died 1894; union with the kingdom of Sardinia)

BIBLIOGRAPHY

Léonard, E. G., *Les Angevins de Naples* (Paris, 1954).
Storia di Napoli (11 vols. in 15 pts., Naples, 1967–78).

THE ESTE IN FERRARA AND MODENA

Lords of Ferrara

1196–1212	Azzo I (marquis of Este as Azzo VI; podestà of Ferrara 1196)
1212–1215	Aldobrandino I (son)
1215–1264	Azzo II, the Younger (brother)
1264–1293	Obizzo I (grandson; lord of Ferrara 1264; of Modena 1289)
1293–1308	Azzo III (son)
1308	Fresco (son; deposed, died 1309; Venetian, then papal rule 1308–17)
1317–1335	Rinaldo (grandson of Obizzo I)
1317–1344	Niccolò I (brother)
1317–1352	Obizzo II (brother)
1352–1361	Aldobrandino III (son)
1361–1388	Niccolò II, the Lame (brother)
1388–1393	Alberto (brother)
1393–1441	Niccolò III (son)
1441–1450	Leonello (son)

Dukes of Ferrara

1450–1471	Borso (brother; duke of Modena 1452; made duke of Ferrara by pope Paul II 1471)
1471–1505	Ercole I (brother)
1505–1534	Alfonso I (son)
1534–1559	Ercole II (son)
1559–1597	Alfonso II (son)

Dukes of Modena

1597–1628	Cesare (grandson of Alfonso I; union of Ferrara with the papal states 1598)
1628–1629	Alfonso III (son; abdicated, died 1644)
1629–1658	Francis I (son)
1658–1662	Alfonso IV (son)
1662–1694	Francis II (son)
1694–1737	Rinaldo (son of Francis I)
1737–1780	Francis III (son)
1780–1796	Ercole III (son; deposed, died 1803; union with the Cispadane Republic and later regimes 1796–1814)

House of Habsburg-Lorraine

1814–1846	Francis IV (son of Mary Beatrice, daughter of Ercole III, and Ferdinand, son of emperor Francis I)
1846–1859	Francis V (son; deposed, died 1875; union with the kingdom of Sardinia 1860)

BIBLIOGRAPHY

Chiappini, L., *Gli Estensi* (Milan, 1967).
Gundersheimer, W. L., *Ferrara: the Style of a Renaissance Despotism* (Princeton, 1973).

THE MONTEFELTRO AND DELLA ROVERE IN URBINO

Counts of Urbino

1226–1241	Buonconte (count of Montefeltro; invested with Urbino 1226)
1241–1253	Montefeltrano (son)
1253–1296	Guido (son; papal rule 1285–94; abdicated, died 1298)
1296–1322	Federico I (son)
1322–1360	Nolfo (son; papal rule 1322–4)
1360–1363	Federico II (son)
1363–1404	Antonio (son; papal rule 1369–75)
1404–1443	Guidantonio (son)
1443–1444	Oddantonio (son; made duke of Urbino by pope Eugenius IV 1443)

Dukes of Urbino

1444–1482	Federico III (bastard brother; made duke by pope Sixtus IV 1474)
1482–1508	Guidubaldo I (son)

House of Della Rovere

1508–1538	Francesco Maria I (son of Giovanna, daughter of Federico III, and Giovanni della Rovere)
1538–1574	Guidubaldo II (son)
1574–1621	Francesco Maria II (son; abdicated)
1621–1623	Federico Ubaldo (son)
1623–1631	Francesco Maria II (again; resigned authority 1624; union with the papal states 1631)

NOTES

Chronology Some dates down to 1363 may vary by a year or so.

BIBLIOGRAPHY

Franceschini, G., *I Montefeltro* (Milan, 1970).
Ugolini, F., *Storia dei conti e duchi d'Urbino* (2 vols., Florence, 1859).

THE VISCONTI AND SFORZA IN MILAN

House of Visconti – Lords of Milan

1287–1302, 1311–1322	Matteo I, the Great (captain of the people 1287; lord 1313; abdicated, died 1322)
1322–1327	Galeazzo I (son; deposed, died 1328; republic 1327–9)
1329–1339	Azzone (son)
1339–1349	Luchino (son of Matteo I)
1339–1354	Giovanni (brother)
1354–1355	Matteo II (nephew)
1354–1378	Galeazzo II (brother)
1354–1385	Bernabò (brother; deposed, died 1385)

Dukes of Milan

1378–1402	Gian Galeazzo (son of Galeazzo II; made duke of Milan by Wenceslas, king of the Romans, 1395)
1402–1412	Giovanni Maria (son)
1412–1447	Filippo Maria (brother; Ambrosian Republic 1447–50)

House of Sforza

1450–1466	Francesco I (married Bianca Maria, daughter of Filippo Maria)
1466–1476	Galeazzo Maria (son)
1476–1494	Gian Galeazzo (son)
1494–1499, 1500	Ludovico Maria (son of Francesco I; deposed, died 1508; French occupation 1499–1512)
1512–1515	Massimiliano (son; deposed, died 1530; French occupation 1515–21)
1521–1525, 1529–1535	Francesco II (brother; deposed during imperial occupation 1525–9; union with the empire 1535)

BIBLIOGRAPHY

Cognasso, F., *I Visconti* (Milan, 1966).
Santoro, C., *Gli Sforza* (Milan, 1968).

THE GONZAGA IN MANTUA

Captains-General of Mantua

1328–1360	Luigi (captain-general of Mantua after fall of Bonacolsi rule 1328)
1360–1369	Guido (son)
1369–1382	Ludovico I (son)
1382–1407	Francesco I (son)

Marquises of Mantua

1407–1444	Gianfrancesco (son; made marquis of Mantua by emperor Sigismund 1433)
1444–1478	Ludovico II (son)
1478–1484	Federico I (son)
1484–1519	Francesco II (son)

Dukes of Mantua

1519–1540	Federico II (son; made duke of Mantua by emperor Charles V 1530; marquis of Montferrat 1536)
1540–1550	Francesco III (son)
1550–1587	Guglielmo (brother; duke of Montferrat 1575)
1587–1612	Vincenzo I (son)
1612	Francesco IV (son)
1612–1626	Ferdinando (brother)
1626–1627	Vincenzo II (brother; war of the Mantuan Succession 1628–31)

Line of Nevers

1631–1637	Carlo I (duke of Nevers; grandson of Federico II)
1637–1665	Carlo II (grandson)
1665–1708	Ferdinando Carlo (son; union of Mantua with the empire and of Montferrat with Savoy, 1708)

BIBLIOGRAPHY

Coniglio, G., *I Gonzaga* (Milan, 1967).
—— *Mantova: la storia* (3 vols., Mantua, 1958–63).

THE MEDICI AND THEIR SUCCESSORS IN FLORENCE

House of Medici

1434–1464	Cosimo the Elder (son of Giovanni di Bicci de' Medici; *de facto* ruler of Florence 1434)
1464–1469	Piero I, the Gouty (son)
1469–1492	Lorenzo the Magnificent (son)
1492–1494	Piero II (son; deposed, died 1503; republic 1494–1512)
1512–1513	Giuliano of Nemours (brother; deposed, died 1516)
1513–1519	Lorenzo of Urbino (son of Piero II)
1519–1523	Giulio (grandson of Piero I; pope Clement VII 1523–34)
1524–1527	Ippolito (bastard son of Giuliano; deposed, died 1535; republic 1527–30)

Duchy of Florence

1531–1537	Alessandro (bastard son of Giulio; duke of Florence 1532)

Grand Duchy of Tuscany

1537–1574	Cosimo I (fifth in descent from Giovanni di Bicci; made grand duke of Tuscany by pope Pius V 1569)
1574–1587	Francis I (son)
1587–1609	Ferdinand I (brother)
1609–1621	Cosimo II (son)
1621–1670	Ferdinand II (son)
1670–1723	Cosimo III (son)
1723–1737	Giovanni Gastone (son)

House of Habsburg-Lorraine

1737–1765	Francis II (duke of Lorraine 1729–37; emperor 1745)
1765–1790	Leopold I (son; emperor 1790–2)
1790–1799	Ferdinand III (son; deposed; French occupation 1799, 1800–1; grand duke of Würzburg 1806–14)

House of Bourbon

1801–1803	Louis I (son of Ferdinand, duke of Parma; reconstitution of Tuscany as the kingdom of Etruria 1801–7)
1803–1807	Louis II (Charles Louis) (son; deposed; French rule 1807–9; duke of Parma 1847–9)

House of Bonaparte

1809–1814	Marie Anne (Elisa) (sister of Napoleon I, emperor of the French; deposed, died 1820)

House of Habsburg-Lorraine

1814–1824	Ferdinand III (restored)
1824–1859	Leopold II (son; abdicated, died 1870)
1859–1860	Ferdinand IV (son; deposed, died 1908; union with the kingdom of Sardinia)

BIBLIOGRAPHY

Andrieux, M., *I Medici* (Milan, 1963).
Schevill, F., *History of Florence* (New York, 1961).

THE FARNESE AND BOURBONS IN PARMA

House of Farnese

1545–1547	Pier Luigi (made duke of Parma and Piacenza by his father, Pope Paul III, 1545)
1547–1586	Ottavio (son)
1586–1592	Alessandro (son)
1592–1622	Ranuccio I (son)
1622–1646	Odoardo (son)
1646–1694	Ranuccio II (son)
1694–1727	Francesco (son)
1727–1731	Antonio (brother)

House of Bourbon

1731–1736	Charles I (son of Elizabeth, niece of Antonio, and Philip V of Spain; king of Spain 1759–88; Austrian rule 1736–48)
1748–1765	Philip (brother)
1765–1802	Ferdinand (son; French occupation 1802–8; union with France 1808–14)

House of Habsburg-Lorraine

1814–1847	Marie Louise (daughter of Francis I, emperor of Austria; ex-empress of Napoleon I, emperor of the French)

House of Bourbon

1847–1849	Charles II (grandson of Ferdinand; duke of Lucca 1824–47; abdicated, died 1883)
1849–1854	Charles III (son)
1854–1859	Robert (son; deposed, died 1907; union with the kingdom of Sardinia 1860)

BIBLIOGRAPHY

Bazzi, T., and U. Benassi, *Storia di Parma* (Parma, 1908).
Nasalli Rocca, E., *I Farnese* (Milan, 1969).

THE HOUSE OF SAVOY

Counts of Savoy

1000–1048	Humbert I, Whitehands (count in Savoy and Belley by 1000, in Aosta and Maurienne by 1043)
1048–1051	Amadeus I (son)
1051–1059	Oddone (brother)
1059–1078	Peter I (son)
1078–1080	Amadeus II (brother)
1080–1103	Humbert II, the Fat (son)
1103–1148	Amadeus III (son)
1148–1189	Bl Humbert III (son)
1189–1233	Thomas (son)
1233–1253	Amadeus IV (son)
1253–1263	Boniface (son)
1263–1268	Peter II (son of Thomas)
1268–1285	Philip I (brother)
1285–1323	Amadeus V, the Great (nephew)
1323–1329	Edward the Liberal (son)
1329–1343	Aymon the Pacific (brother)
1343–1383	Amadeus VI, the Green Count (son)
1383–1391	Amadeus VII, the Red Count (son)

Dukes of Savoy

1391–1440	Amadeus VIII (son; duke of Savoy 1416; abdicated, died 1451; antipope as Felix V 1440–9)
1440–1465	Louis (son)
1465–1472	Bl Amadeus IX (son)
1472–1482	Philibert I, the Hunter (son)
1482–1490	Charles I, the Warrior (brother)
1490–1496	Charles John Amadeus (son)
1496–1497	Philip II of Bresse (son of Louis)
1497–1504	Philibert II, the Handsome (son)
1504–1553	Charles II, the Good (brother)
1553–1580	Emmanuel Philibert (son)
1580–1630	Charles Emmanuel I, the Great (son)
1630–1637	Victor Amadeus I (son)
1637–1638	Francis Hyacinth (son)
1638–1675	Charles Emmanuel II (brother)

Kings of Sardinia

1675–1730	Victor Amadeus II (son; king of Sardinia 1720; abdicated, died 1732)
1730–1773	Charles Emmanuel III (son)
1773–1796	Victor Amadeus III (son)
1796–1802	Charles Emmanuel IV (son; abdicated, died 1819; French annexation of Savoy and Piedmont 1792/8–1814)
1802–1821	Victor Emmanuel I (brother; abdicated, died 1824)
1821–1831	Charles Felix (brother)

Line of Carignano

1831–1849	Charles Albert (prince of Carignano; seventh in descent from Charles Emmanuel I; abdicated, died 1849)

Kings of Italy

1849–1878	Victor Emmanuel II (son; kingdom of Italy 1861)
1878–1900	Humbert I (son)
1900–1946	Victor Emmanuel III (son; abdicated, died 1947)
1946	Humbert II (son; deposed, died 1983; proclamation of the republic)

NOTES

Chronology Dates down to 1059 are approximate.

Names and Titles The use of the title 'count of Savoy' dates from 1125. Victor Emmanuel III was styled emperor of Ethiopia from 1936 to 1943, king of Albania from 1939 to 1943.

BIBLIOGRAPHY

Cognasso, F., *Umberto Biancamano* (Turin, 1929).
—— *I Savoia* (Milan, 1971).

5 THE IBERIAN PENINSULA

THE KINGDOMS OF LEÓN AND CASTILE

Kings of Asturias

718–737	Pelayo (leader of revolt against the Muslims; elected king 718)
737–739	Fáfila (son)
739–757	Alfonso I, the Catholic (son-in-law of Pelayo)
757–768	Fruela I (son)
768–774	Aurelio (nephew of Alfonso I)
774–783	Silo (son-in-law of Alfonso I)
783–788	Mauregato (bastard son of Alfonso I)
788–791	Vermudo I, the Deacon (brother of Aurelio; abdicated)
791–842	Alfonso II, the Chaste (son of Fruela I)
842–850	Ramiro I (son of Vermudo I)
850–866	Ordoño I (son)
866–910	Alfonso III, the Great (son; deposed, died 910)

Kings of León

910–914	García (son)
914–924	Ordoño II (brother)
924–925	Fruela II (brother)
926–931	Alfonso IV, the Monk (son of Ordoño II; abdicated, died 933)
931–951	Ramiro II (brother)
951–956	Ordoño III (son)
956–958	Sancho I, the Fat (brother; deposed)
958–959	Ordoño IV, the Bad (son of Alfonso IV; deposed, died 962)
959–966	Sancho I (restored)
966–985	Ramiro III (son)
985–999	Vermudo II, the Gouty (son of Ordoño III)
999–1028	Alfonso V (son)
1028–1037	Vermudo III (son)

House of Navarre

1038–1065	Ferdinand I (count of Castile 1029; married Sancha, daughter of Alfonso V)
1065–1072	Sancho II, the Strong (son; Castile)
1065–1109	Alfonso VI (brother; León; Castile 1072)
1109–1126	Urraca (daughter)

House of Burgundy

1126–1157	Alfonso VII, the Emperor (son of Urraca and Raymond of Burgundy; co-regent 1111)

Kings of Castile

1157–1158	Sancho III, the Desired (son)
1158–1214	Alfonso VIII (son)
1214–1217	Henry I (son)
1217	Berengaria (sister; abdicated, died 1246)

Kings of León

1157–1188	Ferdinand II (son of Alfonso VII)
1188–1230	Alfonso IX (son)

Kings of Castile and León

1217–1252	St Ferdinand III (son of Berengaria and Alfonso IX; León 1230)
1252–1284	Alfonso X, the Learned (son)
1284–1295	Sancho IV, the Fierce (son)
1295–1312	Ferdinand IV, the Summoned (son)
1312–1350	Alfonso XI (son)
1350–1369	Peter the Cruel (son)

House of Trastámara

1369–1379	Henry II (bastard brother; count of Trastámara)
1379–1390	John I (son)
1390–1406	Henry III, the Sickly (son)
1406–1454	John II (son)
1454–1474	Henry IV, the Impotent (son)

House of Aragon

1474–1504	Ferdinand V, the Catholic (king of Aragon 1479–1516; regent of Castile 1507; king of Navarre 1512)
1474–1504	Isabel I, the Catholic (daughter of John II; married Ferdinand V)

House of Habsburg

1504–1506	Philip I, the Handsome (son of emperor Maximilian I; ruler of the Low Countries 1482)
1504–1506	Joan the Crazy (daughter of Isabel I and Ferdinand V; married Philip I; nominal queen 1506–55 (Aragon 1516))

THE KINGDOM OF NAVARRE (PAMPLONA)

House of Iñigo

824–851	Iñigo Arista (leader of revolt against the Franks; elected king *c.*824)
851–880	García Iñiguez (son)
880–905	Fortún Garcés (son)

House of Jimeno

905–925	Sancho I (son of García Jiménez)
925–931	Jimeno (brother)
931–970	García I (son of Sancho I)
970–994	Sancho II, Abarca (son)
994–1004	García II, the Tremulous (son)
1004–1035	Sancho III, the Great (son)
1035–1054	García III of Nájera (son)
1054–1076	Sancho IV of Peñalén (son)
1076–1094	Sancho V (grandson of Sancho III)
1094–1104	Peter I (son)
1104–1134	Alfonso I, the Battler (brother)
1134–1150	García IV, the Restorer (great-grandson of García III)
1150–1194	Sancho VI, the Wise (son)
1194–1234	Sancho VII, the Strong (son)

House of Champagne

1234–1253	Thibaut I, the Posthumous (son of Blanche, daughter of Sancho VI, and Thibaut III of Champagne)
1253–1270	Thibaut II (son)
1270–1274	Henry I, the Fat (brother)

House of France

1284–1305	Philip I, the Fair (king of France as Philip IV 1285–1314)
1274–1305	Joan I (daughter of Henry I; married Philip I)
1305–1316	Louis (son; king of France as Louis X 1314; union with France 1314–28)

House of Evreux

1328–1343	Philip III (count of Evreux)
1328–1349	Joan II (daughter of Louis; married Philip III)
1349–1387	Charles II, the Bad (son)
1387–1425	Charles III, the Noble (son)

House of Aragon

1425–1479	John II (king of Aragon 1458)
1425–1441	Blanche (daughter of Charles III; married John II)
1479	Eleanor (daughter)

House of Foix

1479–1483	Francis Phoebus (grandson of Eleanor and Gaston IV, count of Foix)

House of Albret

1484–1516	John III (son of Alan, lord of Albret)
1483–1517	Catherine (sister of Francis; married John III; Aragonese conquest of southern Navarre 1512)
1517–1555	Henry II (son)

House of Bourbon

1555–1562	Anthony (duke of Vendôme)
1555–1572	Joan III (daughter of Henry II; married Anthony)
1572–1610	Henry III (son; king of France as Henry IV 1589; union with France)

NOTES

Chronology The early history of Pamplona is obscure; dates down to 880 are approximate. The designation 'kingdom of Navarre' was in use from the late eleventh century.

THE COUNTY OF BARCELONA

House of Urgell

878–897	Wilfred I, the Hairy (son of Sunifred of Urgell; count of Barcelona and Girona 878)
897–911	Wilfred II (Borrell I) (son)
911–947	Sunyer (brother; abdicated, died 950)
947–966	Miró (son)
947–992	Borrell II (brother)
992–1017	Raymond Borrell III (son)
1017–1035	Berengar Raymond I, the Crooked (son)
1035–1076	Raymond Berengar I, the Elder (son)
1076–1082	Raymond Berengar II, Towhead (son)
1076–1097	Berengar Raymond II, the Fratricide (brother)
1097–1131	Raymond Berengar III, the Great (son of Raymond Berengar II; co-regent 1086)
1131–1162	Raymond Berengar IV, the Saint (son)
1162–1196	Alfonso (son; king of Aragon as Alfonso II 1164; union with Aragon)

THE COUNTY OF CASTILE

House of Lara

931–970	Fernán González (son of Gonzalo Fernández of Lara; count of Castile 931)
970–995	García I (son)
995–1017	Sancho (son)
1017–1029	García II (son)

House of Navarre

1029–1065	Ferdinand the Great (son of Sancho III of Navarre; maternal grandson of Sancho; king of León 1038)

THE KINGDOM OF SOBRARBE

House of Navarre

1035–1043	Gonzalo (son of Sancho III of Navarre; deposed, died 1045; union with Aragon)

THE KINGDOM OF ARAGON

House of Navarre

1035–1069	Ramiro I (son of Sancho III of Navarre; succeeded to Aragon upon partition of his father's territories)
1069–1094	Sancho Ramírez (son; co-regent 1062; king of Navarre 1076)
1094–1104	Peter I (son; co-regent 1085)
1104–1134	Alfonso I, the Battler (brother)
1134–1137	Ramiro II, the Monk (brother; abdicated, died 1157)
1137–1164	Petronilla (daughter; abdicated, died 1173)

House of Barcelona

1164–1196	Alfonso II, the Chaste (son of Petronilla and Raymond Berengar IV, count of Barcelona)
1196–1213	Peter II, the Catholic (son)
1213–1276	James I, the Conqueror (son)
1276–1285	Peter III, the Great (son)
1285–1291	Alfonso III, the Liberal (son)
1291–1327	James II, the Just (brother)
1327–1336	Alfonso IV, the Benign (son)
1336–1387	Peter IV, the Ceremonious (son)
1387–1396	John I, the Hunter (son)
1396–1410	Martin the Humane (brother; interregnum 1410–12)

House of Trastámara

1412–1416	Ferdinand I of Antequera (son of Eleanor, daughter of Peter IV, and John I of Castile)
1416–1458	Alfonso V, the Magnanimous (son)
1458–1479	John II (brother)
1479–1516	Ferdinand II, the Catholic (son; married Isabel I of Castile; union with Castile 1479–1504 and from 1516)

NOTES

Names and Titles As vassals of Navarre, Gonzalo of Sobrarbe and Ramiro I of Aragon could not lay claim to royal style; the title of king was not employed in Aragon until its union with Navarre (1076). Ubieto, 'Estudios', 163–82.

THE KINGDOM OF GALICIA

House of León

1065–1071	García (son of Ferdinand I of León; deposed, died 1090; union with Castile)

THE KINGDOM OF MAJORCA

House of Aragon

1276–1311	James II (son of James I of Aragon; succeeded to Majorca upon partition of his father's territories)
1311–1324	Sancho (son)
1324–1343	James III (nephew; deposed, died 1349; Aragonese conquest of Majorca)

THE KINGDOM OF SPAIN

House of Habsburg

1516–1556	Charles I (son of Joan and Philip I of Castile; emperor 1519–58; abdicated, died 1558)
1556–1598	Philip II (son)
1598–1621	Philip III (son)
1621–1665	Philip IV (son)
1665–1700	Charles II (son)

House of Bourbon

1700–1724	Philip V (grandson of Maria Theresa, daughter of Philip IV, and Louis XIV of France; abdicated)
1724	Louis I (son)
1724–1746	Philip V (again)
1746–1759	Ferdinand VI (son)
1759–1788	Charles III (brother)
1788–1808	Charles IV (son; abdicated, died 1819)
1808	Ferdinand VII (son; deposed)

House of Bonaparte

1808–1813	Joseph Napoleon (brother of Napoleon I, emperor of the French; deposed, died 1844)

House of Bourbon

1813–1833	Ferdinand VII (restored)
1833–1868	Isabel II (daughter; deposed, died 1904)
1868–1870	Provisional Government

House of Savoy

1870–1873	Amadeus I (son of Victor Emmanuel II, king of Italy; abdicated, died 1890)
1873–1874	First Republic

House of Bourbon

1874–1885	Alfonso XII (son of Isabel II and Francis of Asís, grandson of Charles IV, king consort 1846–68 (died 1902))
1886–1931	Alfonso XIII (son; deposed, died 1941)
1931–1939	Second Republic
1939–1975	Spanish State: Francisco Franco Bahamonde, chief of state

House of Bourbon

1975–	Juan Carlos I (grandson of Alfonso XIII)

BIBLIOGRAPHY FOR THE SPANISH KINGDOMS

Abadal, R. d', *Els primers comtes catalans* (3rd edn., Barcelona, 1980).

Diccionario de historia de España, ed. G. Bleiberg (2nd edn., 3 vols., Madrid, 1968–9).

Floriano, A. C., 'Cronología y genealogía de los reyes de Asturias', *Archivum*, VI (1956), 251–85.

Lacarra, J. M., *Historia política del reino de Navarra desde sus orígenes hasta su incorporación a Castilla* (3 vols., Pamplona, 1972–3).
Pérez de Urbel, J., *Sampiro: su crónica y la monarquía leonesa en el siglo X* (Madrid, 1952).
Sobrequés, S., *Els grans comtes de Barcelona* (3rd edn., Barcelona, 1980).
Ubieto, A., 'Estudios en torno a la división del reino por Sancho el Mayor de Navarra', *Príncipe de Viana*, XXI (1960), 5–56, 163–236.
—— 'Los reyes pamploneses entre 905 y 970: notas cronológicas', *Príncipe de Viana*, XXIV (1963), 77–82.

THE KINGDOM OF PORTUGAL

House of Burgundy

1097–1112	Henry (grandson of Robert I, duke of Burgundy; count of Portugal by 1097)

Kings of Portugal

1112–1185	Afonso I (son; assumed the title of king 1139)
1185–1211	Sancho I (son)
1211–1223	Afonso II, the Fat (son)
1223–1248	Sancho II, Capêlo (son)
1248–1279	Afonso III (brother)
1279–1325	Denis the Farmer (son)
1325–1357	Afonso IV (son)
1357–1367	Pedro I, the Justicer (son)
1367–1383	Ferdinand I (son; interregnum 1383–5)

House of Avis

1385–1433	John I (bastard brother; master of Avis)
1433–1438	Duarte (son)
1438–1481	Afonso V, the African (son)
1481–1495	John II, the Perfect Prince (son)
1495–1521	Manuel I, the Fortunate (grandson of Duarte)
1521–1557	John III (son)
1557–1578	Sebastian (grandson)
1578–1580	Henry the Cardinal (son of Manuel I; union with Spain 1580–1640)

House of Braganza

1640–1656	John IV (duke of Braganza; eighth in descent from John I)
1656–1667	Afonso VI (son; deposed, died 1683)
1683–1706	Pedro II (brother; regent 1667–83)
1706–1750	John V, the Magnanimous (son)
1750–1777	Joseph I (son)
1777–1786	Pedro III (brother)
1777–1816	Maria I (daughter of Joseph I; married Pedro III)
1816–1826	John VI (son; regent 1799–1816)
1826–1828	Pedro IV (son; abdicated, died 1834)
1828–1834	Miguel I (brother; deposed, died 1866)
1834–1853	Maria II (daughter of Pedro IV)

House of Saxe-Coburg-Gotha

1853–1861	Pedro V (son of Maria II and Ferdinand of Saxe-Coburg-Gotha, king consort 1837–53 (died 1885))
1861–1889	Luís I (brother)
1889–1908	Carlos I (son)
1908–1910	Manuel II (son; deposed, died 1932; proclamation of the republic)

NOTES

Names and Titles Henry was styled count of Coimbra by 1095, count of Portugal by late 1097; the royal title was in regular use from 1140 (Livermore, 65). From 1815 until Brazilian independence (1822), the monarch had the additional title king or queen of Brazil.

BIBLIOGRAPHY

Livermore, H. V., *A History of Portugal* (Cambridge, 1947).
Serrão, J., *Dicionário de história de Portugal* (4 vols., Lisbon, 1963–71).

6 THE GERMAN-SPEAKING STATES

THE HOLY ROMAN EMPIRE

Carolingian House

800–814	Charles I, the Great (Charlemagne) (king of the Franks 768; crowned emperor 800)
814–840	Louis I, the Pious (son; crowned emperor 813, 816)
840–855	Lothair I (son; crowned emperor 817, 823)
855–875	Louis II (son; crowned emperor 850)
875–877	Charles II, the Bald (son of Louis I; crowned emperor 875; interregnum 877–81)
881–887	Charles III, the Fat (nephew; crowned emperor 881; deposed, died 888)
887–899	Arnulf of Carinthia (nephew; crowned emperor 896)
900–911	Louis III, the Child (son)

House of Franconia

911–918	Conrad I

House of Saxony

919–936	Henry I, the Fowler
936–973	Otto I, the Great (son; crowned emperor 962)
973–983	Otto II (son; co-regent, 961; crowned emperor 967)
983–1002	Otto III (son; co-regent, 983; crowned emperor 996)
1002–1024	St Henry II (great-grandson of Henry I; crowned emperor 1014)

Salian House

1024–1039	Conrad II (great-grandson of Liutgard, daughter of Otto I; crowned emperor 1027)
1039–1056	Henry III (son; co-regent 1028; crowned emperor 1046)
1056–1105	Henry IV (son; co-regent 1054; crowned emperor 1084; deposed, died 1106)
1077–1080	[Rudolf of Swabia]
1081–1088	[Herman of Salm]
1087–1098	Conrad (son of Henry IV; co-regent; deposed, died 1101)
1105–1125	Henry V (brother; co-regent 1099; crowned emperor 1111)

House of Supplinburg

1125–1137	Lothair II of Saxony (crowned emperor 1133)

House of Hohenstaufen

1138–1152	Conrad III (son of Agnes, daughter of Henry IV, and Frederick I of Swabia; rival king 1127–35)
1147–1150	Henry (son; co-regent)
1152–1190	Frederick I, Barbarossa (nephew of Conrad III; crowned emperor, 1155)

1190–1197	Henry VI (son; co-regent 1169; crowned emperor 1191)
1198–1208	Philip of Swabia (brother)

House of Welf

1198–1218	Otto IV of Brunswick (crowned emperor 1209)

House of Hohenstaufen

1212–1250	Frederick II (son of Henry VI; crowned emperor 1220)
1220–1235	Henry (son; co-regent; deposed, died 1242)
1246–1247	[Henry Raspe of Thuringia]
1247–1256	[William of Holland]
1250–1254	Conrad IV (son of Frederick II; co-regent 1237)
1257–1272	[Richard of Cornwall]

House of Habsburg

1273–1291	Rudolf I

House of Nassau

1292–1298	Adolf (deposed, died 1298)

House of Habsburg

1298–1308	Albert I of Austria (son of Rudolf I)

House of Luxemburg

1308–1313	Henry VII (crowned emperor 1312)

House of Wittelsbach

1314–1347	Louis IV of Bavaria (crowned emperor 1328)
1314–1330	[Frederick of Austria] (son of Albert I)

House of Luxemburg

1346–1378	Charles IV (grandson of Henry VII; crowned emperor 1355)
1349	[Günther of Schwarzburg] (abdicated, died 1349)
1378–1400	Wenceslas (son of Charles IV; co-regent 1376; deposed, died 1419)

House of Wittelsbach

1400–1410	Rupert of the Palatinate

House of Luxemburg

1410–1437	Sigismund (son of Charles IV; crowned emperor 1433)
1410–1411	[Jobst of Moravia] (nephew of Charles IV)

House of Habsburg

1438–1439	Albert II of Austria (fourth in descent from Albert I)
1440–1493	Frederick III (second cousin; crowned emperor 1452)
1493–1519	Maximilian I (son; co-regent 1486; emperor 1508)
1519–1558	Charles V (grandson; crowned emperor 1530; abdicated, died 1558)
1558–1564	Ferdinand I (brother)
1564–1576	Maximilian II (son)
1576–1612	Rudolf II (son)
1612–1619	Matthias (brother)

1619–1637	Ferdinand II (grandson of Ferdinand I)
1637–1657	Ferdinand III (son)
1658–1705	Leopold I (son)
1705–1711	Joseph I (son)
1711–1740	Charles VI (brother; interregnum 1740–2)

House of Wittelsbach

1742–1745	Charles VII of Bavaria

House of Habsburg-Lorraine

1745–1765	Francis I of Lorraine (married Maria Theresa, daughter of Charles VI)
1765–1790	Joseph II (son)
1790–1792	Leopold II (brother)
1792–1806	Francis II (son; abdicated; emperor of Austria as Francis I 1804–35)

NOTES

Names and Titles To the Carolingian titles of Imperator and Augustus, Otto II added the epithet 'of the Romans' (Gebhardt, I, 262). From the eleventh century to the sixteenth, the monarch was 'king of the Romans' (*Romanorum rex*) before imperial coronation, thereafter *Romanorum imperator*. Uncrowned by the pope, Maximilian I proclaimed himself 'Roman emperor elect' (1508); this was thenceforth the monarch's strict legal title, the successor-designate being styled 'king of the Romans' (ibid., II, 12).

From the breakup of the Carolingian empire (887), the basic dates given are dates of reign as German king. Except in the case of co-regents, overlapping dates indicate rival claims. Kings elected in opposition to others, and never receiving general recognition, are in square brackets.

With few exceptions, imperial coronations down to Charles V took place in Rome at the hands of the pope. With Ferdinand I, the German coronation had imperial status, and papal participation ceased. For post-Carolingian kings of Italy who obtained the imperial crown, see under that kingdom.

BIBLIOGRAPHY

Gebhardt, B., *Handbuch der deutschen Geschichte* (9th edn., 4 vols. in 5 pts., Stuttgart, 1970–6).

Krones, F., *Grundriss der oesterreichischen Geschichte mit besonderer Rücksicht auf Quellen- und Literaturkunde* (4 pts., Vienna, 1881–2).

THE AUSTRIAN EMPIRE

House of Habsburg-Lorraine

1804–1835	Francis I (Holy Roman emperor as Francis II; emperor of Austria 1804)
1835–1848	Ferdinand I (son; abdicated, died 1875)
1848–1916	Francis Joseph I (nephew)
1916–1918	Charles I (grandnephew; deposed, died 1922; proclamation of the republic)

NOTES

Names and Titles The imperial title, assumed by Francis I in August 1804, was *Kaiser von Österreich*; he retained the titles king of Hungary and of Bohemia.

BIBLIOGRAPHY

Macartney, C. A., *The Habsburg Empire, 1790–1918* (London, 1971).

THE KINGDOM OF BURGUNDY

House of Welf

888–912	Rudolf I (son of Conrad, count of Auxerre; recognized as king of Jurane Burgundy 888)
912–937	Rudolf II (son; king of Italy 922–6)
937–993	Conrad the Pacific (son; inherited Provence 948)
993–1032	Rudolf III, the Sluggard (son; union with the Holy Roman empire 1033)

BIBLIOGRAPHY

Poupardin, R., *Le royaume de Bourgogne (888–1038)* (Paris, 1907) (*Bibliothèque de l'école des hautes études*, CLXIII).

Previté-Orton, C. W., 'Italy and Provence, 900–950', *English Historical Review*, XXXII (1917), 335–47.

THE DUCHY OF BAVARIA

Liutpolding House

907–937	Arnulf (son of margrave Liutpold; attested as duke from 907)
937–938	Eberhard (son; deposed)
938–947	Berthold (son of Liutpold)

House of Saxony

947–955	Henry I (son of Henry I, king of Germany)
955–976	Henry II, the Quarrelsome (son; deposed)
976–982	Otto I of Swabia (grandson of emperor Otto I)

Liutpolding House

983–985	Henry III (son of Berthold; abdicated, died 989)

House of Saxony

985–995	Henry II (restored)
995–1004	Henry IV (son; emperor Henry II 1002–24)

House of Luxemburg

1004–1009	Henry V (deposed)

House of Saxony

1009–1017	Henry IV (emperor Henry II, again)

House of Luxemburg

1017–1026	Henry V (restored)

Salian House

1027–1042	Henry VI (emperor Henry III 1039–56)

House of Luxemburg

1042–1047	Henry VII (nephew of Henry V)

Salian House

1047–1049	Henry VI (emperor Henry III, again)

Ezzonid House

1049–1053	Conrad I of Zütphen (deposed, died 1055)

Salian House

1053–1054	Henry VIII (son of Henry VI; emperor Henry IV 1056–1105)
1054–1055	Conrad II, the Child (brother)
1055–1061	Agnes of Poitiers (mother; abdicated, died 1077)

House of Nordheim

1061–1070	Otto II (deposed, died 1083)

House of Welf

1070–1077	Welf I (son of Azzo II of Este; deposed)

Salian House

1077–1096	Henry VIII (emperor Henry IV, again)

House of Welf

1096–1101	Welf I (restored)
1101–1120	Welf II, the Fat (son)
1120–1126	Henry IX, the Black (brother)
1126–1138	Henry X, the Proud (son; duke of Saxony 1137; deposed, died 1139)

House of Austria

1139–1141	Leopold

House of Hohenstaufen

1141–1143	Conrad III (king of the Romans 1138–52)

House of Austria

1143–1156	Henry XI, Jasomirgott (brother of Leopold; abdicated, died 1177)

House of Welf

1156–1180	Henry XII, the Lion (son of Henry X; Saxony 1142; deposed, died 1195; end of Welf rule)

BIBLIOGRAPHY

Reindel, K., *Die bayerischen Luitpoldinger, 893–989* (Munich, 1953).

Spindler, M., ed., *Handbuch der bayerischen Geschichte* (4 vols. in 6 pts., Munich, 1968–75).

THE DUCHY OF LORRAINE

House of the Moselle

959–978	Frederick I (son of Wigeric; duke of Upper Lorraine as a vassal of the empire 959)
978–1027	Thierry I (son)
1027–1033	Frederick II (grandson)

House of Verdun

1033–1044	Gozelo (count of Verdun; great-grandson of Wigeric; duke of Lower Lorraine, 1023)
1044–1047	Godfrey the Bearded (son; deposed; Lower Lorraine 1065–9)

House of Châtenois

1047–1048	Adalbert (probable son of Gerard, count of Metz)
1048–1070	Gerard (brother)
1070–1115	Thierry II (son)
1115–1139	Simon I (son)
1139–1176	Matthew I (son)
1176–1206	Simon II (son)
1206–1213	Ferry II of Bitsch (nephew)
1213–1220	Thiébaut I (son)
1220–1251	Matthew II (brother)
1251–1303	Ferry III (son)
1303–1312	Thiébaut II (son)
1312–1329	Ferry IV (son)
1329–1346	Rudolf (son)
1346–1390	John I (son)
1390–1431	Charles II (son)

House of Anjou

1431–1453	René I, the Good (duke of Anjou 1434–80; married Isabel, daughter of Charles II (died 1453))
1453–1470	John II (son)
1470–1473	Nicholas (son)

House of Vaudémont

1473–1508	René II (son of Yolanda, daughter of René I, and Ferry II of Vaudémont, great-grandson of John I)
1508–1544	Anthony (son)
1544–1545	Francis I (son)
1545–1608	Charles III, the Great (son)
1608–1624	Henry II (son)
1624–1625	Nicola (daughter; deposed, died 1657)
1625	Francis II of Vaudémont (son of Charles III; abdicated, died 1632)
1625–1675	Charles IV (son; married Nicola; French occupation of Lorraine 1633–63, 1670–98)

1675–1690	Charles V (nephew)
1690–1729	Leopold (son)
1729–1737	Francis III (son; exchanged Lorraine for Tuscany 1737; emperor 1745–65)

House of Leszczyński

1737–1766	Stanislas (ex-king of Poland; father-in-law of Louis XV of France; union with France 1766)

NOTES

Chronology Dates down to 1027 may be subject to revision; those above follow Poull, *Maison ducale de Bar*, ch. i. On Adalbert and Gerard, not 'of Alsace', see E. Hlawitschka, *Die Anfänge des Hauses Habsburg-Lothringen* (Saarbrucken, 1969), ch. iv. No duke Ferry I, 1205–6: M. de Pange, *Mémoires de la société d'archéologie lorraine*, XLII (1892), 51–81.

BIBLIOGRAPHY

Poull, G., *La maison ducale de Bar* (Rupt-sur-Moselle, 1977).
——*La maison ducale de Lorraine* (Rupt-sur-Moselle, 1968).

THE MARK AND DUCHY OF AUSTRIA

House of Babenberg

976–994	Leopold I (probable grandson of Arnulf, duke of Bavaria; margrave of Austria 975/6)
994–1018	Henry I (son)
1018–1055	Adalbert (brother)
1055–1075	Ernest (son)
1075–1095	Leopold II, the Handsome (son)
1095–1136	St Leopold III (son)
1136–1141	Leopold IV (son; duke of Bavaria 1139)

Dukes of Austria

1141–1177	Henry II, Jasomirgott (brother; Bavaria 1143–56; duke of Austria 1156)
1177–1194	Leopold V (son; duke of Styria 1192)
1194–1198	Frederick I (son)
1198–1230	Leopold VI, the Glorious (brother; Styria 1194)
1230–1246	Frederick II, the Warlike (son; union of Austria and Styria with the empire 1246)

House of Habsburg

1276–1282	Rudolf I (count of Habsburg as Rudolf IV; king of the Romans 1273–91; duke of Austria and Styria 1276)
1282–1283	Rudolf II (son; abdicated, died 1290)
1282–1298	Albert I (brother; king of the Romans 1298–1308)
1298–1307	Rudolf III (son; king of Bohemia 1306)
1298–1326	Leopold I (brother)
1298–1330	Frederick III, the Handsome (brother; king of the Romans 1314)
1326–1358	Albert II, the Lame (brother; duke of Carinthia 1335)
1330–1339	Otto (brother)
1358–1365	Rudolf IV, the Founder (son of Albert II; count of Tyrol 1363)

Albertine Line

1365–1395	Albert III (brother; received Austria by partition 1379)
1395–1404	Albert IV, the Patient (son)
1404–1439	Albert V (son; king of the Romans 1438)
1440–1457	Ladislas Posthumus (son; king of Hungary 1445; union with Styria 1458)

Leopoldine Line

1365–1386	Leopold III (son of Albert II; Tyrol, Styria and Carinthia 1379)
1386–1406	William (son)
1386–1411	Leopold IV, the Fat (brother)

Line of Tyrol

1406–1439	Frederick IV (brother; received Tyrol by partition 1411)
1439–1490	Sigismund (son; archduke 1477; abdicated, died 1496; union with Styria)

Line of Styria

1406–1424	Ernest the Iron (son of Leopold III; Styria and Carinthia 1411)
1424–1463	Albert VI (son; archduke 1453)
1424–1493	Fréderick V (brother; king of the Romans 1440; archduke 1453; reunion of the Habsburg lands 1490)

NOTES

Names and Titles In view of Leopold I's apparent descent from duke Arnulf, the Babenbergs – a designation due to Otto of Freising – were in fact members of the Liutpolding house; see Lechner, ch. iii.

BIBLIOGRAPHY

Huber, A., *Geschichte Österreichs* (5 vols., Gotha, 1885–96).
Lechner, K., *Die Babenberger* (Vienna, 1976).

THE HOUSE OF BRUNSWICK-LÜNEBURG

House of Welf – Dukes of Brunswick-Lüneburg

1235–1252	Otto I, the Child (grandson of Henry XII of Bavaria; made duke of Brunswick and Lüneburg 1235)

Old Line of Lüneburg

1252–1277	John (son; received Lüneburg by partition 1267)
1277–1330	Otto II, the Severe (son)
1330–1352	Otto III (son)
1330–1369	William (brother; Lüneburg succession in dispute 1369–88)

Old Line of Brunswick

1252–1279	Albert I, the Great (son of Otto I; Brunswick 1267)
1279–1286	Henry I, the Singular (son; Grubenhagen 1286–1322)
1279–1292	William (brother; Brunswick 1286)
1279–1318	Albert II, the Fat (brother; Göttingen 1286; Brunswick 1292)
1318–1344	Otto the Mild (son)
1344–1345	Ernest (brother; Göttingen 1345–67)
1344–1369	Magnus I, the Pious (brother; Brunswick 1345)
1369–1373	Magnus II, the Younger (son; co-regent 1345)
1373–1400	Frederick (son; union of Brunswick with Lüneburg 1400)

Middle Line of Lüneburg

1388–1416	Henry II (brother; shared Lüneburg 1388; shared Brunswick 1400; received Lüneburg by partition 1409)
1416–1428	William I, the Victorious (son; Brunswick 1428)
1428–1434	Bernard I (son of Magnus II; Brunswick 1409–28)
1434–1441	Frederick the Pious (son; abdicated)
1434–1446	Otto I, the Lame (brother)
1446–1458	Frederick the Pious (again; abdicated, died 1478)
1458–1464	Bernard II (son)
1464–1471	Otto II (brother)
1471–1522	Henry the Middle (son; abdicated, died 1532)
1522–1527	Otto III (son; Harburg 1527–49)
1522–1546	Ernest I, the Confessor (brother)
1536–1539	Francis (brother; Gifhorn 1539–49)
1546–1559	Francis Otto (son of Ernest I)
1559–1598	Henry (brother; received Dannenberg by partition 1569)

Middle Line of Brunswick

1388–1428	Bernard I (son of Magnus II; shared Lüneburg 1388; shared Brunswick 1400; Brunswick 1409; Lüneburg 1428)
1428–1482	William I, the Victorious (nephew; Lüneburg 1416–28; Calenberg 1432)
1432–1473	Henry the Pacific (brother; Wolfenbüttel)
1482–1484	Frederick (son of William I; Calenberg 1483; deposed, died 1495)
1482–1495	William II, the Younger (brother; Göttingen 1483; abdicated, died 1503)

Line of Calenberg-Göttingen

1495–1540	Erik I, the Elder (son; received Calenberg-Göttingen by partition 1495)
1540–1584	Erik II, the Younger (son; union with Wolfenbüttel 1585)

Line of Wolfenbüttel

1495–1514	Henry I, the Elder (son of William II; Wolfenbüttel 1495)
1514–1568	Henry II, the Younger (son)
1568–1589	Julius (son; Calenberg 1585)
1589–1613	Henry Julius (son)
1613–1634	Frederick Ulrich (son; Calenberg to Lüneburg and Wolfenbüttel to Dannenberg 1635)

New Line of Lüneburg

1559–1592	William the Younger (son of Ernest I; Lüneburg (Celle) 1569)
1592–1611	Ernest II (son)
1611–1633	Christian (brother)
1633–1636	Augustus the Elder (brother; Calenberg (Hanover) 1635)
1636–1641	George (brother; Hanover)
1636–1648	Frederick (brother; Celle)
1641–1665	Christian Louis (son of George; Hanover 1641–8; Celle 1648)
1648–1705	George William (brother; Hanover 1648–65; Celle 1665)
1665–1679	John Frederick (brother; Hanover)

Electors of Hanover

1679–1698	Ernest Augustus (brother; Hanover; elector 1692)
1698–1727	George Louis (son; Celle 1705; king of England as George I 1714; union with England until 1837)

Kings of Hanover

1837–1851	Ernest Augustus (son of George III, king of England)
1851–1866	George V (son; deposed, died 1878; union with Prussia)

New Line of Brunswick – Dukes of Brunswick

1635–1666	Augustus the Younger (son of Henry of Dannenberg (died 1598); Wolfenbüttel (Brunswick) 1635)
1666–1704	Rudolf Augustus (son)
1704–1714	Anthony Ulrich (brother; co-regent 1685)
1714–1731	Augustus William (son)
1731–1735	Louis Rudolf (brother)

Line of Bevern

1735	Ferdinand Albert (grandson of Augustus the Younger)
1735–1780	Charles I (son)
1780–1806	Charles William Ferdinand (son)
1806–1815	Frederick William (son; union with the kingdom of Westphalia 1807–13)
1815–1830	Charles II (son; deposed, died 1873)
1830–1884	William (brother)
1885–1906	Albert of Prussia (regent)
1907–1913	John Albert of Mecklenburg-Schwerin (regent; resigned, died 1920)

Line of Hanover

1913–1918 Ernest Augustus (grandson of George V, king of Hanover; deposed, died 1953; proclamation of the republic)

NOTES

Names and Titles With the exception of the kings of Hanover, reigning members of the dynasty in all its branches were styled dukes of Brunswick and Lüneburg. Hanover was proclaimed a kingdom in October 1814.

BIBLIOGRAPHY

Heinemann, O. von, *Geschichte von Braunschweig und Hannover* (3 vols., Gotha, 1882–92).

Schnath, G., *Geschichte des Landes Niedersachsen* (new edn., Würzburg, 1973).

THE HOUSE OF HESSE

Landgraves of Hesse

1264–1308	Henry I, the Child (son of Henry II, duke of Brabant; recognized as landgrave 1264)
1284–1298	Henry the Younger (son; co-regent)
1308–1311	John (brother; Lower Hesse)
1308–1328	Otto (brother; Upper Hesse)
1328–1376	Henry II, the Iron (son)
1376–1413	Herman the Learned (nephew; co-regent 1367)
1413–1458	Louis II, the Peaceful (son)

Line of Upper Hesse

1458–1483	Henry III, the Rich (son; received Upper Hesse by partition 1458)
1483–1500	William III, the Younger (son); union with Lower Hesse 1500)

Line of Lower Hesse

1458–1471	Louis III, the Frank (son of Louis II; Lower Hesse 1458)
1471–1493	William I, the Elder (son; abdicated, died 1515)

Landgraves of Hesse

1493–1509	William II, the Middle (brother; co-regent 1487; Upper Hesse 1500)
1509–1567	Philip the Magnanimous (son)

Line of Hesse-Cassel

1567–1592	William IV, the Wise (son; received Hesse-Cassel by partition 1567)
1592–1627	Maurice the Learned (son; abdicated, died 1632)
1627–1637	William V, the Constant (son)
1637–1663	William VI, the Just (son)
1663–1670	William VII (son)
1670–1730	Charles (brother)
1730–1751	Frederick I (son; king of Sweden 1720)
1751–1760	William VIII (brother; regent 1730–51)
1760–1785	Frederick II (son)

Electors of Hesse

1785–1821	William IX(I) (son; elector of Hesse 1803; union with the kingdom of Westphalia 1807–13)
1821–1847	William II (son)
1847–1866	Frederick William I (son; co-regent 1831; deposed, died 1875; union with Prussia)

Line of Hesse-Darmstadt

1567–1596	George I, the Pious (son of Philip; Hesse-Darmstadt 1567)
1596–1626	Louis V, the Faithful (son)
1626–1661	George II (son)
1661–1678	Louis VI (son)
1678	Louis VII (son)

1678–1739	Ernest Louis (brother)
1739–1768	Louis VIII (son)
1768–1790	Louis IX (son)

Grand Dukes of Hesse

1790–1830	Louis X(I) (son; grand duke of Hesse 1806)
1830–1848	Louis II (son)
1848–1877	Louis III (son; co-regent 1848)
1877–1892	Louis IV (nephew)
1892–1918	Ernest Louis (son; deposed, died 1937; proclamation of the republic)

BIBLIOGRAPHY

Knetsch, K. G. P., *Das Haus Brabant: Genealogie der Herzoge von Brabant und der Landgrafen von Hessen* (2 vols., Darmstadt, 1931).

Münscher, F., *Geschichte von Hessen für Jung und Alt erzählt* (Marburg, 1894).

THE HOUSE OF HOHENZOLLERN

Electors of Brandenburg

1415–1440	Frederick I (burgrave of Nuremberg as Frederick VI; margrave of Brandenburg with electoral rights 1415)
1440–1463	Frederick the Fat (son; margrave only; Old Mark and Prignitz)
1440–1470	Frederick II, the Iron Margrave (brother; Middle and New Marks; abdicated, died 1471)
1470–1486	Albert Achilles (brother)
1486–1499	John Cicero (son)
1499–1535	Joachim I, Nestor (son)
1535–1571	John (son; margrave only; New Mark)
1535–1571	Joachim II, Hector (brother; Old Mark and Prignitz, Middle Mark)
1571–1598	John George (son)
1598–1608	Joachim Frederick (son)
1608–1620	John Sigismund (son; duke of Prussia 1618)
1620–1640	George William (son)
1640–1688	Frederick William, the Great Elector (son)

Kings of Prussia

1688–1713	Frederick III(I) (son; king of Prussia 1701)
1713–1740	Frederick William I (son)
1740–1786	Frederick II, the Great (son)
1786–1797	Frederick William II (nephew)
1797–1840	Frederick William III (son)
1840–1861	Frederick William IV (son)

German Emperors

1861–1888	William I (brother; regent 1858–61; German emperor 1871)
1888	Frederick III (son)
1888–1918	William II (son; deposed, died 1941; proclamation of the republic)

Dukes of Prussia

1525–1568	Albert (grandson of Albert Achilles; grand master of the Teutonic order 1511; duke of Prussia 1525)
1568–1618	Albert Frederick (son; union of Prussia with Brandenburg 1618)

NOTES

Names and Titles The royal title assumed by Frederick I at his coronation in January 1701 was king *in* Prussia; Frederick II became king *of* Prussia in 1772. The imperial title, assumed by William I in January 1871, was German emperor (*deutscher Kaiser*); he retained the title king of Prussia.

BIBLIOGRAPHY

Heinrich, G., *Geschichte Preussens* (Frankfurt-am-Main, 1981).
Schultze, J., *Die Mark Brandenburg* (5 vols., Berlin, 1961–9).

THE HOUSE OF WETTIN

Electors of Saxony

1423–1428	Frederick I, the Warlike (margrave of Meissen as Frederick IV; duke of Saxe-Wittenberg with electoral rights 1423)
1428–1464	Frederick II, the Gentle (son)

Ernestine Line – Electors of Saxony

1464–1486	Ernest (son; elector; received Saxe-Wittenberg and Thuringia by partition 1485)
1486–1525	Frederick III, the Wise (son)
1525–1532	John the Constant (brother)
1532–1547	John Frederick the Magnanimous (son; deprived of the electorate, died 1554)

Albertine Line – Dukes of Saxony

1464–1500	Albert the Bold (son of Frederick II; Meissen and Osterland 1485)
1500–1539	George the Bearded (son)
1539–1541	Henry the Pious (brother)

Electors of Saxony

1541–1553	Maurice (son; awarded the electorate by emperor Charles V 1547)
1553–1586	Augustus (brother)
1586–1591	Christian I (son)
1591–1611	Christian II (son)
1611–1656	John George I (brother)
1656–1680	John George II (son)
1680–1691	John George III (son)
1691–1694	John George IV (son)
1694–1733	Frederick Augustus I, the Strong (brother)
1733–1763	Frederick Augustus II (son)
1763	Frederick Christian (son)

Kings of Saxony

1763–1827	Frederick Augustus III(I) (son; king of Saxony 1806; duke of Warsaw 1807–13)
1827–1836	Anthony (brother)
1836–1854	Frederick Augustus II (nephew; co-regent 1830)
1854–1873	John (brother)
1873–1902	Albert (son)
1902–1904	George (brother)
1904–1918	Frederick Augustus III (son; deposed, died 1932; proclamation of the republic)

BIBLIOGRAPHY

Böttiger, K. W., and T. Flathe, *Geschichte des Kurstaates und Königreiches Sachsen* (3 vols., Gotha, 1867–73).

Kötzschke, R., and H. Kretzschmar, *Sächsische Geschichte* (Frankfurt-am-Main, 1965).

THE WITTELSBACHS OF BAVARIA

Dukes of Bavaria

1180–1183	Otto I (count of Wittelsbach as Otto VI; made duke of Bavaria by emperor Frederick I 1180)
1183–1231	Louis I, the Kelheimer (son)
1231–1253	Otto II, the Noble (son; inherited the Palatinate 1214)

Line of Lower Bavaria

1253–1290	Henry XIII (son; received Lower Bavaria by partition 1255)
1290–1296	Louis III (son)
1290–1309	Stephen I (brother)
1290–1312	Otto III (brother; king of Hungary 1305–7)
1309–1334	Otto IV (son of Stephen I)
1309–1339	Henry XIV, the Elder (brother)
1312–1333	Henry XV, the Natternberger (son of Otto III)
1339–1340	John I, the Child (son of Henry XIV; union with Upper Bavaria 1341)

Line of Upper Bavaria

1253–1294	Louis II, the Severe (son of Otto II; Upper Bavaria and the Palatinate 1255)
1294–1317	Rudolf I (son; deposed, died 1319)

Dukes of Bavaria

1294–1347	Louis IV, the Bavarian (brother; king of the Romans 1314; resigned the Palatinate 1329; Lower Bavaria 1341)

Line of Upper Bavaria

1347–1351	Louis VI, the Roman (son; shared Upper Bavaria by partition 1349; abdicated, died 1365)
1347–1351	Otto V (brother; shared Upper Bavaria 1349; abdicated; shared Lower Bavaria-Landshut 1376–9)
1347–1361	Louis V, the Brandenburger (brother; shared Upper Bavaria 1349)
1361–1363	Meinhard (son; union with Lower Bavaria-Landshut 1363)

Line of Lower Bavaria-Straubing

1347–1358	William I (son of Louis IV; shared Lower Bavaria 1349; shared Lower Bavaria-Straubing 1353; deposed, died 1389)
1347–1404	Albert I (brother; shared Lower Bavaria 1349; shared Lower Bavaria-Straubing 1353)
1387–1397	Albert II, the Younger (son; co-regent)
1404–1425	John III (brother; co-regent 1397; partition among the remaining lines 1429)

Line of Lower Bavaria-Landshut

1347–1375	Stephen II (son of Louis IV; shared Lower Bavaria 1349; Lower Bavaria-Landshut 1353; Upper Bavaria 1363)
1375–1393	Frederick (son; shared Lower Bavaria-Landshut 1376; received Lower Bavaria-Landshut by partition 1392)
1393–1450	Henry XVI, the Rich (son; Upper Bavaria-Ingolstadt 1447)

1450–1479	Louis IX, the Rich (son)
1479–1503	George the Rich (son; union with Upper Bavaria-Munich 1504)

Line of Upper Bavaria-Ingolstadt

1375–1413	Stephen III, the Magnificent (son of Stephen II; shared Upper Bavaria 1376; Upper Bavaria-Ingolstadt 1392)
1413–1443	Louis VII, the Bearded (son; deposed, died 1447)
1443–1445	Louis VIII, the Younger (son; union with Lower Bavaria-Landshut 1447)

Line of Upper Bavaria-Munich

1375–1397	John II (son of Stephen II; shared Upper Bavaria 1376; Upper Bavaria-Munich 1392)
1397–1435	William III (son)
1397–1438	Ernest (brother)
1438–1460	Albert III, the Pious (son)
1460–1463	John IV (son)
1460–1467	Sigismund (brother; abdicated, died 1501)

Dukes of Bavaria

1465–1508	Albert IV, the Wise (brother; Lower Bavaria-Landshut 1504)
1508–1550	William IV (son)
1516–1545	Louis X (brother)
1550–1579	Albert V (son of William IV)
1579–1597	William V, the Pious (son; abdicated, died 1626)

Electors of Bavaria

1597–1651	Maximilian I (son; regent 1595–7; elector 1623)
1651–1679	Ferdinand Maria (son)
1679–1726	Maximilian II Emanuel (son)
1726–1745	Charles Albert (son; emperor 1742)
1745–1777	Maximilian III Joseph (son)

Line of Sulzbach

1777–1799	Charles Theodore (fourteenth in descent from Rudolf I; elector palatine 1742)

Line of Zweibrücken – Kings of Bavaria

1799–1825	Maximilian IV(I) Joseph (duke of Zweibrücken; fourteenth in descent from Rudolf I; king of Bavaria 1806)
1825–1848	Louis I (son; abdicated, died 1868)
1848–1864	Maximilian II (son)
1864–1886	Louis II (son)
1886–1912	Luitpold (son of Louis I; regent)
1886–1913	Otto (son of Maximilian II; deposed, died 1916)
1913–1918	Louis III (son of Luitpold; regent 1912–13; deposed, died 1921; proclamation of the republic)

BIBLIOGRAPHY

Riezler, S., *Geschichte Baierns* (8 vols., Gotha, 1878–1914).

Spindler, M., ed., *Handbuch der bayerischen Geschichte* (4 vols. in 6 pts., Munich, 1968–75).

THE WITTELSBACHS OF THE PALATINATE

Electors of the Palatinate

1329–1353	Rudolf II (son of Rudolf I, duke of Upper Bavaria; count palatine with electoral rights 1329)
1353–1390	Rupert I (brother)
1390–1398	Rupert II (nephew)
1398–1410	Rupert III (son; king of the Romans 1400)
1410–1436	Louis III (son)
1436–1449	Louis IV, the Gentle (son)
1452–1476	Frederick I, the Victorious (brother; regent 1449–52)
1476–1508	Philip the Upright (son of Louis IV)
1508–1544	Louis V, the Pacific (son)
1544–1556	Frederick II (brother)
1556–1559	Otto Henry (nephew)

Line of Simmern

1559–1576	Frederick III, the Pious (duke of Simmern; fifth in descent from Rupert III)
1576–1583	Louis VI (son)
1583–1610	Frederick IV (son)
1610–1623	Frederick V, the Winter King (son; king of Bohemia 1619–20; deposed, died 1632; award of the electorate to Bavaria)
1648–1680	Charles I Louis (son; recovered the electorate at the peace of Westphalia 1648)
1680–1685	Charles II (son)

Line of Neuburg

1685–1690	Philip William (duke of Neuburg; eighth in descent from Rupert III)
1690–1716	John William (son)
1716–1742	Charles III Philip (brother)

Line of Sulzbach

1742–1799	Charles IV Theodore (duke of Sulzbach; eleventh in descent from Rupert III; union with Bavaria 1777)

BIBLIOGRAPHY

Häusser, L., *Geschichte der rheinischen Pfalz* (2nd edn., 2 vols., Heidelberg, 1856).
Spindler, M., ed., *Handbuch der bayerischen Geschichte* (4 vols. in 6 pts., Munich, 1968–75).

THE HOUSE OF WÜRTTEMBERG

Counts of Württemberg

1241–1265	Ulrich I, the Founder (attested as count of Württemberg by 1241)
1265–1279	Ulrich II (son)
1279–1325	Eberhard I, the Noble (brother)
1325–1344	Ulrich III (son)
1344–1362	Ulrich IV (son; abdicated, died 1366)
1344–1392	Eberhard II, the Quarrelsome (brother)
1392–1417	Eberhard III, the Mild (grandson)
1417–1419	Eberhard IV, the Younger (son)

Line of Stuttgart

1419–1480	Ulrich V, the Beloved (son; received Württemberg-Stuttgart by partition 1442)
1480–1482	Eberhard VI, the Younger (son; abdicated; union with Urach 1482)

Line of Urach

1419–1450	Louis I, the Elder (son of Eberhard IV; Württemberg-Urach 1442)
1450–1457	Louis II, the Younger (son)

Dukes of Württemberg

1457–1496	Eberhard V(I), the Bearded (brother; Stuttgart 1482; made duke of Württemberg by emperor Maximilian I 1495)
1496–1498	Eberhard II, the Younger (formerly Eberhard VI of Stuttgart; deposed, died 1504)
1498–1550	Ulrich (nephew; imperial occupation of the duchy 1519–34)
1550–1568	Christopher (son)
1568–1593	Louis (son)
1593–1608	Frederick I of Mömpelgard (nephew of Ulrich)
1608–1628	John Frederick (son)
1628–1674	Eberhard III (son)
1674–1677	William Louis (son)
1677–1733	Eberhard Louis (son)
1733–1737	Charles Alexander (grandson of Eberhard III)
1737–1793	Charles Eugene (son)
1793–1795	Louis Eugene (brother)
1795–1797	Frederick Eugene (brother)

Kings of Württemberg

1797–1816	Frederick II(I) (son; elector 1803; king of Württemberg 1806)
1816–1864	William I (son)
1864–1891	Charles (son)
1891–1918	William II (great-grandson of Frederick I; deposed, died 1921; proclamation of the republic)

BIBLIOGRAPHY

Schneider, E., *Württembergische Geschichte* (Stuttgart, 1896).
Stälin, P. F., *Geschichte Württembergs* (2 vols., Gotha, 1882–7).

THE HOUSE OF ZÄHRINGEN

Margraves of Baden

1064–1073	Herman I (son of Berthold I of Zähringen; count of Breisgau with lands in Baden 1064; abdicated, died 1074)
1073–1130	Herman II (son)
1130–1160	Herman III (son)
1160–1190	Herman IV (son)
1190–1243	Herman V (son)
1243–1250	Herman VI (son)
1243–1288	Rudolf I (brother)
1250–1268	Frederick I (son of Herman VI)
1288–1291	Herman VII (son of Rudolf I)
1288–1295	Rudolf II (brother)
1288–1297	Hesso (brother)
1288–1332	Rudolf III (brother)
1291–1333	Frederick II (son of Herman VII)
1291–1348	Rudolf IV (brother)
1297–1335	Rudolf Hesso (son of Hesso)
1333–1353	Herman VIII (son of Frederick II)
1348–1353	Frederick III, the Pacific (son of Rudolf IV)
1348–1361	Rudolf V (brother)
1353–1372	Rudolf VI (son of Frederick III)
1372–1391	Rudolf VII (son)
1372–1431	Bernard I (brother)
1431–1453	James I (son)
1453–1454	George (son; abdicated, died 1484)
1453–1458	Bl Bernard II (brother)
1453–1475	Charles I (brother)
1475–1515	Christopher I (son; abdicated, died 1527)
1515–1533	Philip I (son)

Margraves of Baden-Baden

1515–1536	Bernard III (brother; received Baden-Baden by partition 1535)
1536–1556	Christopher II (son; abdicated, died 1575)
1536–1569	Philibert (brother)
1569–1588	Philip II (son)
1588–1594	Edward Fortunatus (son of Christopher II; deposed, died 1600; union with Baden-Durlach 1594–1622)
1622–1677	William (son)
1677–1707	Louis William (grandson)
1707–1761	Louis George (son)
1761–1771	Augustus George (brother; union with Baden-Durlach 1771)

Margraves of Baden-Durlach

1515–1552	Ernest (son of Christopher I; Baden-Durlach 1535; abdicated, died 1553)
1552–1553	Bernard IV (son)
1552–1577	Charles II (brother)
1577–1590	James III (son)
1577–1604	Ernest Frederick (brother)

1577–1622	George Frederick (brother; abdicated, died 1638)
1590–1591	Ernest James (son of James III)
1622–1659	Frederick V (son of George Frederick)
1659–1677	Frederick VI (son)
1677–1709	Frederick Magnus (son)
1709–1738	Charles William (son)

Grand Dukes of Baden

1738–1811	Charles Frederick (grandson; Baden-Baden 1771; elector 1803; grand duke of Baden 1806)
1811–1818	Charles (grandson)
1818–1830	Louis I (son of Charles Frederick)
1830–1852	Leopold (brother)
1852–1856	Louis II (son; deposed, died 1858)
1856–1907	Frederick I (brother; regent 1852–6)
1907–1918	Frederick II (son; deposed, died 1928; proclamation of the republic)

NOTES

Names and Titles The use of the title 'margrave of Baden' dates from 1112 (Weech, 14).

BIBLIOGRAPHY

Becker, J., *Badische Geschichte vom Grossherzogtum bis zur Gegenwart* (Stuttgart, 1979).

Weech, F. von, *Badische Geschichte* (Karlsruhe, 1896).

THE HOUSE OF LIECHTENSTEIN

Lordship of Vaduz and Schellenberg

1699–1712	John Adam (prince of Liechtenstein 1684; bought the lordships of Schellenberg 1699, and Vaduz 1712)
1712–1718	Joseph Wenceslas (nephew of Anthony Florian (below); abdicated)

Principality of Liechtenstein

1718–1721	Anthony Florian (second cousin of John Adam; principality formed from union of Vaduz and Schellenberg 1719)
1721–1732	Joseph John (son)
1732–1748	John Charles (son)
1748–1772	Joseph Wenceslas (again)
1772–1781	Francis Joseph I (nephew)
1781–1805	Aloysius I (son)
1805–1836	John I (brother; sovereign prince of Liechtenstein 1806)
1836–1858	Aloysius II (son)
1858–1929	John II, the Good (son)
1929–1938	Francis I (brother)
1938–	Francis Joseph II (fourth in descent from John I; regent 1938)

BIBLIOGRAPHY

Falke, J. von, *Geschichte des fürstlichen Hauses Liechtenstein* (3 vols., Vienna, 1868–82).

Ritter, R., *Kurze Geschichte und Stammbaum des fürstlichen Hauses Liechtenstein* (Schaan, Liechtenstein, n.d.).

THE KINGDOM OF WESTPHALIA

House of Bonaparte

1807–1813	Jerome Napoleon (brother of Napoleon I, emperor of the French; deposed, died 1860)

The kingdom was formed from electoral Hesse, the duchy of Brunswick, southern Hanover, and other territories. On Jerome's deposition these lands reverted to their former possessors.

THE GRAND DUCHY OF FRANKFURT

House of Dalberg

1810–1813 Charles Theodore (elector of Mainz 1802–3; ruled Frankfurt 1806; grand duke 1810; deposed, died 1817)

BIBLIOGRAPHY FOR WESTPHALIA AND FRANKFURT

Connelly, O., ed., *Historical Dictionary of Napoleonic France* (Westport, Conn., 1985).

7 SCANDINAVIA

THE KINGDOM OF NORWAY

House of Westfold

858–928	Harald I, Fairhair (son of Halfdan the Black, king of Westfold; abdicated, died 932?)
928–933	Eirik I, Bloodaxe (son; deposed, died 954)
933–959	Haakon I, the Good (brother)
959–974	Harald II, Graycloak (son of Eirik I)
974–994	Earl Haakon Sigurdsson
994–999	Olav I (great-grandson of Harald I)
999–1015	Earl Eirik (son of Earl Haakon; abdicated, died 1023?)
1015–1016	Earl Svein (brother; deposed, died 1016)
1016–1030	St Olav II (fourth in descent from Harald I)
1030–1035	Svein Alfivason (son of Knud I of Denmark; deposed, died 1036)
1035–1046	Magnus I, the Good (son of Olav II)
1045–1066	Harald III, Hardrada (fourth in descent from Harald I)
1066–1069	Magnus II (son)
1067–1093	Olav III, the Gentle (brother)
1093–1095	Haakon Magnusson (son of Magnus II)
1093–1103	Magnus III, Barelegs (son of Olav III)
1103–1115	Olav Magnusson (son)
1103–1123	Eystein I (brother)
1103–1130	Sigurd I, the Crusader (brother)
1130–1135	Magnus IV, the Blind (son; deposed, died 1139)
1130–1136	Harald IV, Gille (son of Magnus III)
1136–1155	Sigurd II, Mouth (son)
1136–1161	Inge I, the Hunchback (brother)
1142–1157	Eystein II (brother)
1157–1162	Haakon II, the Broadshouldered (son of Sigurd II; rival king)
1161–1184	Magnus V (son of Christina, daughter of Sigurd I, and Erling Ormsson; rival king)
1177–1202	Sverre (supposed son of Sigurd II; rival king)
1202–1204	Haakon III (son)
1204	Guttorm (nephew)
1204–1217	Inge II (son of Cecilia, daughter of Sigurd II, and Baard of Rein)
1217–1263	Haakon IV, the Elder (son of Haakon III)
1240–1257	Haakon the Younger (son; co-regent)
1263–1280	Magnus VI, the Law-mender (brother; co-regent 1257)
1280–1299	Eirik II, the Priest-hater (son; co-regent 1273)
1299–1319	Haakon V, Longlegs (brother)

House of Sweden

1319–1355	Magnus VII (son of Ingeborg, daughter of Haakon V, and Erik, son of Magnus I of Sweden; abdicated, died 1374)
1355–1380	Haakon VI (son; co-regent 1343)
1380–1387	Olav IV (son; king of Denmark 1376; union with Denmark 1380–1814)

House of Denmark

1814	Christian Frederick (grandson of Frederick V of Denmark; abdicated, died 1848; union with Sweden 1814–1905)

House of Denmark

1905–1957	Haakon VII (son of Frederick VIII of Denmark; in exile 1940–5)
1957–	Olav V (son)

NOTES

Chronology Dates down to 994 are approximate. Those above follow Einarsdóttir, ch. x; for a lower chronology, cf. G. Jones, *A History of the Vikings* (New York, 1968), 89. On a 1 January year, Olav I died in 999 (not 1000), Magnus I in 1046 (not 1047). Einarsdóttir, chs. vii, xiii (English summary).

For Sverre's claim to be the son of Sigurd II, see H. Koht, *Historisk Tidsskrift*, XLI (1961–2), 293–302.

BIBLIOGRAPHY

Einarsdóttir, O., *Studier i kronologisk metode i tidlig islandsk historieskrivning* (Stockholm, 1964).

Norsk biografisk Leksikon (19 vols., Christiania/Oslo, 1923–83).

THE KINGDOM OF DENMARK

First House of Denmark

940–986	Harald I, Bluetooth (son of Gorm the Old, king in north Jutland)
986–1014	Svend I, Forkbeard (son; king of England 1013)
1014–1018	Harald II (son)
1019–1035	Knud I, the Great (brother; England 1016)
1035–1042	Hardeknud (son; England 1040)
1042–1046	Magnus the Good (king of Norway 1035)

House of Svend Estridsen

1046–1074	Svend II Estridsen (son of Astrid, daughter of Svend I, and earl Ulf)
1074–1080	Harald III, Hén (son)
1080–1086	St Knud II (brother)
1086–1095	Oluf I, Hunger (brother)
1095–1103	Erik I, the Evergood (brother)
1104–1134	Niels (brother)
1134–1137	Erik II, the Memorable (son of Erik I)
1137–1146	Erik III, the Lamb (maternal grandson of Erik I)
1146–1157	Knud III (grandson of Niels)
1146–1157	Svend III, Grathe (son of Erik II; rival king)
1157–1182	Valdemar I, the Great (grandson of Erik I)
1182–1202	Knud IV (son; co-regent 1165)
1202–1241	Valdemar II, the Victorious (brother)
1215–1231	Valdemar the Younger (son; co-regent)
1241–1250	Erik IV, Ploughpenny (brother; co-regent 1232)
1250–1252	Abel (brother)
1252–1259	Christopher I (brother)
1259–1286	Erik V, Klipping (son)
1286–1319	Erik VI, Menved (son)
1320–1326	Christopher II (brother; deposed)
1321–1326	Erik (son; co-regent; deposed)
1326–1330	Valdemar III (fourth in descent from Abel; deposed, died 1364)
1330–1332	Christopher II (restored)
1330–1332	Erik (co-regent; restored; interregnum 1332–40)
1340–1375	Valdemar IV, Atterdag (brother)

House of Norway

1376–1387	Oluf II (son of Margaret, daughter of Valdemar IV, and Haakon VI of Norway)
1387–1396	Margaret I (mother; abdicated, died 1412)

House of Pomerania

1396–1439	Erik VII (maternal grandson of Ingeborg, sister of Margaret; deposed, died 1459)

House of the Palatinate

1440–1448	Christopher III of Bavaria (son of Catherine, sister of Erik VII, and John, count of Neumarkt)

House of Oldenburg

1448–1481	Christian I (count of Oldenburg; sixth in descent, through females, from Erik V; interregnum 1481–3)
1483–1513	John (Hans) (son)
1513–1523	Christian II (son; deposed, died 1559)
1523–1533	Frederick I (son of Christian I)
1534–1559	Christian III (son)
1559–1588	Frederick II (son)
1588–1648	Christian IV (son)
1648–1670	Frederick III (son)
1670–1699	Christian V (son)
1699–1730	Frederick IV (son)
1730–1746	Christian VI (son)
1746–1766	Frederick V (son)
1766–1808	Christian VII (son)
1808–1839	Frederick VI (son; regent 1784–1808)
1839–1848	Christian VIII (grandson of Frederick V)
1848–1863	Frederick VII (son)

Line of Glücksburg

1863–1906	Christian IX (duke of Glücksburg; ninth in descent from Christian III)
1906–1912	Frederick VIII (son)
1912–1947	Christian X (son)
1947–1972	Frederick IX (son)
1972–	Margaret II (daughter)

NOTES

Chronology Dates down to 986 are approximate; for a lower chronology, with Gorm reigning in the 950s, cf. Ousager. Svend II may have died in 1076; cf. *Historisk Tidsskrift*, seventh series, II (1899–1900), 229–39, 407–16.

BIBLIOGRAPHY

Dansk biografisk Leksikon, ed. P. Engelstoft (27 vols., Copenhagen, 1933–44).

Ousager, B., 'Gorm konge: et retoucheret portraet', *Skalk*, II (1957), 19–30.

THE KINGDOM OF SWEDEN

Yngling House

980–995	Erik the Victorious (king of the Swedes at Uppsala by *c*.980)
995–1022	Olof Skötkonung (son)
1022–1050	Anund (Jacob) (son)
1050–1060	Emund the Old (brother)

House of Stenkil

1060–1066	Stenkil Ragnvaldsson
1066–1070	Halsten (son; deposed)
1070–?	Håkan the Red
?–1080	Inge I, the Elder (son of Stenkil; deposed)
1080–1083	Blot-Sven (brother-in-law)
1083–1110	Inge I (restored)
1110–1118	Philip (son of Halsten)
1118–1130	Inge II, the Younger (brother)

Houses of Sverker and Erik

1130–1156	Sverker I, the Elder
1156–1160	St Erik Jedvardsson
1160–1161	Magnus Henriksson
1161–1167	Charles Sverkersson (son of Sverker I)
1167–1173	Kol Jonsson (nephew)
1173–1196	Knut Eriksson (son of St Erik)
1196–1208	Sverker II, the Younger (son of Charles; deposed, died 1210)
1208–1216	Erik Knutsson (son of Knut)
1216–1222	John I (son of Sverker II)
1222–1229	Erik Eriksson (son of Erik Knutsson; deposed)
1229–1234	Knut the Tall (great-grandson of St Erik?)
1234–1250	Erik Eriksson (restored)

Folkung House

1250–1275	Valdemar (son of Ingeborg, daughter of Erik Knutsson, and Birger of Bjälbo; deposed, died 1302)
1275–1290	Magnus I, Ladulås (brother)
1290–1318	Birger (son; deposed, died 1321)
1319–1364	Magnus II (nephew; king of Norway 1319–55; deposed, died 1374)
1344–1359	Erik Magnusson (son; co-regent)
1362–1364	Håkan Magnusson (brother; co-regent; deposed; Norway 1355–80)

House of Mecklenburg

1364–1389	Albert (son of Euphemia, sister of Magnus II, and Albert of Mecklenburg; deposed, died 1412; Danish rule 1389–1448)

House of Denmark

1448–1457	Charles VIII Knutsson (regent 1438–41; deposed)
1457–1464	Christian I (king of Denmark 1448–81; deposed)
1464–1465	Charles VIII (restored; deposed)
1465–1467	Christian I (restored; deposed)

1467–1470	Charles VIII (restored)
1471–1497	Sten Sture the Elder (regent; deposed)
1497–1501	John II (king of Denmark 1483–1513; deposed)
1501–1503	Sten Sture the Elder (restored)
1504–1512	Svante Nilsson (Sture) (regent)
1512–1520	Sten Sture the Younger (son; regent)
1520–1521	Christian II (king of Denmark 1513–23; deposed)
House of Vasa	
1523–1560	Gustavus I (Gustavus Vasa) (regent 1521–3)
1560–1568	Erik XIV (son; deposed, died 1577)
1568–1592	John III (brother)
1592–1599	Sigismund (son; deposed; king of Poland 1587–1632)
1604–1611	Charles IX (son of Gustavus I; regent 1599–1604)
1611–1632	Gustavus II Adolphus (son)
1632–1654	Christina (daughter; abdicated, died 1689)
House of the Palatinate	
1654–1660	Charles X Gustavus (son of Catherine, daughter of Charles IX, and John Casimir, count of Kleeburg)
1660–1697	Charles XI (son)
1697–1718	Charles XII (son)
1718–1720	Ulrica Eleonora (sister; abdicated, died 1741)
House of Hesse	
1720–1751	Frederick I (husband)
House of Holstein-Gottorp	
1751–1771	Adolphus Frederick (grandnephew of Hedwig Eleonora, queen of Charles X)
1771–1792	Gustavus III (son)
1792–1809	Gustavus IV Adolphus (son; deposed, died 1837)
1809–1818	Charles XIII (son of Adolphus Frederick)
House of Bernadotte	
1818–1844	Charles XIV John (adopted son)
1844–1859	Oscar I (son)
1859–1872	Charles XV (son)
1872–1907	Oscar II (brother)
1907–1950	Gustavus V (son)
1950–1973	Gustavus VI Adolphus (son)
1973–	Charles XVI Gustavus (grandson)

NOTES

Chronology According to tradition, Sverker I was killed in 1156 and St Erik in 1160; Philip died in 1118. Remaining dates through the twelfth century range from approximate to highly uncertain. See the pertinent articles in *Svenskt biografiskt Lexikon*.

BIBLIOGRAPHY

Scott, F. D., *Sweden: the Nation's History* (Minneapolis, 1977).
Svenskt biografiskt Lexikon (25 vols. to date, Stockholm, 1918–87).

8 EASTERN EUROPE

MEDIEVAL BULGARIA

First Bulgarian Empire – House of Dulo

680–700	Asparukh (supposed descendant of Attila; crossed the Danube into Bulgaria 680)
700–721	Tervel
721–738	Kormisoš
738–753	Sevar

House of Ukil

753–760	Vinekh
760–763	Telets
763–766	Sabin (deposed)
766	Umar (deposed)
766–767	Toktu
767–768	Pagan
768–777	Telerig (deposed)
777–803	Kardam

House of Krum

803–814	Krum
814	Dukum (brother)
814–815	Ditseng (brother)
815–831	Omurtag (son of Krum)
831–836	Malamir (son)
836–852	Presian (nephew)
852–889	Boris I (Michael) (son; abdicated, died 907)
889–893	Vladimir (son; deposed)
893–927	Simeon I (brother; crowned emperor 913)
927–969	Peter I (son)
969–971	Boris II (son; deposed, died 976; Byzantine rule 971–6)

Macedonian Empire

976–1014	Samuel (crowned emperor 997)
1014–1015	Gabriel Radomir (son)
1015–1018	Ivan Vladislav (nephew of Samuel; Byzantine rule 1018–1185)

Second Bulgarian Empire – House of Asen

1185–1187	Peter II (deposed)
1187–1196	Asen I (brother)
1196–1197	Peter II (restored)
1197–1207	Kaloyan (brother)
1207–1218	Boril (sister's son; deposed)
1218–1241	Ivan Asen II (son of Asen I)
1241–1246	Koloman I (son)
1246–1256	Michael II (brother)

1256–1257	Koloman II (grandson of Asen I)
1257–1277	Constantine Tikh
1277–1279	Ivajlo (deposed, died 1280)
1279–1280	Ivan Asen III (maternal grandson of Ivan Asen II; deposed)

House of Terter

1280–1292	George I Terter (deposed)
1292–1298	Smilets
1299–1300	Čaka (son-in-law of George I; deposed)
1300–1322	Theodore Svetoslav (son of George I)
1322–1323	George II (son)

House of Šišman

1323–1330	Michael III Šišman
1330–1331	Ivan Stephen (son; deposed)
1331–1371	Ivan Alexander (son of Keratsa, sister of Michael III, and Sratsimir)
1371–1393	Ivan Šišman (son; ruled at Trnovo; deposed, died 1395)
1356–1396	Ivan Sratsimir (brother; ruled at Vidin; in exile 1365–9; deposed; Turkish conquest of Bulgaria)

NOTES

Chronology Dates down to Kardam, most of which are approximate, follow the *Istoria na Bŭlgaria*, II. Some scholars hold that Malamir and Presian are two names for the same ruler; Boris I would then be his nephew. For the start of the Second Bulgarian Empire, cf. Cankova-Petkova; for Ivajlo and Ivan Asen III, cf. Failler, 234–42.

Names and Titles The pagan title of khan gave way to that of prince (*knyaz*) under Boris I; the imperial title was the Greek *basileus*, rendered in Slavonic as tsar.

BIBLIOGRAPHY

Biographisches Lexikon zur Geschichte Südosteuropas, ed. M. Bernath (4 vols., Munich, 1974–81).

Cankova-Petkova, G., 'La libération de la Bulgarie de la domination byzantine', *Byzantinobulgarica*, V (1978), 95–121.

Failler, A., 'Chronologie et composition dans l'histoire de Georges Pachymère', *Revue des études byzantines*, XXXIX (1981), 145–249.

Istoria na Bŭlgaria, ed. V. I. Velkov (6 vols. to date, Sofia, 1979–87).

THE KINGDOM OF BOHEMIA

House of Přemysl

870–895	Bořivoj I (prince or duke; according to tradition, eighth in descent from Přemysl)
895–912	Spytihněv I (son)
912–921	Vratislav I (brother)
921–929	St Wenceslas I (son)
929–972	Boleslav I, the Cruel (brother)
972–999	Boleslav II, the Pious (son)
999–1002	Boleslav III, the Red (son; deposed)
1002–1003	Vladivoj (son of Dobravy, daughter of Boleslav I, and Mieszko I of Poland)
1003	Jaromír (son of Boleslav II; deposed)
1003	Boleslav III (restored; deposed, died 1037)
1003–1004	Bolesław I (duke of Poland; deposed)
1004–1012	Jaromír (restored; deposed)
1012–1033	Ulrich (brother; deposed, died 1034)
1033–1034	Jaromír (restored; deposed, died 1035)
1034–1055	Břetislav I (son of Ulrich)
1055–1061	Spytihněv II (son)
1061–1092	Vratislav II (I) (brother; crowned king of Bohemia 1085)
1092	Conrad (brother)
1092–1100	Břetislav II (son of Vratislav II)
1100–1107	Bořivoj II (brother; deposed, died 1124)
1107–1109	Svatopluk (grandson of Břetislav I)
1109–1125	Vladislav I (son of Vratislav II; abdicated in favour of Bořivoj II 1117–20)
1125–1140	Soběslav I (brother)
1140–1173	Vladislav II (I) (son of Vladislav I; crowned king 1158; abdicated, died 1174)
1173	Frederick (son; deposed)
1173–1178	Soběslav II (son of Soběslav I; deposed, died 1180)
1178–1189	Frederick (restored)
1189–1191	Conrad Otto (great-grandson of Conrad)
1191–1192	Wenceslas II (son of Soběslav I; deposed)
1192–1193	Přemysl Ottokar I (son of Vladislav II; deposed)
1193–1197	Henry Břetislav (grandson of Vladislav I)
1197	Vladislav III Henry (son of Vladislav II; abdicated, died 1222)

Kings of Bohemia

1197–1230	Přemysl Ottokar I (restored; crowned king 1198)
1230–1253	Wenceslas I (son; co-regent 1228)
1253–1278	Přemysl Ottokar II, the Great (son)
1278–1305	Wenceslas II (son; king of Poland 1300)
1305–1306	Wenceslas III (son)

House of Habsburg

1306–1307	Rudolf of Austria (married Elizabeth, widow of Wenceslas II)

House of Carinthia

1307–1310	Henry (married Anne, daughter of Wenceslas II; deposed, died 1335)

House of Luxemburg

1310–1346	John the Blind (married Elizabeth, daughter of Wenceslas II)
1346–1378	Charles (son)
1378–1419	Wenceslas IV (son; co-regent 1363)
1419–1437	Sigismund (brother)

House of Habsburg

1437–1439	Albert of Austria (married Elizabeth, daughter of Sigismund; interregnum 1439–53)
1453–1457	Ladislas Posthumus (son)

House of Poděbrad

1458–1471	George of Poděbrad

House of Poland

1471–1516	Vladislav II (son of Elizabeth, daughter of Albert, and Casimir IV of Poland)
1516–1526	Louis (son; co-regent 1509)

House of Habsburg

1526–1564	Ferdinand I (married Anne, daughter of Vladislav II; emperor 1558; union with the Habsburg lands)

NOTES

Chronology Dates down to 972 are approximate. Bořivoj I was baptized *c.*870; Spytihněv I is attested in 895. St Wenceslas died in 929 or 935, Boleslav I between 967 and 972. Z. Fiala, *Sborník historický*, IX (1962), 5–65; German summary.

Names and Titles The title of king was not hereditary until Přemysl Ottokar I (1198).

BIBLIOGRAPHY

Bachmann, A., *Geschichte Böhmens* (2 vols., Gotha, 1899–1905).
Bosl, K., ed., *Handbuch der Geschichte der böhmischen Länder* (4 vols., Stuttgart, 1967–70).

THE KINGDOM OF POLAND

House of Piast – Dukes of Poland

960?–992	Mieszko I (prince or duke; fourth in descent from Piast, traditional founder of Polish ruling house)
992–1025	Bolesław I, the Brave (son; crowned king of Poland 1025)
1025–1034	Mieszko II (Lambert) (son; king)
1034–1058	Casimir I, the Restorer (son)
1058–1079	Bolesław II, the Bold (son; crowned king 1076; deposed, died 1081)
1079–1102	Władysław I (Herman) (brother)
1102–1107	Zbigniew (son; deposed)
1102–1138	Bolesław III, Wrymouth (brother)

Dukes of Cracow

1138–1146	Władysław II, the Exile (son; deposed, died 1159)
1146–1173	Bolesław IV, the Curly (brother)
1173–1177	Mieszko III, the Elder (brother; deposed)
1177–1194	Casimir II, the Just (brother)
1194–1199	Leszek I, the White (son; deposed)
1199–1202	Mieszko III (restored)
1202	Władysław III, Spindleshanks (son; deposed)
1202–1227	Leszek I (restored)
1228	Władysław III (restored; deposed, died 1231)
1228–1229	Henry I, the Bearded (grandson of Władysław II; deposed)
1229–1232	Conrad of Mazovia (son of Casimir II; deposed)
1232–1238	Henry I (restored)
1238–1241	Henry II, the Pious (son)
1241–1243	Conrad (restored; deposed, died 1247)
1243–1279	Bolesław V, the Chaste (son of Leszek I)
1279–1288	Leszek II, the Black (grandson of Conrad)
1288–1290	Henry IV, Probus (grandson of Henry II)
1290–1291	Przemysł (fourth in descent from Mieszko III; abdicated; king 1295–6)

House of Bohemia

1291–1305	Wacław II (married Elizabeth, daughter of Przemysł; crowned king 1300)

House of Piast – Kings of Poland

1305–1333	Władysław I, the Short (brother of Leszek II; crowned king 1320)
1333–1370	Casimir III, the Great (son)

House of Anjou

1370–1382	Louis the Great (son of Elizabeth, daughter of Władysław I, and Charles I of Hungary)
1383–1399	Jadwiga (daughter)

House of Lithuania

1386–1434	Władysław II Jagiełło (Jogaila, grand duke of Lithuania; married Jadwiga)

1434–1444	Władysław III (son; interregnum 1444–6)
1446–1492	Casimir IV (brother)
1492–1501	John I Albert (son)
1501–1506	Alexander (brother)
1506–1548	Sigismund I, the Elder (brother)
1548–1572	Sigismund II Augustus (son; co-regent 1529)

House of France

1573–1575	Henry (deposed; king of France 1574–89)

House of Transylvania

1575–1586	Stephen Bathory (prince of Transylvania; married Anne, daughter of Sigismund I)

House of Sweden

1587–1632	Sigismund III (son of Catherine, daughter of Sigismund I, and John III of Sweden)
1632–1648	Władysław IV (son)
1648–1668	John II Casimir (brother; abdicated, died 1672)

House of Wiśniowiecki

1669–1673	Michael

House of Sobieski

1674–1696	John III

House of Saxony

1697–1704, 1709–1733	Augustus II, the Strong (elector of Saxony as Frederick Augustus I; deposed; restored)

House of Leszczyński

1704–1709, 1733–1736	Stanislas I (deposed; restored; abdicated; duke of Lorraine 1737–66)

House of Saxony

1733–1763	Augustus III (son of Augustus II; rival king; elector of Saxony)

House of Poniatowski

1764–1795	Stanislas II Augustus (abdicated, died 1798; partition of Poland by Russia, Prussia and Austria)

NOTES

Names and Titles The title of king was not hereditary until Władysław I (1320).

BIBLIOGRAPHY

The Cambridge History of Poland, ed. W. F. Reddaway (2 vols., Cambridge, 1950–1).

Łowmiański, H., ed., *Historia Polski do roku 1764* (2 vols., Łódź, 1957) (*Historia Polski*, ed. T. Manteuffel, I: 1–2).

THE KINGDOM OF HUNGARY

House of Árpád

970?–997	Géza (prince or duke; great-grandson of Árpád, who led the Magyars into Hungary *c.*895)
997–1038	St Stephen I (son; crowned king of Hungary 1001)
1038–1041	Peter (son-in-law of Géza; deposed)
1041–1044	Samuel Aba (son-in-law of Géza)
1044–1046	Peter (restored; deposed, died 1047?)
1046–1060	Andrew I (grandnephew of Géza)
1060–1063	Béla I (brother)
1063–1074	Salamon (son of Andrew I; deposed, died 1087)
1074–1077	Géza I (son of Béla I)
1077–1095	St Ladislas I (brother)
1095–1116	Koloman (son of Géza I)
1116–1131	Stephen II (son)
1131–1141	Béla II, the Blind (nephew of Koloman)
1141–1162	Géza II (son)
1162–1172	Stephen III (son)
1162–1163	Ladislas II (son of Béla II; rival king)
1163–1165	Stephen IV (brother; rival king)
1172–1196	Béla III (son of Géza II)
1196–1204	Emeric (son; co-regent 1185)
1204–1205	Ladislas III (son; co-regent 1204)
1205–1235	Andrew II (son of Béla III)
1235–1270	Béla IV (son; co-regent 1214)
1270–1272	Stephen V (son; co-regent 1245)
1272–1290	Ladislas IV, the Cumanian (son)
1290–1301	Andrew III, the Venetian (grandson of Andrew II)

House of Bohemia

1301–1305	Wenceslas (fourth in descent from Constance, daughter of Béla III; king of Bohemia 1305–6)

House of Bavaria

1305–1307	Otto (son of Elizabeth, daughter of Béla IV, and Henry XIII of Bavaria; deposed, died 1312)

House of Anjou

1307–1342	Charles I (grandson of Mary, daughter of Stephen V, and Charles II of Naples)
1342–1382	Louis I, the Great (son; king of Poland 1370)
1382–1385	Mary (daughter; deposed)
1385–1386	Charles II of Durazzo (great-grandson of Charles II of Naples)
1386–1395	Mary (restored)

House of Luxemburg

1387–1437	Sigismund (married Mary; king of Bohemia 1419)

House of Habsburg

1437–1439	Albert of Austria (married Elizabeth, daughter of Sigismund; king of Bohemia)

House of Poland

1440–1444	Vladislas I (king of Poland 1434)

House of Habsburg

1445–1457	Ladislas V, Posthumus (son of Albert; king of Bohemia 1453)

House of Hunyadi

1458–1490	Matthias I, Corvinus

House of Poland

1490–1516	Vladislas II (son of Elizabeth, daughter of Albert, and Casimir IV of Poland; king of Bohemia 1471)
1516–1526	Louis II (son; co-regent 1508; king of Bohemia)

House of Habsburg

1526–1564	Ferdinand I (married Anne, daughter of Vladislas II; emperor 1558; union with the Habsburg lands)

House of Zápolyai

1526–1540	John (rival king)
1540–1570	John Sigismund (son; rival king; abdicated; prince of Transylvania 1570–1)

BIBLIOGRAPHY

Hóman, B., *Geschichte des ungarischen Mittelalters* (2 vols., Berlin, 1940–3).
Sinor, D., *History of Hungary* (Westport, Conn., 1976).

MEDIEVAL SERBIA

House of Nemanja

1167–1196	Stephen Nemanja (St Simeon) (grand župan of Rascia 1167; conquered Zeta; abdicated, died 1200)
1196–1228	St Stephen the First-Crowned (son; king of Serbia 1217)
1228–1234	Stephen Radoslav (son; deposed)
1234–1243	Stephen Vladislav (brother; deposed)
1243–1276	Stephen Uroš I (brother; deposed, died 1277?)
1276–1282	Stephen Dragutin (son; abdicated; north Serbia 1282–1316)
1282–1321	Stephen (Uroš II) Milutin (brother)
1321–1331	Stephen Uroš III, Dečanski (son; deposed, died 1331)

Empire of Serbia

1331–1355	Stephen Dušan (son; co-regent 1322; emperor 1345)
1355–1371	Stephen Uroš IV (son)

House of Hrebeljanović

1371–1389	Lazar Hrebeljanović (prince only; ruled in north Serbia)
1389–1427	Stephen (son; despot 1402)

House of Branković

1427–1456	George Branković (son of Mara, daughter of Lazar, and Vuk Branković; despot 1429)
1456–1458	Lazar (son; co-regent 1446)
1458–1459	Stephen the Blind (brother; deposed, died 1476)
1459	Stephen Tomašević (son-in-law of Lazar; deposed, died 1463; Turkish conquest of Serbia)

NOTES

Chronology Dates for Stephen Nemanja and his son may vary by a year or so; see, besides the relevant articles in *Biographisches Lexikon*, G. Ostrogorsky, *History of the Byzantine State* (rev. edn., New Brunswick, NJ, 1969), 388, 409.

Names and Titles The imperial title was the Greek *basileus*, rendered in Slavonic as tsar.

BIBLIOGRAPHY

Biographisches Lexikon zur Geschichte Südosteuropas, ed. M. Bernath (4 vols., Munich, 1974–81).

Jireček, J. K., *Geschichte der Serben* (2 vols., Gotha, 1911–18).

THE GRAND DUCHY OF LITHUANIA

House of Liutauras

1295–1316	Vytenis (son of Liutauras; grand prince or duke of Lithuania by 1295)
1316–1341	Gediminas (brother)
1341–1345	Jaunutis (son; deposed)
1345–1377	Algirdas (brother)
1345–1382	Kęstutis (brother; deposed, died 1382)
1377–1392	Jogaila (son of Algirdas; abdicated; king of Poland 1386–1434)
1392–1430	Vytautas the Great (son of Kęstutis)
1430–1432	Švitrigaila (son of Algirdas; deposed, died 1452)
1432–1440	Sigismund (son of Kęstutis)
1440–1492	Casimir (son of Jogaila; king of Poland 1446)
1492–1506	Alexander (son; king of Poland 1501; union of Lithuania with Poland)

NOTES

Chronology Dates down to 1345 may vary by a year or so.

BIBLIOGRAPHY

Hellmann, M., *Grundzüge der Geschichte Litauens und des litauischen Volkes* (Darmstadt, 1986).

Jurgėla, C. R., *History of the Lithuanian Nation* (New York, 1948).

THE KINGDOM OF MONTENEGRO

House of Petrović-Njegoš

1697–1735	Danilo I (hereditary prince-bishop (*vladika*) of Montenegro 1697)
1735–1750	Sava (first cousin; abdicated)
1750–1766	Vasilije (nephew of Danilo I)
1766–1781	Sava (again)
1781–1830	Peter I (grandnephew of Danilo I)
1830–1851	Peter II (nephew)
1851–1860	Danilo II (grandnephew of Peter I; secular prince of Montenegro 1852)

Kingdom of Montenegro

1860–1921	Nicholas I (nephew; recognition of Montenegrin independence 1878; king 1910; union with Serbia 1918)
1921	Danilo I (son; nominal king; abdicated, died 1939)
1921–1922	Michael I (nephew; nominal king; resigned his rights, died 1986; continued Montenegrin–Serbian union)

BIBLIOGRAPHY

Biographisches Lexikon zur Geschichte Südosteuropas, ed. M. Bernath (4 vols., Munich, 1974–81).

Ivić, A., *Rodoslovne tablice srpskikh dinastija i vlastele* (Novi Sad, 1928).

MODERN SERBIA AND YUGOSLAVIA

Houses of Obrenović and Karadjordjević

1815–1839	Miloš Obrenović (prince of Serbia 1815; recognition of Serbian autonomy 1830; abdicated)
1839	Milan (son)
1839–1842	Michael (brother; deposed)
1842–1858	Alexander Karadjordjević (deposed, died 1885)
1858–1860	Miloš (again)
1860–1868	Michael (restored)

Kingdom of Serbia

1868–1889	Milan I (grandnephew of Miloš; recognition of Serbian independence 1878; king 1882; abdicated, died 1901)
1889–1903	Alexander I (son)
1903–1921	Peter I (son of Alexander Karadjordjević; kingdom of the Serbs, Croats and Slovenes 1918)

Kingdom of Yugoslavia

1921–1934	Alexander I (son; regent 1914–21; kingdom of Yugoslavia 1929)
1934–1945	Peter II (son; in exile 1941; deposed, died 1970; proclamation of the People's Republic)

BIBLIOGRAPHY

Darby, H. C., *A Short History of Yugoslavia from Early Times to 1966* (Cambridge, 1966).

Petrovich, M. B., *A History of Modern Serbia, 1804–1918* (2 vols., New York, 1976).

MODERN GREECE

House of Bavaria

1832–1862	Otho (son of Louis I of Bavaria; king of Greece 1832; deposed, died 1867)

House of Denmark

1863–1913	George I (son of Christian IX of Denmark; king of the Hellenes 1863)
1913–1917	Constantine I (son; deposed)
1917–1920	Alexander (son)
1920–1922	Constantine I (restored; abdicated, died 1923)
1922–1923, 1935–1947	George II (son; deposed; republic 1924–35; restored; in exile 1941–6)
1947–1964	Paul (brother)
1964–1973	Constantine II (son; in exile 1967; deposed; proclamation of the republic)

BIBLIOGRAPHY

Campbell, J., and P. Sherrard, *Modern Greece* (New York, 1968).
Dakin, D., *The Unification of Greece, 1770–1923* (London, 1972).

THE KINGDOM OF ROMANIA

House of Cuza

1859–1866	Alexander John (autonomous prince of Moldavia and Wallachia 1859; deposed, died 1873)

House of Hohenzollern-Sigmaringen

1866–1914	Carol I (autonomous prince of Romania 1866; recognition of Romanian independence 1878; king 1881)
1914–1927	Ferdinand (nephew)
1927–1930	Michael (grandson; deposed)
1930–1940	Carol II (father; deposed, died 1953)
1940–1947	Michael (restored; deposed; proclamation of the People's Republic)

BIBLIOGRAPHY

Giurescu, C. C., ed., *Chronological History of Romania* (Bucharest, 1972).
Jelavich, B., *Russia and the Formation of the Romanian National State, 1821–1878* (Cambridge, 1984).

MODERN BULGARIA

House of Battenberg

1879–1886 Alexander (autonomous prince of Bulgaria 1879; deposed, died 1893)

House of Saxe-Coburg-Gotha

1887–1918 Ferdinand I (king of independent Bulgaria 1908; abdicated, died 1948)

1918–1943 Boris III (son)

1943–1946 Simeon II (son; deposed; proclamation of the People's Republic)

BIBLIOGRAPHY

Crampton, R. J., *Bulgaria, 1878–1918: a History* (Boulder, Colo., 1983).
Miller, M. L., *Bulgaria during the Second World War* (Stanford, 1975).

THE KINGDOM OF ALBANIA

House of Wied

1914 William (independent prince of Albania 1914; deposed, died 1945; regency 1914–25)

House of Zogu

1928–1939 Zog I (Ahmed Zogu) (president 1925; king 1928; deposed, died 1961; Italian rule 1939–43)

BIBLIOGRAPHY

Murmullaku, R., *Albania and the Albanians* (London, 1975).
Swire, J., *Albania: the Rise of a Kingdom* (London, 1929).

9 RUSSIA

THE PRINCEDOM OF KIEV

House of Rurik

893–924	Oleg (viking prince of Novgorod; captured Kiev and made it his capital *c*.893)
924–945	Igor I (son or descendant of Rurik)
945–972	Svyatoslav I (son)
972–978	Yaropolk I (son)
978–1015	St Vladimir I (brother)
1015–1019	Svyatopolk I (son)
1019–1054	Yaroslav I, the Wise (brother)
1054–1068	Izyaslav I (son; deposed)
1068–1069	Vseslav (great-grandson of Vladimir I; deposed, died 1101)
1069–1073	Izyaslav I (restored; deposed)
1073–1076	Svyatoslav II (brother)
1076–1077	Vsevolod I (brother; deposed)
1077–1078	Izyaslav I (restored)
1078–1093	Vsevolod I (restored)
1093–1113	Svyatopolk II (son of Izyaslav I)
1113–1125	Vladimir II, Monomakh (son of Vsevolod I)
1125–1132	Mstislav I (son)
1132–1139	Yaropolk II (brother)
1139	Vyacheslav (brother; deposed, died 1154)
1139–1146	Vsevolod II (grandson of Svyatoslav II)
1146	Igor II (brother; deposed, died 1147)
1146–1154	Izyaslav II (son of Mstislav I)
1154–1155	Izyaslav III (grandson of Svyatoslav II; deposed)
1155–1157	Yurii I, Dolgorukii (son of Vladimir II)
1157–1158	Izyaslav III (restored; deposed)
1158–1159	Mstislav II (son of Izyaslav II; deposed)
1159–1161	Rostislav I (son of Mstislav I; deposed)
1161	Izyaslav III (restored)
1161–1167	Rostislav I (restored)
1167–1169	Mstislav II (restored; deposed, died 1170)
1169–1171	Gleb (son of Yurii I; confusion and civil war till Mongol conquest 1240)

THE GRAND PRINCEDOM OF VLADIMIR

House of Rurik

1176–1212	Vsevolod III, Big Nest (son of Yurii I of Kiev; prince of Vladimir 1176; styled grand prince from 1195)
1212–1216	Yurii II (son; deposed)
1216–1218	Constantine (brother)
1218–1238	Yurii II (restored)
1238–1246	Yaroslav II (brother)
1247	Svyatoslav (brother; deposed, died 1253)
1247–1252	Andrew II (son of Yaroslav II; deposed, died 1264)
1252–1263	St Alexander I, Nevskii (brother)
1264–1271	Yaroslav III (brother)
1272–1277	Vasilii (brother)
1277–1282	Dimitri I (son of Alexander I; deposed)
1282–1283	Andrew III (brother; deposed)
1283–1294	Dimitri I (restored)
1294–1304	Andrew III (restored)
1305–1318	St Michael (son of Yaroslav III)
1318–1322	Yurii III (grandson of Alexander I; prince of Moscow 1303–25; deposed)
1322–1326	Dimitri II (son of Michael)
1326–1327	Alexander II (brother; deposed, died 1339)
1328–1331	Alexander III (great-grandson of Andrew II)
1332–1340	Ivan I, Kalita (brother of Yurii III; prince of Moscow 1325)
1340–1353	Simeon the Proud (son)
1353–1359	Ivan II, the Gentle (brother)
1360–1362	Dimitri III (nephew of Alexander III; deposed, died 1383)
1362–1389	Dimitri IV, Donskoi (son of Ivan II; prince of Moscow 1359; union with Moscow)

THE TSARDOM OF RUSSIA

House of Rurik – Princes of Moscow

1263–1303	Daniel (son of Alexander I of Vladimir; prince of Moscow, 1263 or later)
1303–1325	Yurii (son)
1325–1340	Ivan I, Kalita (brother)
1340–1353	Simeon the Proud (son)
1353–1359	Ivan II, the Gentle (brother)

Grand Princes of Moscow-Vladimir

1359–1389	Dimitri Donskoi (son)
1389–1425	Basil I (son)
1425–1462	Basil II, the Blind (son)
1462–1505	Ivan III, the Great (son)
1471–1490	Ivan the Younger (son; co-regent)
1505–1533	Basil III (brother; co-regent 1502)

Tsars of Russia

1533–1584	Ivan IV, the Terrible (son; crowned tsar 1547)
1584–1598	Theodore I (son)

House of Godunov

1598–1605	Boris Godunov
1605	Theodore II (son)
1605–1606	Dimitri (pretended son of Ivan IV)

House of Shuiskii

1606–1610	Basil IV Shuiskii (deposed, died 1612; interregnum 1610–13)

House of Romanov

1613–1645	Michael Romanov
1645–1676	Alexis (son)
1676–1682	Theodore III (son)
1682–1696	Ivan V (brother)
1682–1725	Peter I, the Great (brother; emperor 1721)
1725–1727	Catherine I (Martha) (widow)
1727–1730	Peter II (grandson of Peter I)
1730–1740	Anne (daughter of Ivan V)
1740–1741	Ivan VI (maternal grandson of Catherine, sister of Anne; deposed, died 1764)
1741–1762	Elizabeth (daughter of Catherine I and Peter I)

House of Holstein-Gottorp-Romanov

1762	Peter III (son of Anne, sister of Elizabeth, and Charles Frederick of Holstein-Gottorp; deposed, died 1762)
1762–1796	Catherine II, the Great (Sophia of Anhalt) (widow)
1796–1801	Paul I (son)
1801–1825	Alexander I (son)
1825–1855	Nicholas I (brother)

1855–1881	Alexander II (son)
1881–1894	Alexander III (son)
1894–1917	Nicholas II (son; deposed, died 1918; provisional government, then Soviet rule)

NOTES

Chronology and Calendar Medieval Russian chroniclers employed the Byzantine creation era beginning 1 September 5508 BC, but the year began on 1 March either preceding the Byzantine new year's day (Ultra-March style), or following it (March style). The former count was a year ahead of the latter. To find which of these systems was in use in each of the chronicles, the basic work is N. G. Berezhkov, *Khronologiya russkogo letopisaniya* (Moscow, 1963).

In the later fifteenth century, the beginning of the year was shifted to 1 September. Dating by the Christian era began on 1 January 1700, but the Julian year remained in use down to the fall of the monarchy.

According to tradition, Oleg ruled at Kiev from 878 to 913, Igor from 913 to 945; dates given above, which are approximate, are those of Taube.

Names and Titles For the title of grand prince (*velikii knyaz'*), first used by Vsevolod III, see A. Poppe, *Harvard Ukrainian Studies*, III–IV (1979–80), 684–9; for the titles of tsar and emperor, see M. Szeftel, 'The Title of the Muscovite Monarch up to the End of the Seventeenth Century', *Canadian-American Slavic Studies*, XIII (1979), 59–81.

BIBLIOGRAPHY FOR RUSSIAN DYNASTIES

Baumgarten, N. de, *Généalogies et mariages occidentaux des Rurikides russes du Xe au XIIIe siècle* (Rome, 1927) (*Orientalia Christiana*, IX: 1).

——*Généalogies des branches régnantes des Rurikides du XIIIe au XVIe siècle* (Rome, 1934) (*Orientalia Christiana*, XXXV: 1).

Fennell, J. L. I., *The Crisis of Medieval Russia, 1200–1304* (London, 1983).

——*The Emergence of Moscow, 1304–1359* (Berkeley, 1968).

Taube, M. de, 'Nouvelles recherches sur l'histoire politique et religieuse de l'Europe orientale à l'époque de la formation de l'état russe (IXe et Xe siècles)', *Istina*, IV (1957), 9–32, 265–78; V (1958), 7–16.

10 CRUSADER STATES

THE COUNTY OF EDESSA

House of Boulogne

1098–1100	Baldwin I (captured Edessa 1098; king of Jerusalem 1100–18)

House of Rethel

1100–1118	Baldwin II of Bourg (Jerusalem 1118–31)

House of Courtenay

1119–1131	Joscelin I
1131–1146	Joscelin II (son; deposed, died 1159; Turkish capture of Edessa)

THE PRINCIPALITY OF ANTIOCH

House of Hauteville

1099–1111	Bohemond I (son of Robert Guiscard, duke of Apulia; captured Antioch 1098)
1111–1112	Tancred (sister's son; regent 1105–11)
1112–1119	Roger of Salerno (grandnephew of Robert Guiscard)
1119–1126	Baldwin II of Jerusalem
1126–1130	Bohemond II (son of Bohemond I)
1130–1163	Constance (daughter; deposed, died 1164?)
1136–1149	Raymond of Poitiers (son of William IX of Aquitaine; married Constance)
1153–1160	Reginald of Châtillon (second husband of Constance; deposed, died 1187)

House of Poitiers

1163–1201	Bohemond III, the Stammerer (son of Constance and Raymond of Poitiers)
1201–1216	Bohemond IV, the One-eyed (son; count of Tripoli 1187; deposed)
1216–1219	Raymond Rupen (nephew; deposed, died 1222)
1219–1233	Bohemond IV (restored)
1233–1252	Bohemond V (son)
1252–1275	Bohemond VI (son; Mamluk capture of Antioch 1268)
1275–1287	Bohemond VII (son)
1288–1289	Lucy (sister; deposed; Mamluk capture of remaining Christian strongholds)

THE KINGDOM OF JERUSALEM

House of Boulogne

1099–1100	Godfrey of Bouillon (duke of Lower Lorraine; captured Jerusalem 1099; defender of the Holy Sepulchre)
1100–1118	Baldwin I (brother; king)

House of Rethel

1118–1131	Baldwin II of Bourg

House of Anjou

1131–1143	Fulk of Anjou
1131–1152	Melisend (daughter of Baldwin II; married Fulk; deposed, died 1161)
1143–1163	Baldwin III (son)
1163–1174	Amalric (brother)
1174–1185	Baldwin IV, the Leper (son)
1185–1186	Baldwin V (son of Sibyl, daughter of Amalric, and William of Montferrat; co-regent 1183)
1186–1190	Sibyl (daughter of Amalric)
1186–1192	Guy of Lusignan (second husband of Sibyl; deposed, died 1194)
1192–1205	Isabel I (daughter of Amalric)
1192	Conrad I of Montferrat (second husband of Isabel I)
1192–1197	Henry I of Champagne (third husband of Isabel I)
1197–1205	Aimery of Lusignan (brother of Guy; fourth husband of Isabel I; king of Cyprus 1197)

House of Montferrat

1205–1212	Mary (daughter of Isabel I and Conrad I)

House of Brienne

1210–1212	John I (married Mary; regent 1212–25; emperor of Constantinople 1231–7)
1212–1228	Isabel II (daughter)

House of Hohenstaufen

1225–1228	Frederick (king of the Romans 1212–50; married Isabel II; regent 1228–43)
1228–1254	Conrad II (son; king of the Romans 1250)
1254–1268	Conradin (son)

House of Cyprus

1269–1284	Hugh (maternal grandson of Alice, daughter of Isabel I and Henry I; king of Cyprus 1267)
1284–1285	John II (son; Cyprus)
1285–1291	Henry II (brother; Cyprus 1285–1324; Mamluk conquest of Palestine 1291)

THE COUNTY OF TRIPOLI

House of Toulouse

1102–1105	Raymond I of St Gilles (count of Toulouse as Raymond IV; captured Tortosa 1102)
1105–1109	William of Cerdagne (distant cousin)
1109–1112	Bertram (son of Raymond I; Toulouse 1105; captured Tripoli 1109)
1112–1137	Pons (son)
1137–1152	Raymond II (son)
1152–1187	Raymond III (son; bequeathed Tripoli to the house of Antioch)

THE KINGDOM OF CYPRUS

House of Lusignan

1192–1194	Guy (former king of Jerusalem; lord of Cyprus after purchase from the Templars 1192)
1194–1205	Aimery (brother; crowned king 1197)
1205–1218	Hugh I (son)
1218–1253	Henry I (son)
1253–1267	Hugh II (son)

House of Antioch-Lusignan

1267–1284	Hugh III (son of Isabel, daughter of Hugh I, and Henry, son of Bohemond IV of Antioch)
1284–1285	John I (son)
1285–1306	Henry II (brother; deposed)
1306–1310	Amalric (brother; governor only)
1310–1324	Henry II (restored)
1324–1359	Hugh IV (nephew)
1359–1369	Peter I (son; co-regent 1358)
1369–1382	Peter II, the Fat (son)
1382–1398	James I (son of Hugh IV)
1398–1432	Janus (son)
1432–1458	John II (son)
1458–1464	Charlotte (daughter; deposed, died 1487)
1464–1473	James II, the Bastard (brother)
1473–1474	James III (son)
1473–1489	Catherine Cornaro (mother; abdicated, died 1510; Venetian rule of Cyprus)

THE EMPIRE OF CONSTANTINOPLE

House of Flanders

1204–1205	Baldwin I (count of Flanders as Baldwin IX; captured Constantinople 1204; deposed, died 1206?)
1206–1216	Henry (brother; regent 1205–6)

House of Courtenay

1217	Peter of Courtenay (deposed, died 1218?)
1217–1219	Yolanda (sister of Henry; married Peter)
1221–1228	Robert (son)
1231–1237	John of Brienne
1240–1261	Baldwin II (brother of Robert; deposed, died 1273; Byzantine recapture of Constantinople)

BIBLIOGRAPHY

Runciman, S., *A History of the Crusades* (3 vols., Cambridge, 1951–4).
Setton, K. M., ed., *A History of the Crusades* (5 vols., Philadelphia and Madison, 1958–85).

VI

Islamic Dynasties (except India)

THE CALIPHATE

Orthodox Caliphate

632–634	Abū Bakr (father-in-law of Muḥammad the Prophet; acclaimed as his successor on his death in 632)
634–644	ʿUmar (father-in-law of Muḥammad)
644–656	ʿUthmān (son-in-law of Muḥammad)
656–661	ʿAlī (first cousin and son-in-law of Muḥammad)

Umayyad Dynasty

661–680	Muʿāwiya I (great-grandson of Umayya, distant cousin of Muḥammad)
680–683	Yazīd I (son)
683–684	Muʿāwiya II (son)
684–685	Marwān I (great-grandson of Umayya)
685–705	ʿAbd al-Malik (son)
705–715	Al-Walīd I (son)
715–717	Sulaymān (brother)
717–720	ʿUmar II (grandson of Marwān I)
720–724	Yazīd II (son of ʿAbd al-Malik)
724–743	Hishām (brother)
743–744	Al-Walīd II (son of Yazīd II)
744	Yazīd III (son of al-Walīd I)
744	Ibrāhīm (brother; deposed, died 750)
744–750	Marwān II (grandson of Marwān I)

ʿAbbāsid Dynasty

750–754	Abū al-ʿAbbās al-Saffāḥ (fourth in descent from al-ʿAbbās, uncle of Muḥammad)
754–775	Al-Manṣūr (brother)
775–785	Al-Mahdī (son)
785–786	Al-Hādī (son)
786–809	Hārūn al-Rashīd (brother)
809–813	Al-Amīn (son)
813–833	Al-Ma'mūn (brother)
833–842	Al-Muʿtaṣim (brother)
842–847	Al-Wāthiq (son)
847–861	Al-Mutawakkil (brother)
861–862	Al-Muntaṣir (son)
862–866	Al-Mustaʿīn (grandson of al-Muʿtaṣim; deposed, died 866)
866–869	Al-Muʿtazz (son of al-Mutawakkil)
869–870	Al-Muhtadī (son of al-Wāthiq)
870–892	Al-Muʿtamid (son of al-Mutawakkil)
892–902	Al-Muʿtaḍid (nephew)
902–908	Al-Muktafī (son)
908–932	Al-Muqtadir (brother)
932–934	Al-Qāhir (brother; deposed, died 950)
934–940	Al-Rāḍī (son of al-Muqtadir)
940–944	Al-Muttaqī (brother; deposed, died 968)
944–946	Al-Mustakfī (son of al-Muktafī; deposed, died 949)
946–974	Al-Muṭīʿ (son of al-Muqtadir; deposed, died 974)

974–991	Al-Ṭā'iʿ (son; deposed, died 1003)
991–1031	Al-Qādir (son of al-Muttaqī)
1031–1075	Al-Qā'im (son)
1075–1094	Al-Muqtadī (grandson)
1094–1118	Al-Mustaẓhir (son)
1118–1135	Al-Mustarshid (son)
1135–1136	Al-Rāshid (son; deposed, died 1138)
1136–1160	Al-Muqtafī (son of al-Mustaẓhir)
1160–1170	Al-Mustanjid (son)
1170–1180	Al-Mustaḍī' (son)
1180–1225	Al-Nāṣir (son)
1225–1226	Al-Ẓāhir (son)
1226–1242	Al-Mustanṣir (son)
1242–1258	Al-Mustaʿṣim (son; deposed, died 1258; Mongol conquest of Iraq)

NOTES

Calendar and Dating The Muslim year is a lunar year of 354 days, with eleven intercalary days in a cycle of thirty years. The era of the Hijra runs from new year's day, 1 Muḥarram, of the year of the Prophet's emigration (*hijra*) from Mecca to Medina; the corresponding Julian date is 15 or 16 July 622. Conversion tables, of which the most widely used are the *Vergleichungs-Tabellen* of H. F. Wüstenfeld (many editions), are based on the second of these dates. Grohmann, 9–12.

Names and Titles The caliph (*khalīfa*, 'successor') was *imām* as supreme head of the Muslim community; as political leader, he was *amīr al-mu'minīn*, 'commander of the believers'. The ʿAbbāsids and their rivals in Spain and north Africa took an honorific (*laqab*), such as al-Manṣūr, 'aided [by God]', or al-Muʿtaṣim-billāh, 'holding fast to God'. On Arabic names and titles, see the *Encyclopaedia of Islam*, arts. 'ism', 'laḳab'.

GENERAL BIBLIOGRAPHY

Bosworth, C. E., *The Islamic Dynasties: a Chronological and Genealogical Handbook* (Edinburgh, 1967).

Burke's Royal Families of the World, Volume II: Africa and the Middle East (London, 1980).

Encyclopaedia of Islam, ed. H. A. R. Gibb *et al.* (5 vols. to date, Leiden, 1960–86).

Freeman-Grenville, G. S. P., *The Muslim and Christian Calendars* (2nd edn., London, 1977).

Grohmann, A., *Arabische Chronologie und arabische Papyruskunde* (Leiden, 1966) (*Handbuch der Orientalistik*, ed. B. Spuler, suppl. II: 1).

THE CALIPHATE OF CORDOBA

Umayyad Dynasty

756–788	ʿAbd al-Raḥmān I (grandson of the caliph Hishām; amir of al-Andalus 756)
788–796	Hishām I (son)
796–822	Al-Ḥakam I (son)
822–852	ʿAbd al-Raḥmān II (son)
852–886	Muḥammad I (son)
886–888	Al-Mundhir (son)
888–912	ʿAbd Allāh (brother)
912–961	ʿAbd al-Raḥmān III, al-Nāṣir (grandson; assumed the title of *amīr al-muʾminīn* 929)
961–976	Al-Ḥakam II, al-Mustanṣir (son)
976–1009	Hishām II, al-Muʾayyad (son; deposed)
1009	Muḥammad II, al-Mahdī (great-grandson of ʿAbd al-Raḥmān III; deposed)
1009–1010	Sulaymān al-Mustaʿīn (great-grandson of ʿAbd al-Raḥmān III; deposed)
1010	Muḥammad II (restored)
1010–1013	Hishām II (restored)
1013–1016	Sulaymān (restored)
1016–1018	ʿAlī b. Ḥammūd al-Nāṣir
1018	ʿAbd al-Raḥmān IV, al-Murtaḍā (great-grandson of ʿAbd al-Raḥmān III)
1018–1021	Al-Qāsim al-Maʾmūn (brother of ʿAlī; deposed)
1021–1023	Yahyā al-Muʿtalī (son of ʿAlī; deposed)
1023	Al-Qāsim (restored; deposed, died 1036)
1023–1024	ʿAbd al-Raḥmān V, al-Mustaẓhir (brother of Muḥammad II)
1024–1025	Muḥammad III, al-Mustakfī (great-grandson of ʿAbd al-Raḥmān III)
1025–1027	Yahyā (restored; deposed, died 1035)
1027–1031	Hishām III, al-Muʿtadd (brother of ʿAbd al-Raḥmān IV; deposed, died 1036; breakup of the caliphate into petty kingdoms)

NOTES

Chronology Dates above are those of rule in Cordoba; for Ḥammūdid rule in Malaga and Algeciras, see Seco de Lucena.

BIBLIOGRAPHY

Lévi-Provençal, E., *Histoire de l'Espagne musulmane* (3 vols., Paris, 1950–67).
Seco de Lucena, L., *Los Hammūdíes, señores de Málaga y Algeciras* (Malaga, 1955).

THE KINGDOM OF GRANADA

Naṣrid Dynasty

1232–1273	Muḥammad I (son of Yūsuf b. Naṣr; sultan 1232; occupied Granada 1237)
1273–1302	Muḥammad II (son)
1302–1309	Muḥammad III (son, deposed, died 1314)
1309–1314	Naṣr (brother; deposed, died 1322)
1314–1325	Ismāʿīl I (great-grandson of Yūsuf b. Naṣr)
1325–1333	Muḥammad IV (son)
1333–1354	Yūsuf I (brother)
1354–1359	Muḥammad V (son; deposed)
1359–1360	Ismāʿīl II (brother)
1360–1362	Muḥammad VI (grandnephew of Ismāʿīl I; deposed, died 1362)
1362–1391	Muḥammad V (restored)
1391–1392	Yūsuf II (son)
1392–1408	Muḥammad VII (son)
1408–1417	Yūsuf III (brother)
1417–1419	Muḥammad VIII (son; deposed)
1419–1427	Muḥammad IX (grandson of Muḥammad V; deposed)
1427–1429	Muḥammad VIII (restored; deposed, died 1431)
1429–1431	Muḥammad IX (restored; deposed)
1432	Yūsuf IV (maternal grandson of Muḥammad VI)
1432–1445	Muḥammad IX (restored; deposed)
1445	Muḥammad X (nephew; deposed)
1445–1446	Yūsuf V (grandson of Yūsuf II; deposed)
1446–1448	Muḥammad X (restored; deposed)
1448–1453	Muḥammad IX (restored)
1453–1455	Muḥammad XI (son of Muḥammad VIII; deposed)
1455–1462	Saʿd (grandson of Yūsuf II; deposed)
1462	Yūsuf V (restored; deposed)
1462–1464	Saʿd (restored; deposed, died 1465)
1464–1482	ʿAlī (son; deposed)
1482–1483	Muḥammad XII (son; deposed)
1483–1485	ʿAlī (restored; deposed)
1485–1487	Muḥammad XIII (brother; deposed)
1487–1492	Muḥammad XII (restored; deposed, died 1494; Castilian conquest of Granada)

NOTES

Chronology From Muḥammad II, dates of reign refer to possession of the capital. Much of later Naṣrid history is obscure; for Muḥammad XI, see H. V. Livermore, *Al-Andalus*, XXVIII (1963), 331–48. For the death of Muḥammad XII, see M. C. Brosselard, *Journal asiatique*, seventh series, VII (1876), 174–8.

BIBLIOGRAPHY

Arié, R., *L'Espagne musulmane au temps des naṣrides (1232–1492)* (Paris, 1973).
Seco de Lucena, L., 'Más rectificaciones a la historia de los últimos naṣrīes', *Al-Andalus*, XXIV (1959), 275–95.

THE AGHLABID DYNASTY

800–812	Ibrāhīm I (son of al-Aghlab; amir of Tunisia under nominal ʿAbbāsid suzerainty 800)
812–817	ʿAbd Allāh I (son)
817–838	Ziyādat Allāh I (brother)
838–841	Al-Aghlab (brother)
841–856	Muḥammad I (son)
856–863	Aḥmad (nephew)
863–864	Ziyādat Allāh II (brother)
864–875	Muḥammad II (son of Aḥmad)
875–902	Ibrāhīm II (brother)
902–903	ʿAbd Allāh II (son)
903–909	Ziyādat Allāh III (son; deposed, died 916?; Fāṭimid conquest of Tunisia)

BIBLIOGRAPHY

Talbi, M., *L'émirat aghlabide, 184–296/800–909: histoire politique* (Paris, 1966).

THE ALMORAVID EMPIRE

Tāshufīnid Dynasty

1071–1106	Yūsuf b. Tāshufīn (independent ruler in Marrakesh 1071; assumed the title of *amīr al-muslimīn* 1073)
1106–1143	ʿAlī (son)
1143–1145	Tāshufīn (son)
1145	Ibrāhīm (son; deposed)
1145–1147	Isḥāq (son of ʿAlī; Almohad capture of Marrakesh 1147)

NOTES

Names and Titles For the title of *amīr al-muslimīn*, 'commander of the Muslims', see M. van Berchem, *Journal asiatique*, tenth series, IX (1907), 270–5, 293–305.

BIBLIOGRAPHY

Codera, F., *Decadencia y desaparición de los Almorávides en España* (Zaragoza, 1899).

Huici Miranda, A., 'La salida de los Almorávides del desierto y el reinado de Yūsuf b. Tāšfīn', *Hespéris*, XLVI (1959), 155–82.

THE ALMOHAD EMPIRE

1121–1130	Muḥammad b. Tūmart (messianic leader in southern Morocco 1121)

Mu'minid Dynasty

1133–1163	ʿAbd al-Mu'min (disciple of b. Tūmart; assumed the title of *amīr al-mu'minīn* 1133)
1163–1184	Yūsuf I (son; amir only 1163–8)
1184–1199	Yaʿqūb al-Manṣūr (son)
1199–1213	Muḥammad al-Nāṣir (son)
1213–1224	Yūsuf II, al-Mustanṣir (son)
1224	ʿAbd al-Wāḥid I (son of Yūsuf I)
1224–1227	ʿAbd Allāh al-ʿĀdil (son of Yaʿqūb)
1227–1232	Idrīs I, al-Ma'mūn (brother)
1232–1242	ʿAbd al-Wāḥid II, al-Rashīd (son)
1242–1248	ʿAlī al-Saʿīd (brother)
1248–1266	ʿUmar al-Murtaḍā (grandson of Yūsuf I)
1266–1269	Idrīs II, al-Wāthiq (great-grandson of ʿAbd al-Mu'min; Marīnid conquest of Morocco 1269)

BIBLIOGRAPHY

Bourouiba, R., 'Chronologie d'Ibn Tumart', *Revue d'histoire et de civilisation du Maghreb*, III (1967), 39–47.

Huici Miranda, A., *Historia política del imperio almohade* (2 vols., Tetuán, 1956–7).

THE MARĪNID KINGDOM

Marīnid Dynasty

1195–1217	ʿAbd al-Ḥaqq I (amir of the Banū-Marīn in eastern Morocco 1195)
1217–1240	ʿUthmān I (son)
1240–1244	Muḥammad I (brother)
1244–1258	Abū Bakr (brother)
1258–1259	ʿUmar (son; deposed)
1259–1286	Yaʿqūb (son of ʿAbd al-Ḥaqq I; assumed the title of *amīr al-muslimīn* 1269)
1286–1307	Yūsuf (son)
1307–1308	ʿĀmir (grandson)
1308–1310	Sulaymān (brother)
1310–1331	ʿUthmān II (son of Yaʿqūb)
1331–1351	ʿAlī (son)
1351–1358	Fāris (son)
1358–1359	Muḥammad II (son; deposed)
1359–1361	Ibrāhīm (son of ʿAlī)
1361	Tāshufīn (brother; deposed)
1361–1362	ʿAbd al-Ḥalīm (grandson of ʿUthmān II; deposed)
1362–1366	Muḥammad III (grandson of ʿAlī)
1366–1372	ʿAbd al-ʿAzīz I (son of ʿAlī)
1372–1374	Muḥammad IV (son; deposed)
1374–1384	Aḥmad (son of Ibrāhīm; deposed)
1384–1386	Mūsā (son of Fāris)
1386	Muḥammad V (son of Aḥmad; deposed)
1386–1387	Muḥammad VI (grandson of ʿAlī)
1387–1393	Aḥmad (restored)
1393–1396	ʿAbd al-ʿAzīz II (son)
1396–1398	ʿAbd Allāh (brother)
1398–1420	ʿUthmān III (brother)
1420–1465	ʿAbd al-Ḥaqq II (son; interregnum 1465–71, then Waṭṭāsid rule)

BIBLIOGRAPHY

Hazard, H. W., *Numismatic History of Late Medieval North Africa* (New York, 1952).

Ibn al-Aḥmar, Ismāʿīl b. Yūsuf, *Histoire des Benī Merīn, rois de Fās*, tr. G. Bouali and G. Marçais (Paris, 1917).

THE ʿALAWĪ DYNASTY

Sultanate of Morocco

1640–1664	Muḥammad I (son of al-Sharīf, supposed descendant of Muḥammad; independent ruler in the Tafilalt 1640)
1664–1672	Al-Rashīd (brother; proclaimed sultan 1666)
1672–1727	Ismāʿīl (brother)
1727–1728	Aḥmad (son; deposed)
1728	ʿAbd al-Malik (brother; deposed, died 1729)
1728–1729	Aḥmad (restored)
1729–1734	ʿAbd Allāh (brother; deposed)
1734–1736	ʿAlī (brother; deposed)
1736	ʿAbd Allāh (restored; deposed)
1736–1738	Muḥammad II (brother; deposed)
1738–1740	Al-Mustaḍī' (brother; deposed)
1740–1741	ʿAbd Allāh (restored; deposed)
1741	Zayn al-ʿĀbidīn (brother; deposed)
1741–1742	ʿAbd Allāh (restored; deposed)
1742–1743	Al-Mustaḍī' (restored; deposed)
1743–1747	ʿAbd Allāh (restored; deposed)
1747–1748	Al-Mustaḍī' (restored; deposed, died 1760)
1748–1757	ʿAbd Allāh (restored)
1757–1790	Muḥammad III (son)
1790–1792	Yazīd (son)
1792–1798	Hishām (brother; deposed, died 1799)
1798–1822	Sulaymān (brother)
1822–1859	ʿAbd al-Raḥmān (son of Hishām)
1859–1873	Muḥammad IV (son)
1873–1894	Al-Ḥasan I (son)
1894–1908	ʿAbd al-ʿAzīz (son; deposed, died 1943)
1908–1912	ʿAbd al-Ḥāfiẓ (brother; deposed, died 1937)
1912–1927	Yūsuf (brother; French protectorate 1912–56)
1927–1953	Muḥammad V (son; deposed)
1953–1955	Muḥammad VI (grandson of Muḥammad IV; deposed, died 1976)

Kingdom of Morocco

1955–1961	Muḥammad V (restored; assumed the title of king 1957)
1961–	Al-Ḥasan II (son)

BIBLIOGRAPHY

Abun-Nasr, J. M., *A History of the Maghrib in the Islamic Period* (Cambridge, 1987).

Cigar, N., ed., *Muhammad al-Qadiri's Nashr al-mathani: the Chronicles* (London, 1981).

THE ḤAFṢID KINGDOM

Ḥafṣid Dynasty

1229–1249	Yaḥyā I (grandson of Abū Ḥafṣ ʿUmar; independent amir of Tunisia 1229)
1249–1277	Muḥammad I (son; assumed the title of *amīr al-mu'minīn* 1253)
1277–1279	Yaḥyā II (son; deposed, died 1280)
1279–1283	Ibrāhīm I (son of Yaḥyā I; deposed, died 1283)
1283	ʿAbd al-ʿAzīz I (son)
1283–1284	Aḥmad b. Marzūq (pretended son of Yaḥyā II)
1284–1295	ʿUmar I (son of Yaḥyā I)
1295–1309	Muḥammad II (son of Yaḥyā II)
1309	Abū Bakr I (great-grandson of Yaḥyā I)
1309–1311	Khālid I (grandson of Ibrāhīm I; deposed, died 1313)
1311–1317	Zakariyā' I (grandnephew of Yaḥyā I; deposed, died 1326)
1317–1318	Muḥammad III (son; deposed)
1318–1346	Abū Bakr II (brother of Khālid I)
1346–1347	Aḥmad I (son)
1347	ʿUmar II (brother; Marīnid rule 1347–50)
1350	Al-Faḍl (brother)
1350–1369	Ibrāhīm II (brother)
1369–1370	Khālid II (son; deposed, died 1370)
1370–1394	Aḥmad II (grandson of Abū Bakr II)
1394–1434	ʿAbd al-ʿAzīz II (son)
1434–1435	Muḥammad IV (grandson)
1435–1488	ʿUthmān (brother)
1488–1489	Yaḥyā III (grandson)
1489–1490	ʿAbd al-Mu'min (grandson of ʿUthmān; deposed)
1490–1494	Zakariyā' II (son of Yaḥyā III)
1494–1526	Muḥammad V (nephew of Yaḥyā III)
1526–1542	Muḥammad VI (son; deposed)
1542–1569	Aḥmad III (son; deposed; Turkish rule 1569–73)
1573–1574	Muḥammad VII (brother; deposed; Turkish conquest of Tunisia)

NOTES

Names and Titles The Ḥafṣid monarchs, though officially caliphs, were commonly known as sultans. For titles, see Brunschvig, II, 7–17.

BIBLIOGRAPHY

Brunschvig, R., *La Berbérie orientale sous les Ḥafṣides des origines à la fin du XVe siècle* (2 vols., Paris, 1940–7).

Hazard, H. W., *Numismatic History of Late Medieval North Africa* (New York, 1952).

THE BEYLIK OF TUNISIA

Ḥusaynid Dynasty

1705–1735	Ḥusayn I (bey of Tunisia under Turkish suzerainty 1705; deposed, died 1740)
1735–1756	ʿAlī I (nephew)
1756–1759	Muḥammad I (son of Ḥusayn I)
1759–1782	ʿAlī II (brother)
1782–1814	Ḥamūda (son)
1814	ʿUthmān (brother)
1814–1824	Maḥmūd (son of Muḥammad I)
1824–1835	Ḥusayn II (son)
1835–1837	Muṣṭafā (brother)
1837–1855	Aḥmad I (son)
1855–1859	Muḥammad II (son of Ḥusayn II)
1859–1882	Muḥammad III, al-Ṣādiq (brother; French protectorate 1881–1956)
1882–1902	ʿAlī III (brother)
1902–1906	Muḥammad IV, al-Hādī (son)
1906–1922	Muḥammad V, al-Nāṣir (son of Muḥammad II)
1922–1929	Muḥammad VI, al-Ḥabīb (grandson of Ḥusayn II)
1929–1942	Aḥmad II (son of ʿAlī III)
1942–1943	Muḥammad VII, al-Munṣif (son of Muḥammad V; deposed, died 1948)
1943–1957	Muḥammad VIII, al-Amīn (son of Muḥammad VI; deposed, died 1962; republic of Tunisia)

BIBLIOGRAPHY

Brown, L. C., *The Tunisia of Ahmad Bey, 1837–1855* (Princeton, 1974).

Grandchamp, P., 'Tableau généalogique des beys husseinites (1705–1944)', *Cahiers de Tunisie*, XIII (1965), 132–3.

THE KINGDOM OF LIBYA

Sanūsī Dynasty

1837–1859	Muḥammad al-Sanūsī (founder of the Sanūsī order 1837; resident in Cyrenaica 1841)
1859–1902	Muḥammad al-Mahdī (son)
1902–1916	Aḥmad al-Sharīf (nephew; resigned political authority, died 1933)

Kingdom of Libya

1916–1969	Muḥammad Idrīs (son of al-Mahdī; amir of Cyrenaica 1949; king as Idrīs I 1951; deposed, died 1983; Libyan Arab Republic)

BIBLIOGRAPHY

Evans-Pritchard, E. E., *The Sanusi of Cyrenaica* (Oxford, 1963).
Wright, J., *Libya* (New York, 1969).

ISLAMIC EGYPT

Ṭūlūnid Dynasty

868–884	Aḥmad b. Ṭūlūn (governor of Egypt under nominal ʿAbbāsid suzerainty 868)
884–896	Khumārawayh (son)
896	Jaysh (son)
896–904	Hārūn (brother)
904–905	Shaybān (son of Aḥmad; deposed; direct ʿAbbāsid rule 905–35)

Ikhshīdid Dynasty

935–946	Muḥammad b. Ṭughj (governor of Egypt 935; granted the title of *ikhshīd* by the caliph 939)
946–960	Unūjūr (son)
960–966	ʿAlī (brother)
966–968	Kāfūr (slave of Muḥammad)
968–969	Aḥmad (son of ʿAlī; deposed, died 987; Fāṭimid conquest of Egypt)

Fāṭimid Dynasty

910–934	ʿUbayd Allāh al-Mahdī (claimed descent from Fāṭima, daughter of Muḥammad; imam and caliph in Tunisia 910)
934–946	Al-Qā'im (son?)
946–953	Al-Manṣūr (son)
953–975	Al-Muʿizz (son)
975–996	Al-ʿAzīz (son)
996–1021	Al-Ḥākim (son)
1021–1036	Al-Ẓāhir (son)
1036–1094	Al-Mustanṣir (son)
1094–1101	Al-Mustaʿlī (son)
1101–1130	Al-Āmir (son)
1132–1149	Al-Ḥāfiẓ (grandson of al-Mustanṣir; regent 1130–2)
1149–1154	Al-Ẓāfir (son)
1154–1160	Al-Fā'iz (son)
1160–1171	Al-ʿĀḍid (grandson of al-Ḥāfiẓ; nominal ʿAbbāsid rule 1171–5)

Ayyūbid Dynasty

1175–1193	Al-Nāṣir Yūsuf (Saladin) (son of Ayyūb; invested with Egypt and Syria by the caliph 1175)
1193–1198	Al-ʿAzīz ʿUthmān (son)
1198–1200	Al-Manṣūr Muḥammad I (son; deposed)
1200–1218	Al-ʿĀdil Abū Bakr I (son of Ayyūb)
1218–1238	Al-Kāmil Muḥammad II (son)
1238–1240	Al-ʿĀdil Abū Bakr II (son; deposed, died 1248)
1240–1249	Al-Ṣāliḥ Ayyūb (brother)
1249–1250	Al-Muʿaẓẓam Tūrānshāh (son)
1250	Shajar al-Durr (widow of al-Ṣāliḥ Ayyūb; abdicated, died 1257)
1250–1254	Al-Ashraf Mūsā (grandson of al-Kāmil Muḥammad II; co-regent with Aybak, first Baḥrī Mamlūk; deposed)

The Baḥrī Mamlūks

1250–1257	Al-Muʿizz Aybak (married Shajar al-Durr, widow of al-Ṣāliḥ Ayyūb)
1257–1259	Al-Manṣūr ʿAlī I (son; deposed)
1259–1260	Al-Muẓaffar Quṭuz
1260–1277	Al-Ẓāhir Baybars I
1277–1279	Al-Saʿīd Baraka Khan (son; deposed)
1279	Al-ʿĀdil Salāmish (brother; deposed)
1279–1290	Al-Manṣūr Qalā'ūn
1290–1293	Al-Ashraf Khalīl (son)
1293–1294	Al-Nāṣir Muḥammad I (brother; deposed)
1294–1296	Al-ʿĀdil Kitbughā (deposed, died 1303)
1296–1299	Al-Manṣūr Lājīn
1299–1309	Al-Nāṣir Muḥammad I (restored; abdicated)
1309–1310	Al-Muẓaffar Baybars II
1310–1341	Al-Nāṣir Muḥammad I (again)
1341	Al-Manṣūr Abū Bakr (son)
1341–1342	Al-Ashraf Kūjūk (brother; deposed)
1342	Al-Nāṣir Aḥmad (brother; deposed, died 1344)
1342–1345	Al-Ṣāliḥ Ismāʿīl (brother)
1345–1346	Al-Kāmil Shaʿbān I (brother)
1346–1347	Al-Muẓaffar Ḥājjī I (brother)
1347–1351	Al-Nāṣir al-Ḥasan (brother; deposed)
1351–1354	Al-Ṣāliḥ Ṣāliḥ (brother; deposed)
1354–1361	Al-Nāṣir al-Ḥasan (restored)
1361–1363	Al-Manṣūr Muḥammad II (son of Ḥājjī I; deposed)
1363–1377	Al-Ashraf Shaʿbān II (grandson of Muhammad I)
1377–1381	Al-Manṣūr ʿAlī II (son)
1381–1382	Al-Ṣāliḥ Ḥājjī II (brother; deposed)
1382–1389	Al-Ẓāhir Barqūq [Burjī] (deposed)
1389–1390	Al-Muẓaffar Ḥājjī II (restored with new honorific; deposed, died 1412)

The Burjī Mamlūks

1390–1399	Al-Ẓāhir Barqūq (restored)
1399–1405	Al-Nāṣir Faraj (son; deposed)
1405	Al-Manṣūr ʿAbd al-ʿAzīz (brother; deposed, died 1406)
1405–1412	Al-Nāṣir Faraj (restored)
1412	Al-ʿĀdil al-Mustaʿīn (ʿAbbāsid caliph in Cairo; deposed, died 1430)
1412–1421	Al-Mu'ayyad Shaykh
1421	Al-Muẓaffar Aḥmad II (son; deposed, died 1430)
1421	Al-Ẓāhir Ṭaṭār
1421–1422	Al-Ṣāliḥ Muḥammad III (son; deposed, died 1430)
1422–1438	Al-Ashraf Barsbay
1438	Al-ʿAzīz Yūsuf (son; deposed)
1438–1453	Al-Ẓāhir Jaqmaq
1453	Al-Manṣūr ʿUthmān (son; deposed)
1453–1461	Al-Ashraf Ināl
1461	Al-Mu'ayyad Aḥmad III (son; deposed)
1461–1467	Al-Ẓāhir Khūshqadam
1467	Al-Ẓāhir Bilbay (deposed, died 1468)

1467–1468	Al-Ẓāhir Timurbughā (deposed, died 1475)
1468–1496	Al-Ashraf Qā'itbay
1496–1498	Al-Nāṣir Muḥammad IV (son)
1498–1500	Al-Ẓāhir Qānṣūh I (deposed)
1500–1501	Al-Ashraf Jānbalāt (deposed, died 1501)
1501	Al-ʿĀdil Tūmānbay I (deposed)
1501–1516	Al-Ashraf Qānṣūh II, al-Ghawrī
1516–1517	Al-Ashraf Tūmānbay II (deposed, died 1517; direct Turkish rule 1517–1805)

Muḥammad ʿAlī Dynasty

1805–1848	Muḥammad ʿAlī (viceroy of Egypt under Turkish suzerainty 1805; hereditary viceroy 1841; deposed, died 1849)
1848	Ibrāhīm (son)
1848–1854	ʿAbbās I Ḥilmī (nephew)
1854–1863	Saʿīd (son of Muḥammad ʿAlī)
1863–1879	Ismāʿīl (son of Ibrāhīm; khedive 1867; deposed, died 1895)
1879–1892	Tawfīq (son; British occupation of Egypt 1882–1922)
1892–1914	ʿAbbās II Ḥilmī (son; deposed, died 1944)
1914–1917	Husayn Kāmil (son of Ismāʿīl; sultan)
1917–1936	Aḥmad Fu'ād (brother; king as Fu'ād I 1922)
1936–1952	Farūq (son; deposed, died 1965)
1952–1953	Fu'ād II (son; nominal king; deposed; Arab Republic of Egypt)

NOTES

Names and Titles For the title of sultan, officially used from al-Ṣāliḥ Ayyūb (1249), see Humphreys, 365–9.

BIBLIOGRAPHY

Bacharach, J. L., 'The Career of Muḥammad ibn Ṭughj al-Ikhshīd, a Tenth-Century Governor of Egypt', *Speculum*, L (1975), 586–612.

Hassan, Z. M., *Les Tulunides: étude de l'Egypte musulmane à la fin du IXᵉ siècle, 868–905* (Paris, 1933).

Holt, P. M., *Egypt and the Fertile Crescent, 1516–1922: a Political History* (Ithaca, NY, 1966).

Humphreys, R. S., *From Saladin to the Mongols: the Ayyubids of Damascus, 1193–1260* (Albany, NY, 1977).

Wiet, G., *L'Egypte arabe* (Paris, 1937) (*Histoire de la nation égyptienne*, ed. G. Hanotaux, IV).

THE OTTOMAN EMPIRE

Osmanli Dynasty

1280–1324	Osman I (son of Ertuğrul; Turkoman chieftain in western Anatolia *c.*1280)
1324–1362	Orhan (son)
1362–1389	Murad I (son)
1389–1402	Bayezid I, the Thunderbolt (son; deposed, died 1403)
1402–1403	Isa (son; claimed Anatolia)
1402–1411	Süleyman (brother; claimed Rumelia)
1409–1413	Musa (brother; claimed Rumelia)
1413–1421	Mehmed I (brother; claimed Anatolia 1402–13)
1421–1451	Murad II (son; abdicated in favour of Mehmed II 1444–6)
1451–1481	Mehmed II, the Conqueror (son)
1481–1512	Bayezid II (son; deposed, died 1512)
1512–1520	Selim I, the Grim (son)
1520–1566	Süleyman I, the Magnificent (son)
1566–1574	Selim II, the Sot (son)
1574–1595	Murad III (son)
1595–1603	Mehmed III (son)
1603–1617	Ahmed I (son)
1617–1618	Mustafa I (brother; deposed)
1618–1622	Osman II (son of Ahmed I)
1622–1623	Mustafa I (restored; deposed, died 1639)
1623–1640	Murad IV (son of Ahmed I)
1640–1648	Ibrahim (brother; deposed, died 1648)
1648–1687	Mehmed IV (son; deposed, died 1693)
1687–1691	Süleyman II (brother)
1691–1695	Ahmed II (brother)
1695–1703	Mustafa II (son of Mehmed IV; deposed, died 1703)
1703–1730	Ahmed III (brother; deposed, died 1736)
1730–1754	Mahmud I (son of Mustafa II)
1754–1757	Osman III (brother)
1757–1774	Mustafa III (son of Ahmed III)
1774–1789	Abdülhamid I (brother)
1789–1807	Selim III (son of Mustafa III; deposed, died 1808)
1807–1808	Mustafa IV (son of Abdülhamid I; deposed, died 1808)
1808–1839	Mahmud II (brother)
1839–1861	Abdülmecid I (son)
1861–1876	Abdülaziz (brother; deposed, died 1876)
1876	Murad V (son of Abdülmecid I; deposed, died 1904)
1876–1909	Abdülhamid II (brother; deposed, died 1918)
1909–1918	Mehmed V Reşad (brother)
1918–1922	Mehmed VI Vahidüddin (brother; deposed, died 1926; republic of Turkey 1923)
1922–1924	Abdülmecid (II) (son of Abdülaziz; caliph only; deposed, died 1944)

NOTES

Chronology Osman I died in 1323 or 1324 (Alderson, 164, n. 5), Orhan in March 1362 (P. Charanis, *Byzantion*, XIII (1938), 349–51).

Names and Titles The dynastic title of sultan was first in use from the reign of Orhan. See A. S. Atiya, *The Crusade of Nicopolis* (London, 1934), 157–60.

BIBLIOGRAPHY

Alderson, A. D., *The Structure of the Ottoman Dynasty* (Oxford, 1956).

THE HĀSHIMID DYNASTY

Kingdom of the Ḥijāz

1916–1924	Ḥusayn (descendant of Hāshim, great-grandfather of Muḥammad; abdicated, died 1931)
1924–1925	ʿAlī (son; deposed, died 1935; Saʿūdī conquest of the Ḥijāz)

Kingdom of Iraq

1921–1933	Fayṣal I (brother; king of Syria 1920; king of Iraq under British mandate 1921–32)
1933–1939	Ghāzī (son)
1939–1958	Fayṣal II (son; Iraqi Republic 1958)

Kingdom of Jordan

1921–1951	ʿAbd Allāh (son of Ḥusayn; amir of Transjordan under British mandate 1921–46; king 1946; Hashemite Kingdom of Jordan 1949)
1951–1952	Ṭalāl (son; deposed, died 1972)
1952–	Ḥusayn (son)

BIBLIOGRAPHY

Morris, J., *The Hashemite Kings* (New York, 1959).
Patai, R., *The Kingdom of Jordan* (Princeton, 1958).

THE SAʿŪDĪ DYNASTY

Imamate of Najd

1744–1765	Muḥammad (son of Saʿūd; imam of the Wahhābī state in Najd 1744)
1765–1803	ʿAbd al-ʿAzīz (son)
1803–1814	Saʿūd I, the Great (son)
1814–1818	ʿAbd Allāh I (son; deposed, died 1818; Turkish occupation 1818–24)
1824–1834	Turkī (grandson of Muḥammad)
1834–1837	Fayṣal (son; deposed)
1837–1841	Khālid (son of Saʿūd I; deposed, died 1861)
1841–1843	ʿAbd Allāh II (fourth in descent from Saʿūd; deposed, died 1843)
1843–1865	Fayṣal (restored)
1865–1871	ʿAbd Allāh III (son; deposed)
1871	Saʿūd II (brother; deposed)
1871–1873	ʿAbd Allāh III (restored; deposed)
1873–1875	Saʿūd II (restored)
1875–1876	ʿAbd al-Raḥmān (brother; abdicated, died 1928)
1876–1887	ʿAbd Allāh III (restored; deposed, died 1889; Rashīdī occupation 1887–1902)

Kingdom of Saʿūdī Arabia

1902–1953	ʿAbd al-ʿAzīz (son of ʿAbd al-Raḥmān; king of the Ḥijāz 1926; of Najd 1927; of Saʿūdī Arabia 1932)
1953–1964	Saʿūd (son; deposed, died 1969)
1964–1975	Fayṣal (brother)
1975–1982	Khālid (brother)
1982–	Fahd (brother)

BIBLIOGRAPHY

Philby, H. St. J. B., *Saʿudi Arabia* (Beirut, 1968).
Winder, R. B., *Saudi Arabia in the Nineteenth Century* (New York, 1965).

THE KINGDOM OF YEMEN

Qāsimī Dynasty

1597–1620	Al-Qāsim I, al-Manṣūr (descendant of Muḥammad; proclaimed imam 1597)
1620–1644	Muḥammad I, al-Mu'ayyad (son)
1644–1676	Ismāʿīl al-Mutawakkil (brother)
1676–1681	Aḥmad I, al-Mahdī (nephew)
1681–1686	Muḥammad II, al-Mu'ayyad (son of Ismāʿīl)
1686–1718	Muḥammad III, al-Mahdī (son of Aḥmad I)
1718–1727	Al-Qāsim II, al-Mutawakkil (nephew)
1727–1748	Ḥusayn al-Manṣūr (son)
1748–1775	ʿAbbās I, al-Mahdī (son)
1775–1809	ʿAlī I, al-Manṣūr (son)
1809–1816	Aḥmad II, al-Mutawakkil (son)
1816–1835	ʿAbd Allāh I, al-Mahdī (son)
1835–1837	ʿAlī II, al-Manṣūr (son; deposed)
1837–1840	ʿAbd Allāh II, al-Nāṣir (great-grandson of ʿAbbās I)
1840–1844	Muḥammad IV, al-Hādī (son of Aḥmad II)
1844–1845	ʿAlī II (restored; deposed)
1845–1849	Muḥammad V, al-Mutawakkil (grandson of ʿAlī I)
1849–1850	ʿAlī II (restored; deposed)
1850	ʿAbbās II, al-Mu'ayyad (sixth in descent from Ismāʿīl; deposed)
1851–1857	Ghālib al-Hādī (son of Muḥammad V; deposed)
1857	ʿAlī II (restored; deposed; period of confusion; Turkish occupation 1872–1918)
1890–1904	Muḥammad VI, al-Manṣūr (eighth in descent from al-Qāsim I)

Kingdom of Yemen

1904–1948	Yaḥyā al-Mutawakkil (son; Mutawakkilite Kingdom of Yemen 1918)
1948	ʿAbd Allāh al-Hādī (usurper; deposed, died 1948)
1948–1962	Ahmad al-Nāsir (son of Yaḥyā)
1962	Muḥammad al-Manṣūr (son; deposed; Yemen Arab Republic)

NOTES

Chronology The imamate was never strictly hereditary, and there were numerous pretenders and rival claimants from the Qāsimī and other ʿAlid families. Dates for the later Qāsimīs refer to possession of the capital, Ṣan'ā'.

BIBLIOGRAPHY

Stookey, R. W., *Yemen* (Boulder, Colo., 1978).
Wenner, M. W., *Modern Yemen, 1918–1966* (Baltimore, 1967).

THE SĀMĀNID KINGDOM

Sāmānid Dynasty

864–892	Naṣr I (great-grandson of Sāmān; governor of Samarkand 864; independent amir of Transoxiana 875)
892–907	Ismāʿīl (brother; conquered Khurasan 900)
907–914	Aḥmad (son)
914–942	Naṣr II (son; deposed, died 943)
942–954	Nūḥ I (son)
954–961	ʿAbd al-Malik I (son)
961–976	Manṣūr I (brother)
976–997	Nūḥ II (son)
997–999	Manṣūr II (son; deposed)
999	ʿAbd al-Malik II (brother; deposed; Ghaznavid conquest of Khurasan)

BIBLIOGRAPHY

Barthold, V. V., *Turkestan down to the Mongol Invasion* (3rd edn., London, 1968).
Cambridge History of Iran, Volume IV, ed. R. N. Frye (Cambridge, 1975).

THE GHAZNAVID EMPIRE

Ghaznavid Dynasty

977–997	Sebüktigin (governor of Ghazna in eastern Afghanistan 977)
997–998	Ismāʿīl (son; deposed)
998–1030	Maḥmūd (brother; conquered Khurasan and northern India)
1030	Muḥammad (son; deposed)
1030–1040	Masʿūd I (brother; deposed, died 1041)
1040–1041	Muḥammad (restored)
1041–1048	Maudūd (son of Masʿūd I)
1048	Masʿūd II (son; deposed)
1048–1049	ʿAlī (son of Masʿūd I; deposed)
1049–1051	ʿAbd al-Rashīd (son of Maḥmūd)
1051–1052	Toghrïl (usurper)
1052–1059	Farrukhzād (son of Masʿūd I)
1059–1099	Ibrāhīm (brother)
1099–1115	Masʿūd III (son)
1115–1116	Shīrzād (son; deposed, died 1116)
1116–1117	Arslanshāh (brother; deposed, died 1118)
1117–1157	Bahrāmshāh (brother)
1157–1160	Khusraushāh (son)
1160–1186	Khusrau Malik (son; deposed, died 1191; Ghūrid conquest of northern India)

NOTES

Names and Titles The title of sultan was in use from the reign of Farrukhzād. Bosworth, *Later Ghaznavids*, 55–6.

BIBLIOGRAPHY

Bosworth, C. E., *The Ghaznavids: their Empire in Afghanistan and Eastern Iran, 994–1040* (2nd edn., Beirut, 1973).

—— *The Later Ghaznavids: Splendour and Decay, 1040–1186* (New York, 1977).

THE SELJUQID DYNASTY

Great Seljuqid Sultanate

1038–1063	Toghrïl Beg (grandson of Seljuq; sultan 1038; conquered Khurasan, Iraq and western Persia)
1063–1072	Alp Arslan (nephew)
1072–1092	Malikshāh I (son)
1092–1094	Maḥmūd I (son)
1094–1104	Berkyaruq (brother)
1104–1105	Malikshāh II (son; deposed)
1105–1118	Muḥammad I (son of Malikshāh I)
1118–1157	Sanjar (brother; ruled Khurasan; Oghuz domination of Khurasan 1157)

Iraq and Western Persia

1118–1131	Maḥmūd II (son of Muḥammad I)
1131–1134	Toghrïl II (brother)
1134–1152	Mas'ūd (brother)
1152–1153	Malikshāh III (son of Maḥmūd II; deposed, died 1160)
1153–1159	Muḥammad II (brother)
1160	Sulaymān (son of Muḥammad I; deposed, died 1161)
1160–1175	Arslan (son of Toghrïl II)
1175–1194	Toghrïl III (son; Khwārazmian conquest of western Persia 1194)

NOTES

Names and Titles For the title of sultan (*al-sulṭān*), first used by Toghrïl Beg, see the *Encyclopaedia of Islam*, I, 20.

BIBLIOGRAPHY

Cambridge History of Iran, Volume V, ed. J. A. Boyle (Cambridge, 1968).
Köymen, M. A., *Selçuklu devri Türk tarihi* (Ankara, 1963).

THE GHŪRID EMPIRE

Shansabānī Dynasty

1117–1146	ʿIzz al-Dīn Ḥusayn I (supposed descendant of Shansab; amir of Ghūr in central Afghanistan 1117)
1146–1149	Sayf al-Dīn Sūrī (son)
1149	Bahāʾ al-Dīn Sām I (brother)
1149–1161	ʿAlāʾ al-Dīn Ḥusayn II (brother; captured Ghazna and assumed the title of sultan 1149)
1161–1163	Sayf al-Dīn Muḥammad I (son)
1163–1203	Ghiyāth al-Dīn Muḥammad II (son of Sām I)
1203–1206	Muʿizz al-Dīn Muḥammad III (brother; Ghazna 1174)
1206–1210	Ghiyāth al-Dīn Maḥmūd (son of Muḥammad II)
1210	Bahāʾ al-Dīn Sām II (son; deposed)
1210–1214	ʿAlāʾ al-Dīn Atsïz (son of Ḥusayn II)
1214–1215	ʿAlāʾ al-Dīn Muḥammad IV (grandson of Ḥusayn I; deposed; Khwārazmian conquest of the Ghūrid empire)

NOTES

Chronology Dates follow Abdul Ghafur; those of the first ruler are approximate.

BIBLIOGRAPHY

Abdul Ghafur, M., *The Gōrids: History, Culture and Administration* (Ph.D. dissertation, University of Hamburg, 1960).

Cambridge History of Iran, Volume V, ed. J. A. Boyle (Cambridge, 1968).

THE KHWĀRAZMIAN EMPIRE

Dynasty of Anūshtigin

1098–1128	Quṭb al-Dīn Muḥammad I (son of Anūshtigin; governor of Khwārazm with the title of Khwārazm-Shāh 1098)
1128–1156	ʿAlāʾ al-Dīn Atsïz (son)
1156–1172	Tāj al-Dunyā Il Arslan (son; assumed the title of sultan 1166)
1172–1193	Jalāl al-Dunyā Sulṭānshāh (son; Khurasan)
1172–1200	ʿAlāʾ al-Dīn Tekish (brother; Khwārazm, later Khurasan; sultan 1187)
1200–1220	ʿAlāʾ al-Dīn Muḥammad II (son)
1220–1231	Jalāl al-Dīn Mingburnu (son; Mongol conquest of the Khwārazmian empire 1231)

NOTES

Names and Titles On the form Mingburnu, which is uncertain, see the *Encyclopaedia of Islam*, II, 392; on titles, see L. Richter-Bernburg, 'Zur Titulatur der Ḫwārezm-Šāhe aus der Dynastie Anūštegīns', *Archäologische Mitteilungen aus Īran*, new series, IX (1976), 179–205.

BIBLIOGRAPHY

Barthold, V. V., *Turkestan down to the Mongol Invasion* (3rd edn., London, 1968).
Kafesoğlu, İ., *Harezmşahlar devleti tarihi (485–617/1092–1229)* (Ankara, 1956).

IL-KHANS OF PERSIA

Chingizid Dynasty

1256–1265	Hülegü (grandson of Chingiz; conquered Persia and Iraq 1256–8)
1265–1282	Abaqa (son)
1282–1284	Tegüder (Aḥmad) (brother)
1284–1291	Arghun (son of Abaqa)
1291–1295	Gaikhatu (brother)
1295	Baidu (grandson of Hülegü)
1295–1304	Ghazan (Maḥmūd) (son of Arghun)
1304–1316	Öljeitü (Muḥammad) (brother)
1316–1335	Abū Saʿīd (son)
1335–1336	Arpa (sixth in descent from Chingiz)
1336–1337	Mūsā (grandson of Baidu)
1336–1338	Muḥammad (fifth in descent from Hülegü)
1338–1339	Sati Beg (daughter of Öljeitü; deposed)
1339–1340	Jahān Temür (grandson of Gaikhatu; deposed)
1339–1343	Sulaymān (fourth in descent from Hülegü; deposed; breakup of the Il-Khanid state into petty kingdoms)

NOTES

Names and Titles The title of *īl-khān*, or subject khan, denoted subordination to the great khan in Mongolia (later China); converts to Islam, beginning with Tegüder, had the title of sultan (*Cambridge History of Iran*, 345, 365).

BIBLIOGRAPHY

Cambridge History of Iran, Volume V, ed. J. A. Boyle (Cambridge, 1968).

Spuler, B., *Die Mongolen in Iran: Politik, Verwaltung und Kultur der Ilchanzeit, 1220–1350* (3rd edn., Berlin, 1968).

THE TĪMŪRID EMPIRE

Tīmūrid Dynasty

1370–1405	Tīmūr the Lame (Tamerlane) (amir of Transoxiana 1370; conquered Iraq, Persia and Afghanistan)
1405–1408	Mīrānshāh (son; western Persia)
1405–1409	Khalīl (son; Transoxiana; western Persia 1409–11)
1405–1447	Shāhrukh (son of Tīmūr; Khurasan; Transoxiana 1409)
1447–1449	Ulugh Beg (son)

Transoxiana

1449–1450	ʿAbd al-Laṭīf (son)
1450–1451	ʿAbd Allāh (grandson of Shāhrukh)
1451–1469	Abū Saʿīd (nephew of Khalīl)
1469–1494	Aḥmad (son)
1494–1495	Maḥmūd (brother)
1495–1497	Bāysunqur (son; deposed, died 1499)
1497–1498	Bābur (grandson of Abū Saʿīd; deposed)
1498–1500	ʿAlī (son of Maḥmūd)
1500–1501	Bābur (restored; deposed, died 1530; Özbeg conquest of Transoxiana)

Khurasan

1449–1457	Bābur (grandson of Shāhrukh)
1457–1459	Maḥmūd (son)
1459–1469	Abū Saʿīd (nephew of Khalīl; Transoxiana 1451)
1469–1506	Ḥusayn Bāyqarā (fourth in descent from Tīmūr)
1506–1507	Badīʿ al-Zamān (son; deposed, died 1517; Özbeg conquest of Khurasan)

NOTES

Names and Titles The title of sultan was in use from the reign of Shāhrukh.

BIBLIOGRAPHY

Barthold, V. V., *Ulugh-beg* (Leiden, 1958) (*Four Studies on the History of Central Asia*, II).

Savory, R. M., 'The Struggle for Supremacy in Persia after the Death of Tīmūr', *Islam*, XL (1964–5), 35–65.

MODERN PERSIA (IRAN)

Ṣafavid Dynasty

1501–1524	Ismāʿīl I (sixth in descent from Ṣafī al-Dīn; proclaimed shah 1501)
1524–1576	Ṭahmāsp I (son)
1576–1577	Ismāʿīl II (son)
1577–1587	Sulṭān Muḥammad (brother; deposed, died 1595)
1587–1629	ʿAbbās I, the Great (son)
1629–1642	Ṣafī I (grandson)
1642–1666	ʿAbbās II (son)
1666–1694	Ṣafī II (son; re-crowned as Sulaymān I 1668)
1694–1722	Sulṭān Ḥusayn (son; deposed, died 1726)

Ghalzay Dynasty

1722–1725	Maḥmūd
1725–1729	Ashraf (first cousin; deposed, died 1730)

Ṣafavid Dynasty

1729–1732	Ṭahmāsp II (son of Sulṭān Ḥusayn; deposed, died 1740)
1732–1736	ʿAbbās III (son; deposed, died 1740)

Afshārid Dynasty

1736–1747	Nādir (regent 1732–6)
1747–1748	ʿĀdil (nephew; deposed, died 1749)
1748–1749	Ibrāhīm (brother)
1748–1749	Shāhrukh (grandson of Nādir; rival claimant; deposed)

Ṣafavid Dynasty

1749–1750	Sulaymān II (maternal grandson of Ṣafī II; deposed, died 1763)
1750–1773	Ismāʿīl III (maternal grandson of Sulṭān Ḥusayn; nominal ruler only, in western Persia)

Afshārid Dynasty

1750–1796	Shāhrukh (restored; nominal ruler only, in Khurasan; deposed, died 1796)

Qājār Dynasty

1796–1797	Āghā Muḥammad
1797–1834	Fatḥ ʿAlī (nephew)
1834–1848	Muḥammad (grandson)
1848–1896	Nāṣir al-Dīn (son)
1896–1907	Muẓaffar al-Dīn (son)
1907–1909	Muḥammad ʿAlī (son; deposed, died 1925)
1909–1925	Aḥmad (son; deposed, died 1930)

Pahlavī Dynasty

1925–1941	Riżā (abdicated, died 1944)
1941–1979	Muḥammad Riżā (son; deposed, died 1980; Islamic Republic of Iran)

NOTES

Chronology For chronological problems in an important Ṣafavid source, and for ʿAbbās I's accession late in 1587, see R. D. McChesney, 'A Note on Iskandar Beg's Chronology', *Journal of Near Eastern Studies*, XXXIX (1980), 53–63.

Names and Titles Karīm Khan Zand and his dynasty, who held power in western Persia from 1751 to 1794, did not assume the royal title of *shāhānshāh*; see J. R. Perry, *Karim Khan Zand* (Chicago, 1979), 214–17.

BIBLIOGRAPHY

Perry, J. R. 'The Last Ṣafavids, 1722–1773', *Iran*, IX (1971), 59–69.

Rabino, H. L., *Coins, Medals and Seals of the Shahs of Iran (1500–1941)* (Hertford, 1945).

THE KINGDOM OF AFGHANISTAN

Durrānī Dynasty

1747–1772	Aḥmad (assumed the title of shah and the epithet Durr-i Durrān 1747)
1772–1793	Tīmūr (son)
1793–1801	Zamān (son; deposed, died 1844)
1801–1803	Maḥmūd (brother; deposed)
1803–1809	Shujāʿ (brother; deposed)
1809–1818	Maḥmūd (restored; deposed, died 1829; period of confusion, 1818–26)

Bārakzay Dynasty

1826–1839	Dūst Muḥammad (assumed the title of amir 1834; deposed)
1839–1842	Shujāʿ (restored)
1842–1863	Dūst Muḥammad (restored)
1863–1866	Shīr ʿAlī (son; deposed)
1866–1867	Muḥammad Afḍal (brother)
1867–1868	Muḥammad Aʿẓam (brother; deposed, died 1869)
1868–1879	Shīr ʿAlī (restored)
1879	Muḥammad Yaʿqūb (son; abdicated, died 1923)
1880–1901	ʿAbd al-Raḥmān (son of Muḥammad Afḍal)
1901–1919	Ḥabīb Allāh (son)
1919	Naṣr Allāh (brother; deposed, died 1920)

Shahs of Afghanistan

1919–1929	Amān Allāh (son of Ḥabīb Allāh; shah 1926; deposed, died 1960)
1929	ʿInāyat Allāh (brother; deposed, died 1946)
1929–1933	Muḥammad Nādir (great-grandnephew of Dūst Muḥammad)
1933–1973	Muḥammad Ẓāhir (son; deposed; republic of Afghanistan)

BIBLIOGRAPHY

Dupree, L., *Afghanistan* (Princeton, 1973).
Gregorian, V., *The Emergence of Modern Afghanistan* (Stanford, 1969).

VII

India

THE MAURYA EMPIRE

Maurya Dynasty

321–297	Chandragupta Maurya (founder of India's first imperial dynasty *c.*321 BC)
297–272	Bindusāra (son; interregnum 272–268)
268–232	Aśoka (son)
232–224	Daśaratha (grandson)
224–215	Samprati (brother?)
215–202	Śāliśuka
202–195	Devavarman
195–187	Śatadhanvan
187–180	Bṛihadratha (overthrown by Pushyamitra, founder of the Śuṅga dynasty *c.*180)

NOTES

Chronology Maurya chronology hinges on Aśoka. Ceylonese sources date his coronation 218 years after the Buddha's death (486 or 483 BC); an eclipse of 249, mentioned in one of his inscriptions, suggests 269/8 as his accession year. Dates, which are approximate, are those of Thapar, ch. i.

BIBLIOGRAPHY

Eggermont, P. H. L., *The Chronology of the Reign of Asoka Moriya* (Leiden, 1956). Review by A. L. Basham, *Studies in Indian History and Culture* (Calcutta, 1964), 88–98.

Thapar, R., *Aśoka and the Decline of the Mauryas* (Oxford, 1963).

THE GUPTA EMPIRE

Gupta Dynasty

275–300	Gupta (local *mahārāja* in the Ganges river valley region *c.*275)
300–320	Ghaṭotkacha (son)
320–350	Chandragupta I (son; founder of the Gupta empire)
350–376	Samudragupta (son)
376–415	Chandragupta II (son)
415–455	Kumāragupta I (son)
455–470	Skandagupta (son)
470–475	Kumāragupta II (son)
475–500	Budhagupta (nephew of Skandagupta)
500–515	Vainyagupta (brother)
515–530	Narasiṁhagupta (brother)
530–540	Kumāragupta III (son)
540–550	Vishṇugupta (son; breakup of the empire into petty kingdoms *c.*550)

NOTES

Chronology and Dating Dates are approximate, and one or two relationships are tentative; rulers doubtfully attested are not given. For Skandagupta, cf. A. L. Basham, *Studies in Indian History and Culture* (Calcutta, 1964), 141–5.

The base year of the Gupta era ran from March 319 to February 320; the accession or coronation of Chandragupta I probably took place at the start of the following (first) year. P. C. Sengupta, 'The Gupta Era', *Journal of the Royal Asiatic Society of Bengal, Letters*, VIII (1942), 41–56.

Names and Titles The first two rulers were styled 'great king' (*mahārāja*); the later imperial title was 'great king of kings' (*mahārājādhirāja*).

BIBLIOGRAPHY

Goyal, S. R., *History of the Imperial Guptas* (Allahabad, 1967).
Gupta, P. L., *The Imperial Guptas* (Benares, 1974).

THE DELHI SULTANATE

Muʿizzī Dynasty

1206–1210	Aybak (lieutenant of Muʿizz al-Dīn Muḥammad of Ghūr; captured Delhi 1193; *de facto* sultan 1206)
1210–1211	Ārām Shāh
1211–1236	Iltutmish (Iletmish) (son-in-law of Aybak)
1236	Fīrūz I (son)
1236–1240	Raḍiyya (sister; deposed, died 1240)
1240–1242	Bahrām (brother; deposed, died 1242)
1242–1246	Masʿūd (son of Fīrūz I)
1246–1266	Maḥmūd I (son of Iltutmish)
1266–1287	Balban
1287–1290	Kayqubādh (grandson)
1290	Kayūmarth (son; deposed)

Khaljī Dynasty

1290–1296	Fīrūz II
1296	Ibrāhīm I (son; deposed)
1296–1316	Muḥammad I (nephew of Fīrūz II)
1316	ʿUmar (son; deposed)
1316–1320	Mubārak I (brother)
1320	Khusrau

Tughluqid Dynasty

1320–1325	Tughluq I
1325–1351	Muḥammad II (son)
1351–1388	Fīrūz III (nephew of Tughluq I)
1387–1388	Muḥammad III (son; co-regent; deposed)
1388–1389	Tughluq II (nephew)
1389–1390	Abū Bakr (grandson of Fīrūz III; deposed)
1390–1394	Muḥammad III (restored)
1394	Sikandar I (son)
1394–1413	Maḥmūd II (brother)
1413–1414	Daulat Khan Lōdī (deposed)

Sayyid Dynasty

1414–1421	Khiḍr Khan
1421–1434	Mubārak II (son)
1434–1445	Muḥammad IV (nephew)
1445/6–1451	ʿĀlam Shāh (son; deposed, died 1478)

Lōdī Dynasty

1451–1489	Bahlūl Lōdī
1489–1517	Sikandar II (son)
1517–1526	Ibrāhīm II (son; Mogul conquest of the Delhi sultanate 1526)

NOTES

Names and Titles Iltutmish, not Iletmish: S. Digby, *Iran*, VIII (1970), 57–64.

BIBLIOGRAPHY

ʿAzīz Aḥmad, M., *Political History and Institutions of the Early Turkish Empire of Delhi (AD 1206–1290)* (New Delhi, 1972).
Habib, M., and K. A. Nizami, eds., *The Delhi Sultanate (AD 1206–1526)* (New Delhi, 1970) (*Comprehensive History of India*, V).

THE BAHMANĪ KINGDOM OF THE DECCAN

Bahmanī Dynasty

1347–1359	Ḥasan Bahman Shāh (rebelled against the rule of Delhi; proclaimed sultan 1347)
1359–1375	Muḥammad I (son)
1375–1378	Mujāhid (son)
1378	Dāwūd I (grandson of Bahman Shāh)
1378–1397	Muḥammad II (brother)
1397	Tahamtan (son; deposed)
1397	Dāwūd II (brother; deposed, died 1413)
1397–1422	Fīrūz (grandson of Bahman Shāh; abdicated, died 1422)
1422–1436	Aḥmad I (brother)
1436–1458	Aḥmad II (son)
1458–1461	Humāyūn (son)
1461–1463	Aḥmad III (son)
1463–1482	Muḥammad III (brother)
1482–1518	Maḥmūd (son)
1518–1520	Aḥmad IV (son)
1520–1523	ʿAlāʾ al-Dīn (son; deposed)
1523–1526	Walī Allāh (son of Maḥmūd)
1526–1538	Kalīm Allāh (brother; breakup of the sultanate into petty kingdoms 1538)

BIBLIOGRAPHY

Husaini, S. A. Q., *Bahman Shāh* (Calcutta, 1960).
Sherwani, H. K., *The Bahmanis of the Deccan* (2nd edn., New Delhi, 1985).

THE MOGUL EMPIRE

Mogul Dynasty

1526–1530	Bābur (Tīmūrid ruler of Transoxiana 1497–8 and 1500–1; captured Delhi 1526)
1530–1540	Humāyūn (son; deposed)

Sūrī Dynasty

1540–1545	Shīr Shāh Sūr
1545–1553	Islām Shāh (son)
1553–1555	Muḥammad ʿĀdil (nephew of Shīr Shāh; deposed, died 1557)
1555	Ibrāhīm III (first cousin of Shīr Shāh; deposed, died 1568)
1555	Sikandar III (first cousin; deposed, died 1559)

Mogul Dynasty

1555–1556	Humāyūn (restored)
1556–1605	Akbar I, the Great (son)
1605–1627	Jahāngīr (son)
1628–1658	Shāh Jahān I (son; deposed, died 1666)
1658–1707	Aurangzīb ʿĀlamgīr I (son)
1707–1712	Bahādur Shāh I (Shāh ʿĀlam I) (son)
1712–1713	Jahāndār Shāh (son; deposed, died 1713)
1713–1719	Farrukhsiyar (nephew; deposed, died 1719)
1719	Rafīʿ al-Darajāt (grandson of Bahādur Shāh I; deposed, died 1719)
1719	Shāh Jahān II (Rafīʿ al-Daula) (brother)
1719–1748	Muḥammad Shāh (grandson of Bahādur Shāh I)
1748–1754	Aḥmad Shāh (son; deposed, died 1774)
1754–1759	ʿĀlamgīr II (son of Jahāndār Shāh)
1759–1806	Shāh ʿĀlam II (son)
1806–1837	Akbar II (son)
1837–1858	Bahādur Shāh II (son; deposed, died 1862; direct British rule of India)

NOTES

Chronology For a more detailed chronology of Mogul reigns, including all pretenders and rival claimants, see Hodivala, ch. xxi.

Names and Titles The imperial title, which followed name and honorifics, was *Pādishāh-i-Ghāzī*; the final element signified victor in a holy war. See Hodivala, ch. xxii.

BIBLIOGRAPHY

Hodivala, S. H., *Historical Studies in Mughal Numismatics* (Calcutta, 1923).

Majumdar, R. C., ed., *The Mughul Empire* (Bombay, 1974) (*History and Culture of the Indian People*, VII).

VIII

The Far East

CHINA

Ch'in Dynasty

221–210	Shih Huang Ti (Chao Chêng) (king of the feudal state of Ch'in 247 BC; assumed the title of First Emperor 221)
210–207	Êrh Shih Huang Ti (son)
207	Ch'in Wang (nephew; deposed, died 206)

Western Han Dynasty

207–195	Kao Ti (Liu Chi) (king only 207–202)
195–188	Hui Ti (son)
188–180	Lü Hou (mother; regent)
180–157	Wên Ti (son of Kao Ti)
157–141	Ching Ti (son)
141–87	Wu Ti (son)
87–74	Chao Ti (son)
74–48	Hsüan Ti (great-grandson of Wu Ti)
48–33	Yüan Ti (son)
33–7	Ch'êng Ti (son)
7–1	Ai Ti (nephew)
1 BC–AD 6	P'ing Ti (grandson of Yüan Ti)
6–9	Ju-tzŭ Ying (fourth in descent from Hsüan Ti; deposed, died 25)

Hsin Dynasty

9–23	Chia Huang Ti (Wang Mang) (regent and acting emperor 6–9)
23–25	Huai-yang Wang (Liu Hsüan) (deposed, died 26)

Eastern Han Dynasty

25–57	Kuang Wu Ti (Liu Hsiu) (sixth in descent from Ching Ti of Western Han)
57–75	Ming Ti (son)
75–88	Chang Ti (son)
88–106	Ho Ti (son)
106	Shang Ti (son)
106–125	An Ti (grandson of Chang Ti)
125–144	Shun Ti (son)
144–145	Ch'ung Ti (son)
145–146	Chih Ti (fourth in descent from Chang Ti)
146–168	Huan Ti (great-grandson of Chang Ti)
168–189	Ling Ti (fourth in descent from Chang Ti)
189	Shao Ti (son; deposed, died 190)
189–220	Hsien Ti (brother; deposed, died 234)

THE THREE KINGDOMS

Wei Dynasty

220–226	Wên Ti (Ts'ao P'ei)
226–239	Ming Ti (son)
239–254	Fei Ti (adopted son; deposed, died 274)

254–260	Shao Ti (grandson of Wên Ti)
260–266	Yüan Ti (nephew of Wên Ti; deposed, died 302)

Minor Han Dynasty

221–223	Chao Lieh Ti (Liu Pei)
223–263	Hou Chu (son; deposed, died 271; conquest by Wu)

Wu Dynasty

222–252	Ta Ti (Sun Ch'üan) (king only 222–9)
252–258	Fei Ti (son; deposed, died 260)
258–264	Ching Ti (brother)
264–280	Mo Ti (nephew; deposed, died 281; conquest by Western Chin)

Western Chin Dynasty

266–290	Wu Ti (Ssŭ-ma Yen) (grandson of Ssŭ-ma I)
290–307	Hui Ti (son)
307–311	Huai Ti (brother; deposed, died 313; interregnum 311–13)
313–316	Min Ti (nephew; deposed, died 318; conquest by the Hsiung-nu)

THE SOUTHERN DYNASTIES

Eastern Chin Dynasty

317–323	Yüan Ti (Ssŭ-ma Jui) (great-grandson of Ssŭ-ma I; king only 317–18)
323–325	Ming Ti (son)
325–342	Ch'êng Ti (son)
342–344	K'ang Ti (brother)
344–361	Mu Ti (son)
361–365	Ai Ti (son of Ch'êng Ti)
365–372	Hai-hsi Kung (brother; deposed, died 386)
372	Chien Wên Ti (son of Yüan Ti)
372–396	Hsiao Wu Ti (son)
396–419	An Ti (son)
419–420	Kung Ti (brother; deposed, died 421)

Liu Sung Dynasty

420–422	Wu Ti (Liu Yü)
422–424	Shao Ti (son)
424–453	Wên Ti (brother)
453–464	Hsiao Wu Ti (son)
464–466	Ch'ien Fei Ti (son)
466–472	Ming Ti (son of Wên Ti)
472–477	Hou Fei Ti (son)
477–479	Shun Ti (brother; deposed, died 479)

Southern Ch'i Dynasty

479–482	Kao Ti (Hsiao Tao-ch'êng)
482–493	Wu Ti (son)
493–494	Yü-lin Wang (grandson)
494	Hai-ling Wang (brother; deposed, died 494)
494–498	Ming Ti (nephew of Kao Ti)

498–501 Tung-hun Hou (son; deposed, died 501)
501–502 Ho Ti (brother; deposed, died 502)

Liang Dynasty

502–549 Wu Ti (Hsiao Yen)
549–551 Chien Wên Ti (son; deposed, died 551)
551 Yü-chang Wang (great-grandson of Wu Ti; deposed, died 552)
552–555 Yüan Ti (son of Wu Ti)
555–557 Ching Ti (son; deposed, died 558)

Ch'ên Dynasty

557–559 Wu Ti (Ch'ên Pa-hsien)
559–566 Wên Ti (nephew)
566–568 Lin-hai Wang (son; deposed, died 570)
569–582 Hsüan Ti (brother of Wên Ti)
582–589 Hou Chu (son; deposed, died 604; conquest by Sui)

THE NORTHERN DYNASTIES

Northern Wei Dynasty (Hsien-pei)

386–409 Tao Wu Ti (T'o-pa Kuei) (king only 386–96)
409–423 Ming Yüan Ti (son)
423–452 T'ai Wu Ti (son)
452 Nan-an Wang (son)
452–465 Wên Ch'êng Ti (nephew)
465–471 Hsien Wên Ti (son; abdicated, died 476)
471–499 Hsiao Wên Ti (son)
499–515 Hsüan Wu Ti (son)
515–528 Hsiao Ming Ti (son)
528 Lin-t'ao Wang (great-grandson of Hsiao Wên Ti)
528–530 Hsiao Chuang Ti (grandson of Hsien Wên Ti; deposed, died 531)
530–531 Tung-hai Wang (fourth in descent from T'ai Wu Ti; deposed, died 532)
531–532 Chieh Min Ti (grandson of Hsien Wên Ti)
531–532 An-ting Wang (fifth in descent from T'ai Wu Ti; rival claimant; deposed, died 532)
532–535 Hsiao Wu Ti (grandson of Hsiao Wên Ti)

Eastern Wei Dynasty (Hsien-pei)

534–550 Hsiao Ching Ti (T'o-pa Shan-chien) (great-grandson of Hsiao Wên Ti of Northern Wei; deposed, died 552)

Northern Ch'i Dynasty

550–559 Wên Hsüan Ti (Kao Yang)
559–560 Fei Ti (son; deposed, died 561)
560–561 Hsiao Chao Ti (brother of Wên Hsüan Ti)
561–565 Wu Ch'êng Ti (brother; abdicated, died 569)
565–577 Hou Chu (son; abdicated, died 577)
577 Yu Chu (son; conquest by Northern Chou, 577)

Western Wei Dynasty (Hsien-pei)

535–551	Wên Ti (T'o-pa Pao-chü) (grandson of Hsiao Wên Ti of Northern Wei)
551–554	Fei Ti (son)
554–557	Kung Ti (brother)

Northern Chou Dynasty (Hsien-pei)

557	Hsiao Min Ti (Yü-wên Chüeh)
557–560	Ming Ti (brother)
560–578	Wu Ti (brother)
578–579	Hsüan Ti (son; abdicated, died 580)
579–581	Ching Ti (son; deposed, died 581)

Sui Dynasty

581–604	Wên Ti (Yang Chien)
604–617	Yang Ti (son; deposed, died 618)
617–618	Kung Ti (grandson; deposed, died 619)

T'ang Dynasty

618–626	Kao Tsu (Li Yüan) (abdicated, died 635)
626–649	T'ai Tsung (son)
649–683	Kao Tsung (son)
684	Chung Tsung (son; deposed)
684–690	Jui Tsung (brother; deposed)
690–705	Wu Hou (mother; Chou Dynasty; deposed, died 705)
705–710	Chung Tsung (restored)
710–712	Jui Tsung (restored; abdicated; regent 712–13; died 716)
712–756	Hsüan Tsung (son; deposed, died 762)
756–762	Su Tsung (son)
762–779	Tai Tsung (son)
779–805	Tê Tsung (son)
805	Shun Tsung (son; abdicated, died 806)
805–820	Hsien Tsung (son)
820–824	Mu Tsung (son)
824–827	Ching Tsung (son)
827–840	Wên Tsung (brother)
840–846	Wu Tsung (brother)
846–859	Hsiuan Tsung (son of Hsien Tsung)
859–873	I Tsung (son)
873–888	Hsi Tsung (son)
888–904	Chao Tsung (brother)
904–907	Ai Ti (son; deposed, died 908)

THE FIVE DYNASTIES

Later Liang Dynasty

907–912	T'ai Tsu (Chu Wên)
912–913	Ying Wang (son)
913–923	Mo Ti (brother)

Later T'ang Dynasty (Turkish)

923–926	Chuang Tsung (Li Ts'un-hsü)
926–933	Ming Tsung (adopted brother)
933–934	Min Ti (son)
934–937	Fei Ti (adopted brother)

Later Chin Dynasty (Turkish)

937–942	Kao Tsu (Shih Ching-t'ang)
942–947	Ch'u Ti (nephew; deposed, died 964)

Later Han Dynasty (Turkish)

947–948	Kao Tsu (Liu Chih-yüan)
948–951	Yin Ti (son)

Later Chou Dynasty

951–954	T'ai Tsu (Kuo Wei)
954–959	Shih Tsung (adopted son)
959–960	Kung Ti (son; deposed, died 973)

THE BORDER EMPIRES

Liao Dynasty (Khitan)

907–926	T'ai Tsu (Yeh-lü A-pao-chi)
927–947	T'ai Tsung (son)
947–951	Shih Tsung (nephew)
951–969	Mu Tsung (son of T'ai Tsung)
969–982	Ching Tsung (son of Shih Tsung)
982–1031	Shêng Tsung (son)
1031–1055	Hsing Tsung (son)
1055–1101	Tao Tsung (son)
1101–1125	T'ien-tso Ti (grandson; deposed, died 1128; conquest by Chin)

Chin Dynasty (Jurchen)

1115–1123	T'ai Tsu (Wan-yen A-ku-ta)
1123–1135	T'ai Tsung (brother)
1135–1150	Hsi Tsung (nephew)
1150–1161	Hai-ling Wang (grandson of T'ai Tsu)
1161–1189	Shih Tsung (grandson of T'ai Tsu)
1189–1208	Chang Tsung (grandson)
1208–1213	Wei-shao Wang (son of Shih Tsung)
1213–1224	Hsüan Tsung (brother of Chang Tsung)
1224–1234	Ai Tsung (son; abdicated, died 1234)
1234	Mo Ti (conquest by Yüan 1234)

Northern Sung Dynasty

960–976	T'ai Tsu (Chao K'uang-yin)
976–997	T'ai Tsung (brother)
997–1022	Chên Tsung (son)
1022–1063	Jên Tsung (son)
1063–1067	Ying Tsung (great-grandson of T'ai Tsung)
1067–1085	Shên Tsung (son)

1085–1100	Chê Tsung (son)
1100–1126	Hui Tsung (brother; abdicated, died 1135)
1126–1127	Ch'in Tsung (son; deposed, died 1161)

Southern Sung Dynasty

1127–1162	Kao Tsung (brother; abdicated, died 1187)
1162–1189	Hsiao Tsung (seventh in descent from T'ai Tsu; abdicated, died 1194)
1189–1194	Kuang Tsung (son; abdicated, died 1200)
1194–1224	Ning Tsung (son)
1224–1264	Li Tsung (tenth in descent from T'ai Tsu)
1264–1274	Tu Tsung (nephew)
1274–1276	Kung Ti (son; deposed, died 1323)
1276–1278	Tuan Tsung (brother)
1278–1279	Ti Ping (brother; conquest by Yüan 1279)

Yüan Dynasty (Mongol)

1206–1227	T'ai Tsu (Chingiz) (interregnum 1227–9)
1229–1241	T'ai Tsung (Ögödei) (son; interregnum 1241–6)
1246–1248	Ting Tsung (Güyük) (son; interregnum 1248–51)
1251–1259	Hsien Tsung (Möngke) (grandson of T'ai Tsu)
1260–1294	Shih Tsu (Qubilai) (brother)
1294–1307	Ch'êng Tsung (Temür) (grandson)
1307–1311	Wu Tsung (Qaishan) (nephew)
1311–1320	Jên Tsung (Ayurbarwada) (brother)
1320–1323	Ying Tsung (Shidebala) (son)
1323–1328	T'ai-ting Ti (Yesün Temür) (nephew of Ch'êng Tsung)
1328–1329	Wên Tsung (Tugh Temür) (son of Wu Tsung; abdicated)
1329	Ming Tsung (Qoshila) (brother)
1329–1332	Wên Tsung (Tugh Temür) (again)
1332	Ning Tsung (Irinjibal) (son of Ming Tsung)
1333–1368	Shun Ti (Toghon Temür) (brother; deposed, died 1370)

Ming Dynasty

1368–1398	Hung Wu (T'ai Tsu) (Chu Yüan-chang)
1398–1402	Chien Wên (Hui Ti) (grandson)
1402–1424	Yung Lo (Ch'êng Tsu) (son of T'ai Tsu)
1424–1425	Hung Hsi (Jên Tsung) (son)
1425–1435	Hsüan Tê (Hsüan Tsung) (son)
1435–1449	Chêng T'ung (Ying Tsung) (son; deposed)
1449–1457	Ching T'ai (Ching Ti) (brother; deposed, died 1457)
1457–1464	T'ien Shun (Ying Tsung) (restored)
1464–1487	Ch'êng Hua (Hsien Tsung) (son)
1487–1505	Hung Chih (Hsiao Tsung) (son)
1505–1521	Chêng Tê (Wu Tsung) (son)
1521–1567	Chia Ching (Shih Tsung) (grandson of Hsien Tsung)
1567–1572	Lung Ch'ing (Mu Tsung) (son)
1572–1620	Wan Li (Shên Tsung) (son)
1620	T'ai Ch'ang (Kuang Tsung) (son)
1620–1627	T'ien Ch'i (Hsi Tsung) (son)
1627–1644	Ch'ung Chên (Chuang-lieh Ti) (brother)

Ch'ing Dynasty (Manchu)

1644–1661	Shun Chih (Shih Tsu) (Aisin-gioro Fu-lin)
1661–1722	K'ang Hsi (Shêng Tsu) (son)
1722–1735	Yung Chêng (Shih Tsung) (son)
1735–1796	Ch'ien Lung (Kao Tsung) (son; abdicated, died 1799)
1796–1820	Chia Ch'ing (Jên Tsung) (son)
1820–1850	Tao Kuang (Hsüan Tsung) (son)
1850–1861	Hsien Fêng (Wên Tsung) (son)
1861–1875	T'ung Chih (Mu Tsung) (son)
1875–1908	Kuang Hsü (Tê Tsung) (grandson of Hsüan Tsung)
1908–1912	Hsüan T'ung (nephew; deposed, died 1967; republic of China)

(Regency of the dowager empress T'zŭ Hsi, mother of Mu Tsung, 1861–73, 1875–89, and 1898–1908)

NOTES

Chronology In almost all cases, dynasties are dated according to their own claims as presented in their official annals (Kennedy, 285). Overlapping dates show rival claims; minor dynasties, and those which did not rule all China, are indented. Reigns begin with accession or enthronement. Chinese dates for Western Liao (here omitted) are unreliable; see Pelliot, I, 221–4.

Names and Titles The imperial title of *huang ti* (august lord) was assumed by the king of Ch'in following his unification of China. Beginning with the Western Han, emperors were known either by a posthumous memorial title (*shih*), compounded with *chu* (lord), *hou* (marquis), *kung* (duke), *wang* (king), *ti* or *huang ti*, or by a posthumous temple title (*miao hao*), formed with *tsu* (progenitor) or *tsung* (ancestor). The temple title placed the monarch in his ancestral line (Dubs, 31); the designation *tsu* was normally reserved for the founder of a dynasty or of a new line within one, such as the third Ming emperor (Goodrich, I, 317). The last member of a dynasty did not receive temple commemoration, nor did rulers such as Kung Ti of Southern Sung, who died in captivity (Franke, XVI: 3, art. 'Ti Hsien').

In addition, from the Western Han, reigns were designated by a succession of year titles (*nien hao*). These comprised one or more whole calendar years; the first of each reign began on the new year's day following accession (Kennedy, 285). The Ming and Ch'ing emperors are denoted by year title, as each reign had only one.

In the list above, the personal name of a dynasty's founder is given after his title(s); ethnic origin, if non-Chinese, follows the dynasty's name. Mongol personal names of the Yüan emperors follow J. W. Dardess, *Conquerors and Confucians* (New York, 1973).

BIBLIOGRAPHY

Boodberg, P. A., 'Marginalia to the Histories of the Northern Dynasties', *Harvard Journal of Asiatic Studies*, III (1938), 223–53; IV (1939), 230–83.

Dubs, H. H., 'Chinese Imperial Designations', *Journal of the American Oriental Society*, LXV (1945), 26–33.

Franke, H., ed., *Sung Biographies* (4 vols., Wiesbaden, 1976) (*Münchener ostasiatische Studien*, ed. W. Bauer and H. Franke, XVI: 1–3, XVII).

Goodrich, L. C., and C. Fang, eds., *Dictionary of Ming Biography, 1368–1644* (2 vols., New York, 1976).

Kennedy, G. A., 'Dating of Chinese Dynasties and Reigns', *Journal of the American Oriental Society*, LXI (1941), 285–6.

Moule, A. C., and W. P. Yetts, *The Rulers of China, 221 BC–AD 1949* (London, 1957).

Pelliot, P., *Notes on Marco Polo* (3 vols., Paris, 1959–73).

Wittfogel, K. A., and Fêng Chia-shêng, *History of Chinese Society: Liao (907–1125)* (Philadelphia, 1949).

JAPAN

The Yamato Period: c.40 BC–AD 710:

40–10 BC	Jimmu (traditional, semi-legendary founder of Japanese ruling dynasty)
10–AD 20	Suizei (son)
20–50	Annei (son)
50–80	Itoku (son)
80–110	Kōshō (son)
110–140	Kōan (son)
140–170	Kōrei (son)
170–200	Kōgen (son)
200–230	Kaika (son)
230–258	Sujin (son)
258–290	Suinin (son)
290–322	Keikō (son)
322–355	Seimu (son)
355–362	Chūai (nephew)
362–394	Ōjin (son)
394–427	Nintoku (son)
427–432	Richū (son)
432–437	Hanzei (brother)
437–454	Ingyō (brother)
454–457	Ankō (son)
457–489	Yūryaku (brother)
489–494	Seinei (son)
494–497	Kenzō (grandson of Richū)
497–504	Ninken (brother)
504–510	Buretsu (son)
510–527	Keitai (fifth in descent from Ōjin)
527–535	Ankan (son)
535–539	Senka (brother)
539–571	Kimmei (brother)
572–585	Bidatsu (son)
585–587	Yōmei (brother)
587–592	Sushun (brother)
593–628	Suiko (sister)
629–641	Jomei (grandson of Bidatsu)
642–645	Kōgyoku (niece; abdicated)
645–654	Kōtoku (brother)
655–661	Saimei (ex-empress Kōgyoku, again)
661–672	Tenji (son of Jomei)
672	Kōbun (son)
672–686	Temmu (son of Jomei)
686–697	Jitō (daughter of Tenji; abdicated, died 703)
697–707	Mommu (grandson of Temmu)

The Nara Period: 710–784

707–715	Gemmei (daughter of Tenji; abdicated, died 721)
715–724	Genshō (sister of Mommu; abdicated, died 748)
724–749	Shōmu (son of Mommu; abdicated, died 756)

749–758	Kōken (daughter; abdicated)
758–764	Junnin (grandson of Temmu; deposed, died 765)
764–770	Shōtoku (ex-empress Kōken, again)
770–781	Kōnin (grandson of Tenji; abdicated, died 782)

The Heian Period: 794–1185

781–806	Kammu (son)
806–809	Heizei (son; abdicated, died 824)
809–823	Saga (brother; abdicated, died 842)
823–833	Junna (brother; abdicated, died 840)
833–850	Nimmyō (son of Saga)
850–858	Montoku (son)
858–876	Seiwa (son; abdicated, died 881)
876–884	Yōzei (son; deposed, died 949)
884–887	Kōkō (son of Nimmyō)
887–897	Uda (son; abdicated, died 931)
897–930	Daigo (son; abdicated, died 930)
930–946	Suzaku (son; abdicated, died 952)
946–967	Murakami (brother)
967–969	Reizei (son; abdicated, died 1011)
969–984	En'yū (brother; abdicated, died 991)
984–986	Kazan (son of Reizei; abdicated, died 1008)
986–1011	Ichijō (son of En'yū; abdicated, died 1011)
1011–1016	Sanjō (son of Reizei; abdicated, died 1017)
1016–1036	Go-Ichijō (son of Ichijō)
1036–1045	Go-Suzaku (brother; abdicated, died 1045)
1045–1068	Go-Reizei (son)
1068–1073	Go-Sanjō (brother; abdicated, died 1073)
1073–1087	Shirakawa (son; abdicated, died 1129)
1087–1107	Horikawa (son)
1107–1123	Toba (son; abdicated, died 1156)
1123–1142	Sutoku (son; abdicated, died 1164)
1142–1155	Konoe (brother)
1155–1158	Go-Shirakawa (brother; abdicated, died 1192)
1158–1165	Nijō (son; abdicated, died 1165)
1165–1168	Rokujō (son; abdicated, died 1176)
1168–1180	Takakura (son of Go-Shirakawa; abdicated, died 1181)
1180–1185	Antoku (son)

The Kamakura Period: 1185–1333

1183–1198	Go-Toba (brother; abdicated, died 1239)
1198–1210	Tsuchimikado (son; abdicated, died 1231)
1210–1221	Juntoku (brother; abdicated, died 1242)
1221	Chūkyō (son; deposed, died 1234)
1221–1232	Go-Horikawa (grandson of Takakura; abdicated, died 1234)
1232–1242	Shijō (son)
1242–1246	Go-Saga (son of Tsuchimikado; abdicated, died 1272)
1246–1260	Go-Fukakusa (son; abdicated, died 1304)
1260–1274	Kameyama (brother; abdicated, died 1305)
1274–1287	Go-Uda (son; abdicated, died 1324)
1287–1298	Fushimi (son of Go-Fukakusa; abdicated, died 1317)
1298–1301	Go-Fushimi (son; abdicated, died 1336)

1301–1308	Go-Nijō (son of Go-Uda)
1308–1318	Hanazono (son of Fushimi; abdicated, died 1348)

The Southern Court: 1336–1392

1318–1339	Go-Daigo (son of Go-Uda)
1339–1368	Go-Murakami (son)
1368–1383	Chōkei (son; abdicated, died 1394)
1383–1392	Go-Kameyama (brother; abdicated, died 1424)

The Northern Court: 1336–1392

1331–1333	Kōgon (son of Go-Fushimi; deposed, died 1364)
1336–1348	Kōmyō (brother; abdicated, died 1380)
1348–1351	Sukō (son of Kōgon; abdicated, died 1398)
1352–1371	Go-Kōgon (brother; abdicated, died 1374)
1371–1382	Go-En'yū (son; abdicated, died 1393)

The Muromachi Period: 1392–1573

1382–1412	Go-Komatsu (son; abdicated, died 1433)
1412–1428	Shōkō (son)
1428–1464	Go-Hanazono (great-grandson of Sukō; abdicated, died 1471)
1464–1500	Go-Tsuchimikado (son)
1500–1526	Go-Kashiwabara (son)
1526–1557	Go-Nara (son)
1557–1586	Ōgimachi (son; abdicated, died 1593)

The Tokugawa Period: 1600–1868

1586–1611	Go-Yōzei (grandson; abdicated, died 1617)
1611–1629	Go-Mizunoo (son; abdicated, died 1680)
1629–1643	Meishō (daughter; abdicated, died 1696)
1643–1654	Go-Kōmyō (brother)
1655–1663	Go-Sai (brother; abdicated, died 1685)
1663–1687	Reigen (brother; abdicated, died 1732)
1687–1709	Higashiyama (son; abdicated, died 1710)
1709–1735	Nakamikado (son; abdicated, died 1737)
1735–1747	Sakuramachi (son; abdicated, died 1750)
1747–1762	Momozono (son)
1762–1771	Go-Sakuramachi (sister; abdicated, died 1813)
1771–1779	Go-Momozono (son of Momozono)
1780–1817	Kōkaku (great-grandson of Higashiyama; abdicated, died 1840)
1817–1846	Ninkō (son)
1846–1867	Kōmei (son)
1867–1912	Meiji (son)
1912–1926	Taishō (son)
1926–1989	Shōwa (son; regent 1921–6)
1989–	Akihito (son)

The Kamakura Shogunate

1192–1195	Minamoto Yoritomo (appointed *seii-taishōgun* or generalissimo 1192; abdicated, died 1199)
1202–1203	Yoriie (son; deposed, died 1204)
1203–1219	Sanetomo (brother)

1226–1244	Kujō Yoritsune (deposed, died 1256)
1244–1252	Yoritsugu (son; deposed, died 1256)
1252–1266	Munetaka (son of emperor Go-Saga; deposed, died 1274)
1266–1289	Koreyasu (son; deposed, died 1326)
1289–1308	Hisaaki (son of emperor Go-Fukakusa; deposed, died 1328)
1308–1333	Morikuni (son; abdicated, died 1333; suspension of the shogunate)

The Hōjō Regency

1203–1205	Hōjō Tokimasa (appointed *shikken* or shogunal regent 1203; deposed, died 1215)
1205–1224	Yoshitoki (son)
1224–1242	Yasutoki (son)
1242–1246	Tsunetoki (grandson)
1246–1256	Tokiyori (brother; abdicated, died 1263)
1256–1264	Nagatoki (grandson of Yoshitoki)
1264–1268	Masamura (son of Yoshitoki; abdicated, died 1273)
1268–1284	Tokimune (son of Tokiyori)
1284–1301	Sadatoki (son; abdicated, died 1311)
1301–1311	Morotoki (grandson of Tokiyori)
1311–1312	Munenobu (fourth in descent from Tokimasa)
1312–1315	Hirotoki (great-grandson of Masamura)
1316–1326	Takatoki (son of Sadatoki; abdicated, died 1333)
1327–1333	Moritoki (great-grandson of Nagatoki; end of the Hōjō regency 1333)

The Ashikaga Shogunate

1338–1358	Ashikaga Takauji (appointed *seii-taishōgun* or generalissimo 1338)
1359–1367	Yoshiakira (son)
1369–1395	Yoshimitsu (son; abdicated, died 1408)
1395–1423	Yoshimochi (son; abdicated, died 1428)
1423–1425	Yoshikazu (son)
1429–1441	Yoshinori (son of Yoshimitsu)
1442–1443	Yoshikatsu (son)
1449–1474	Yoshimasa (brother; abdicated, died 1490)
1474–1489	Yoshihisa (son)
1490–1493	Yoshitane (nephew of Yoshimasa; deposed)
1495–1508	Yoshizumi (nephew of Yoshimasa; deposed, died 1511)
1508–1522	Yoshitane (restored; deposed, died 1523)
1522–1547	Yoshiharu (son of Yoshizumi; abdicated, died 1550)
1547–1565	Yoshiteru (son)
1568	Yoshihide (nephew of Yoshiharu)
1568–1573	Yoshiaki (son of Yoshiharu; deposed, died 1597; suspension of the shogunate)

The Tokugawa Shogunate

1603–1605	Tokugawa Ieyasu (appointed *seii-taishōgun* 1603; abdicated, died 1616)
1605–1623	Hidetada (son; abdicated, died 1632)
1623–1651	Iemitsu (son)
1651–1680	Ietsuna (son)

1680–1709	Tsunayoshi (brother)
1709–1712	Ienobu (nephew)
1713–1716	Ietsugu (son)
1716–1745	Yoshimune (great-grandson of Ieyasu; abdicated, died 1751)
1745–1760	Ieshige (son; abdicated, died 1761)
1760–1786	Ieharu (son)
1787–1837	Ienari (great-grandson of Yoshimune; abdicated, died 1841)
1837–1853	Ieyoshi (son)
1853–1858	Iesada (son)
1858–1866	Iemochi (grandson of Ienari)
1867–1868	Yoshinobu (Keiki) (tenth in descent from Ieyasu; abdicated, died 1913; end of the shogunate)

NOTES

Chronology Early dates and traditional relationships are those of Reischauer. Kiley, following recent Japanese scholarship, makes Richū the first fully historical Yamato ruler, Keitai the founder of the present imperial line. Dates from *c.*427 to 539 are approximate.

Calendar and Dating Since 701, dates have been expressed in terms of a succession of eras (*nengō*), each comprising one or more whole calendar years. From the start of the Meiji era (1868), the *nengō* is coeval with the reign; see H. Webb, *Research in Japanese Sources: a Guide* (New York, 1965), ch. ii. For a list of *nengō* and the corresponding Julian dates, see P. Y. Tsuchihashi, *Japanese Chronological Tables from 601 to 1872 AD* (Tokyo, 1952). The Gregorian calendar replaced a lunar calendar of Chinese origin on 1 January 1873.

Names and Titles From the early seventh century, the title *tennō* (sovereign, rendered in English as emperor or empress) was in use. An abdicated ruler had the title *dajō-tennō* (retired sovereign) or, if in Buddhist orders, that of *dajō-hōō* (priestly retired sovereign).

In the eighth century, Japan adopted the Chinese practice of giving the rulers posthumous names (*okurina*); those from Jimmu to Jitō were bestowed retroactively. Beginning with the Meiji era (1868), the era name (*nengō*) becomes the emperor's posthumous name. See Reischauer.

BIBLIOGRAPHY

Dokushi sōran (*Handbook of Japanese History*), ed. A. Obata *et al.* (Tokyo, 1966).

Kiley, C. J., 'State and Dynasty in Archaic Yamato', *Journal of Asian Studies*, XXXIII (1973), 25–49.

Kodansha Encyclopedia of Japan (9 vols., Tokyo, 1983).

Reischauer, R. K., *Early Japanese History (c.40 BC–AD 1167)* (2 vols., Princeton, 1937).

THE KINGDOM OF KOREA

Yi Dynasty

1392–1398	T'aejo (Yi Sŏnggye) (*de facto* ruler 1388; king 1392; abdicated, died 1408)
1398–1400	Chŏngjong (son; abdicated, died 1419)
1400–1418	T'aejong (brother; abdicated, died 1422)
1418–1450	Sejong (son)
1450–1452	Munjong (son)
1452–1455	Tanjong (son; deposed, died 1457)
1455–1468	Sejo (son of Sejong)
1468–1469	Yejong (son)
1469–1494	Sŏngjong (nephew)
1494–1506	Yŏnsan-gun (son; deposed, died 1506)
1506–1544	Chungjong (brother)
1544–1545	Injong (son)
1545–1567	Myŏngjong (brother)
1567–1608	Sŏnjo (nephew)
1608–1623	Kwanghae-gun (son; deposed, died 1641)
1623–1649	Injo (nephew)
1649–1659	Hyojong (son)
1659–1674	Hyŏnjong (son)
1674–1720	Sukchong (son)
1720–1724	Kyŏngjong (son)
1724–1776	Yŏngjo (brother)
1776–1800	Chŏngjo (grandson)
1800–1834	Sunjo (son)
1834–1849	Hŏnjong (grandson)
1849–1864	Ch'ŏlchong (grandnephew of Chŏngjo)
1864–1907	Kojong (great-grandnephew of Chŏngjo; emperor 1897; Japanese protectorate 1905; deposed, died 1919)
1907–1910	Sunjong (son; deposed, died 1926; Japanese annexation of Korea)

NOTES

Names and Titles Rulers received posthumous titles in Chinese fashion, usually formed with *jo* (progenitor) or *jong* (ancestor); the founder of the Yi Dynasty was the 'grand progenitor' (Han, 170). The royal title was the Chinese *wang*.

BIBLIOGRAPHY

Han Woo-keun, *The History of Korea* (Honolulu, 1971).
Hatada, T., *A History of Korea* (Santa Barbara, Calif., 1969).

THE KINGDOM OF BURMA

Konbaung Dynasty

1752–1760	Alaungpaya (assumed the title of king, 1752; unified Burma, 1752–57)
1760–1763	Naungdawgyi (son)
1763–1776	Hsinbyushin (brother)
1776–1782	Singu (son; deposed, died 1782)
1782	Maung Maung (son of Naungdawgyi)
1782–1819	Bodawpaya (son of Alaungpaya)
1819–1837	Bagyidaw (grandson; deposed, died 1846)
1837–1846	Tharrawaddy (brother)
1846–1853	Pagan (son; deposed, died 1880)
1853–1878	Mindon (brother)
1878–1885	Thibaw (son; deposed, died 1916; union of Burma with British India, 1886)

BIBLIOGRAPHY

Encyclopedia of Asian History, ed. A. T. Embree (4 vols., New York, 1988).
Pollak, O. B., *Empires in Collision; Anglo-Burmese Relations in the Mid-Nineteenth Century* (Westport, Conn., 1979).

THE KINGDOM OF THAILAND

Chakri Dynasty

1782–1809	Rama I (Chaophraya Chakri) (minister and army commander; proclaimed king 1782)
1809–1824	Rama II (Itsarasunthon) (son)
1824–1851	Rama III (Chetsadabodin) (son)
1851–1868	Rama IV (Mongkut) (brother)
1868–1910	Rama V (Chulalongkorn) (son)
1910–1925	Rama VI (Vajiravudh) (son)
1925–1935	Rama VII (Prajadhipok) (brother; abdicated, died 1941)
1935–1946	Rama VIII (Ananda Mahidol) (nephew)
1946–	Rama IX (Bhumibol Adulyadej) (brother)

BIBLIOGRAPHY

Terwiel, B. J., *A History of Modern Thailand, 1767–1942* (St. Lucia, 1983).
Wyatt, David K., *Thailand: a Short History* (New Haven, 1984).

THE KINGDOM OF LAOS

Kingdom of Luang Prabang

1707–1713	Kingkitsarat (succeeded to Luang Prabang upon partition of Laos *c.*1707)
1713–1723	Ong Nok (cousin; deposed, died 1759)
1723–1749	Inthasom (brother of Kingkitsarat)
1749–1750	Inthaphon (son; abdicated)
1750–1771	Sotikakuman (brother; abdicated)
1771–1791	Suriyavong (brother)
1791–1816	Anuruttha (brother)
1816–1837	Mangthaturat (son)
1837–1850	Suksoem (son)
1850–1870	Chantharat (brother)
1870–1891	Un Kham (brother; deposed, died 1895)
1891–1904	Sakkarin (son; French protectorate over Laos 1893/6–1949)

Kingdom of Laos

1904–1959	Sisavangvong (son; deposed, 1945–6; king of united Laos 1946)
1959–1975	Savangvatthana (son; deposed, died 1978; People's Democratic Republic)

NOTES

Chronology Dates follow the Lao chronicles; those before 1791 are tentative. Savangvatthana died in May 1978; see the *Bangkok Post*, 13 December 1987, 8–9.

BIBLIOGRAPHY

Le Boulanger, P., *Histoire du Laos français* (Paris, 1931).
Viravong, M. S., *History of Laos* (New York, 1964).

MODERN CAMBODIA

Kingdom of Cambodia

1779–1797	Eng (king of Cambodia as a vassal of Thailand; in exile 1783–94)
1797–1835	Chan (son)
1835–1847	Mei (daughter; deposed, died 1875)
1847–1860	Duang (son of Eng)
1860–1904	Norodom (son; French protectorate over Cambodia 1863–1953)
1904–1927	Sisowath (brother)
1927–1941	Monivong (son)
1941–1955	Norodom Sihanouk (maternal grandson; abdicated)
1955–1960	Norodom Suramarit (father; grandson of Norodom)
1960–1970	Norodom Sihanouk (chief of state only; deposed; Khmer Republic 1970–5)

BIBLIOGRAPHY

Chandler, D. P., *A History of Cambodia* (Boulder, Colo., 1983).
Leclère, A., *Histoire du Cambodge* (Paris, 1914).

MODERN VIETNAM

Nguyên Dynasty

1802–1820	Gia Long (Nguyên Phúc-Anh) (king of Cochin-China, Tonkin, and Annam by 1802; emperor 1806)
1820–1841	Minh Mang (son)
1841–1847	Thiêu Tri (son)
1847–1883	Tu Dúc (son; French conquest of Cochin-China 1867)
1883	Duc Dúc (nephew; deposed, died 1883)
1883	Hiêp Hoà (son of Thiêu Tri)
1883–1884	Kiên Phúc (nephew; French protectorate over Tonkin and Annam 1883–1945)
1884–1885	Hàm Nghi (brother; deposed, died 1944)
1885–1889	Dông Khánh (brother)
1889–1907	Thành Thái (son of Duc Dúc; deposed, died 1954)
1907–1916	Duy Tân (son; deposed, died 1945)
1916–1925	Khai Dinh (son of Dông Khánh)
1926–1945	Bao Dai (son; abdicated; chief of the State of Vietnam 1949–55; deposed)

NOTES

Names and Titles Emperors are known by reign title (*niên hiêu*); that of Gia Long began in June 1802. Nguyên Phúc-Anh claimed the title of king from 1780; he assumed that of emperor (*hoàng dê*) in mid-1806. The designation Viêt-Nam was adopted in 1804. See Maybon, 349, 377.

BIBLIOGRAPHY

Bùi Quang Tung, 'Tables synoptiques de chronologie viêtnamienne', *Bulletin de l'école française d'Extrême-Orient*, LI (1963), 1–78.

Maybon, C. B., *Histoire moderne du pays d'Annam (1592–1820)* (Paris, 1919).

IX

Africa

THE ETHIOPIAN EMPIRE

Solomonic Dynasty

1270–1285	Yekuno 'Amlak (founder or, according to legend, restorer of a dynasty claiming descent from Solomon)
1285–1294	Yagbeʿa Seyon (son; period of confusion 1294–9)
1299–1314	Wedem Raʿad (brother)
1314–1344	ʿAmda Seyon I (son)
1344–1371	Newaya Krestos (son)
1371–1380	Newaya Maryam (son)
1380–1412	David I (brother)
1412–1413	Theodore I (son)
1413–1430	Isaac (brother)
1430	Andrew (son)
1430–1433	Takla Maryam (son of David I)
1433	Sarwe Iyasus (son)
1433–1434	ʿAmda Iyasus (brother)
1434–1468	Zar'a Yaʿqob (son of David I)
1468–1478	Ba'eda Maryam I (son)
1478–1494	Alexander (son)
1494	ʿAmda Seyon II (son)
1494–1508	Naʿod (son of Ba'eda Maryam I)
1508–1540	Lebna Dengel (David II) (son)
1540–1559	Claudius (son)
1559–1563	Minas (brother)
1563–1597	Sarsa Dengel (son)
1597–1603	Jacob (son; deposed)
1603–1604	Za Dengel (grandson of Minas)
1604–1607	Jacob (restored)
1607–1632	Susenyos (great-grandson of Lebna Dengel; abdicated, died 1632)
1632–1667	Fasiladas (son)
1667–1682	John I (son)
1682–1706	Iyasu I, the Great (son; deposed, died 1706)
1706–1708	Takla Haymanot I (son)
1708–1711	Theophilus (son of John I)
1711–1716	Justus (maternal grandson of 'Amlakawit, daughter of John I; deposed, died 1716)
1716–1721	David III (son of Iyasu I)
1721–1730	'Asma Giyorgis (brother)
1730–1755	Iyasu II, the Little (son)
1755–1769	Iyo'as I (son; deposed, died 1769)
1769	John II (son of Iyasu I)
1769–1777	Takla Haymanot II (son; deposed, died 1777; period of confusion and divided rule 1777–1855)

Modern Ethiopia

1855–1868	Theodore II (Kassa, governor of Kwara; king only 1854–5)
1868–1871	Takla Giyorgis II (Gobaze) (deposed, died 1872)
1872–1889	John IV (Kassa)
1889–1913	Menelik II (son of Haile Malakot, king of Shoa)

1913–1916	Lij Iyasu (Iyasu V) (maternal grandson; deposed, died 1935)
1916–1930	Zawditu (daughter of Menelik II)
1930–1974	Haile Selassie I (sister's grandson of Haile Malakot; regent 1916–30; king 1928; deposed, died 1975)
1974–1975	Asfa Wossen (son; king only; deposed; Provisional Military Government)

NOTES

Chronology and Calendar Dates down to the mid-fifteenth century may vary by a year or so; for David I and his sons, see Tamrat, 279–80.

The Ethiopian civil year was Julian, beginning 29 August; eras ran from the creation of the world, the birth of Christ, and AD 284, the accession year of Diocletian (era of the Martyrs). D. Buxton, *The Abyssinians* (London, 1970), 182–8.

Names and Titles The royal title was the Amharic *negus*; the imperial title was 'king of kings' (*negusa nagast*).

BIBLIOGRAPHY

Budge, E. A. W., *A History of Ethiopia, Nubia and Abyssinia* (2 vols., London, 1928).

Chaine, M., *La chronologie des temps chrétiens de l'Egypte et de l'Ethiopie* (Paris, 1925).

Tamrat, T., *Church and State in Ethiopia, 1270–1527* (Oxford, 1972).

THE KINGDOM OF MADAGASCAR

Merina (Andriana) Dynasty

1710–1735	Andriantsimitoviaminandriana (king of Ambohimanga in central Madagascar *c.*1710)
1735–1760	Andriambelomasina (distant cousin)
1760–1783	Andrianjafy (son)
1783–1809	Andrianampoinimerina (sister's son)
1809–1828	Radama I (son)
1828–1861	Ranavalona I (widow; grandniece of Andrianjafy)
1861–1863	Radama II (son)
1863–1868	Rasoherina (widow; sister's daughter of Ranavalona I)
1868–1883	Ranavalona II (sister's daughter of Ranavalona I)
1883–1896	Ranavalona III (distant cousin; French protectorate 1895; deposed, died 1917; union with the French empire)

NOTES

Chronology Dates before Andrianampoinimerina are speculative; those above follow Delivré, ch. v. The dynasty did not rule all Madagascar until Radama I.

BIBLIOGRAPHY

Brown, M., *Madagascar Rediscovered: a History from Early Times to Independence* (Hamden, Conn., 1979).

Delivré, A., *L'histoire des rois d'Imerina: interprétation d'une tradition orale* (Paris, 1974).

THE ZULU KINGDOM

1781–1816	Senzangakona (chief of the Zulus in the area of modern Natal *c.*1781)
1816	Sigujana (son)
1816–1828	Shaka (brother)
1828–1840	Dingane (brother)
1840–1872	Mpande (brother)
1872–1884	Cetshwayo (son; in exile 1879–83)
1884–1887	Dinuzulu (son; deposed, died 1913; British annexation of Zululand)

NOTES

Chronology Dates down to 1816 are approximate.

BIBLIOGRAPHY

Binns, C. T., *The Last Zulu King: the Life and Death of Cetshwayo* (London, 1963).

Roberts, B., *The Zulu Kings* (New York, 1974).

THE KINGDOM OF SWAZILAND

Nkosi-Dlamini Dynasty

1815–1839	Sobhuza I (king of the Ngwane in southern Swaziland *c.*1815; unified the chiefdoms to the north)
1839–1865	Mswati II (son)
1865–1874	Ludvonga (son)
1874–1889	Mbandzeni (brother)
1889–1899	Bunu (son; South African protectorate over Swaziland 1894–9)
1921–1982	Sobhuza II (son; regency 1899–1921; British protectorate 1903–68)
1986–	Mswati III (son; regency 1982–6)

NOTES

Chronology For discussion of dates down to 1874, see Bonner.

BIBLIOGRAPHY

Bonner, P., *Kings, Commoners and Concessionaires: the Evolution and Dissolution of the Nineteenth-Century Swazi State* (Cambridge, 1983).
Matsebula, J. S. M., *A History of Swaziland* (Cape Town, 1972).

THE KINGDOM OF LESOTHO

Koena Dynasty

1828–1870	Moshweshwe I (paramount chief of Basutoland *c.*1828; abdicated, died 1870; British protectorate 1868–1966)
1870–1891	Letsie I (son)
1891–1905	Lerotholi (son)
1905–1913	Letsie II (son)
1913–1939	Griffith (brother)
1939–1940	Seeiso (son)
1960–	Moshweshwe II (son; regency 1940–60; kingdom of Lesotho 1966)

BIBLIOGRAPHY

Haliburton, G., *Historical Dictionary of Lesotho* (Metuchen, NJ, 1977).
Sanders, P., *Moshoeshoe, Chief of the Sotho* (London, 1975).

X

The New World

THE INCA EMPIRE

The Kingdom of Cuzco

*c.*1200?	Manco Capac (traditional founder of Cuzco and of the Inca royal house)
	Sinchi Roca (son)
	Lloque Yupanqui (son)
	Mayta Capac (son)
	Capac Yupanqui (son)
	Inca Roca (son)
	Yahuar Huacac (son)
	Viracocha Inca (son)

The Empire

1438–1471	Pachacuti (son; abdicated, died 1472)
1471–1493	Topa Inca (son)
1493–1524	Huayna Capac (son)
1524–1532	Huascar (son; deposed, died 1532)
1532	Atauhuallpa (brother; deposed, died 1533; Spanish conquest of the Inca empire)

The Vilcabamba State

1533	Topa Huallpa (brother)
1533–1545	Manco Inca (brother)
1545–1560	Sayri Tupac (son)
1560–1571	Titu Cusi Yupanqui (brother)
1571–1572	Tupac Amaru (brother; deposed, died 1572; Spanish conquest of the Vilcabamba state)

NOTES

Chronology In Zuidema's view, the Inca rulers preceding Pachacuti are fictitious, contemporary chieftains of Cuzco being presented by later chroniclers as monarchs in a dynasty. Plausible dates for the rulers in the chronicles, in fact, are not found until the accession of Pachacuti in *c.*1438. Zuidema, 52–3, 122–3, 227–35.

Dates down to Huayna Capac are approximate; for his death in 1524, see B. C. Brundage, *Lords of Cuzco* (Norman, Okla., 1967), 373.

BIBLIOGRAPHY

Brundage, B. C., *Empire of the Inca* (Norman, Okla., 1963).

Zuidema, R. T., *The Ceque System of Cuzco: the Social Organization of the Capital of the Inca* (Leiden, 1964).

THE AZTEC EMPIRE

1372–1391	Acamapichtli (Aztec chieftain at Tenochtitlan; traditional founder of Aztec royal house)
1391–1416	Huitzilihuitl (son)
1416–1427	Chimalpopoca (son)
1427–1440	Itzcoatl (son of Acamapichtli)
1440–1468	Moteuczoma I, Ilhuicamina (son of Huitzilihuitl)
1468–1481	Axayacatl (grandson of Itzcoatl)
1481–1486	Tizoc (brother)
1486–1502	Ahuitzotl (brother)
1502–1520	Moteuczoma II, Xoçoyotzin (son of Axayacatl)
1520	Cuitlahuac (brother)
1520–1521	Cuauhtemoc (son of Ahuitzotl; deposed, died 1525; Spanish conquest of the Aztec empire)

NOTES

Chronology and Calendar Dates down to 1468 are approximate; those above follow Davies. For Acamapichtli, ibid., 200–5.

The Aztecs designated each solar year by a number from 1 to 13 and by one of four names, counting the years in cycles of 52 (13 × 4). Although the succession of years within the cycle was fixed, its initial year varied according to the different counts in use in the valley of Mexico; dates in a single source may follow up to seven separate counts. See Davies, 193–7, with a correlation of counts at table A.

BIBLIOGRAPHY

Brundage, B. C., *A Rain of Darts: the Mexica Aztecs* (Austin, 1972).
Davies, C. N., *Los Mexicas: primeros pasos hacia el imperio* (México, 1973).

MEXICO AND BRAZIL

House of Iturbide – Empire of Mexico

1822–1823	Agustín I (proclaimed emperor following Mexican independence 1821; abdicated, died 1824)

House of Habsburg-Lorraine

1864–1867	Maximilian I (brother of Francis Joseph I, emperor of Austria; Republic 1867)

House of Braganza – Empire of Brazil

1822–1831	Pedro I (proclaimed emperor at Brazilian independence; king of Portugal 1826–8; abdicated, died 1834)
1831–1889	Pedro II (son; deposed, died 1891; proclamation of the republic)

BIBLIOGRAPHY

Haring, C. H., *Empire in Brazil: a New World Experiment with Monarchy* (Cambridge, Mass., 1969).

Meyer, M. C., and W. L. Sherman, *The Course of Mexican History* (3rd edn., New York, 1987).

THE KINGDOM OF HAWAII

1795–1819	Kamehameha I (king of part of Hawaii 1782; of all of Hawaii 1791; of all the islands except Kauai 1795)
1819–1824	Kamehameha II (Liholiho) (son)
1825–1854	Kamehameha III (Kauikeaouli) (brother)
1854–1863	Kamehameha IV (Alexander Liholiho) (sister's son)
1863–1872	Kamehameha V (Lot Kamehameha) (brother)
1873–1874	Lunalilo (William C. Lunalilo)
1874–1891	Kalakaua (David Kalakaua)
1891–1893	Liliuokalani (sister; deposed, died 1917; republic of Hawaii 1894)

BIBLIOGRAPHY

Kuykendall, R. S., *The Hawaiian Kingdom* (3 vols., Honolulu, 1938–67).

THE KINGDOM OF TONGA

Tupou Dynasty

1845–1893	George Tupou I (chief of Ha'apai 1820; unified the Tongan group of islands; king 1845)
1893–1918	George Tupou II (son of Fatafehi, maternal grandson of George Tupou I; British protectorate 1900–70)
1918–1965	Sālote Tupou III (daughter)
1965–	Tāufa'āhau Tupou IV (son of Sālote Tupou III and Tungī, prince consort 1918–41)

BIBLIOGRAPHY

Rutherford, N., ed., *Friendly Islands: a History of Tonga* (Melbourne, 1977).
Wood, A. H., *A History and Geography of Tonga* (Nuku'alofa, Tonga, 1932).

INDEX

Bold numbers indicate chapters or major sections of chapters.

Index compiled by Peva Keane